Publisher & Editor
Alan Marcuson
Associate Publisher
Sebastian Ghandchi
Deputy Editor
Daniel Shaffer
Managing Editor
Jill Tilden
Senior Editor
Maria Schlatter
Assistant Editors
Tania Guha, Imogen Tilden
Editorial Archivist & Librarian
Nicholas Purdon
Art Director
Liz Dixon
Art Editor
Anderida Hatch
Advertisement Manager
Julie Wicks
Advertisement Executive
Christiane Di Re
Advertisement Co-Ordinator
Lara Zunino
Projects and Promotions Manager
Matthew Margetts
**Subscriptions Manager
& Administration**
Ashley Spinks
Publisher's Assistant
Wendy Kasabian
Distribution Manager
Marc Thomas
Systems Manager
Veronica Purdey
Receptionist
Zobida Khan

**Hali Publications Limited
Kingsgate House, Kingsgate Place
London NW6 4TA, UK
Telephone (44 71) 328 9341
Fax (44 71) 372 5924**

**USA & Canada Mailing Agents
(correspondence only)
I.M.D. Ltd., P.O. Box 966, Rochdale
Village Station, Jamaica, New York
11434–0966, USA**

Hali Publications Ltd. are the publishers
of HALI, *The International Magazine
of Antique Carpet and Textile Art.*
HALI is published bi-monthly.
For subscription information please
contact our London office.

Hali Publications Ltd. is a member of The
Centaur Communications Ltd. Group.

THE 1994 HALI ANNUAL
**© Worldwide Hali Publications
Ltd., London 1994**

Imagesetting: Disc to Print, London.
Colour Origination: Vision
Reproductions Ltd., Milton Keynes.
Printing & Binding: J. Thomson
Colour Printers Ltd., Glasgow

ISBN 1-898113-00-9

Front cover courtesy E.H. Kirchheim,
Stuttgart, see *Orient Stars: A Carpet
Collection*, 1993, plate 189.
Back cover, private collection,
courtesy Spink & Son, London.

CARPET & TEXTILE ART

THE 1994 HALI ANNUAL

Hali Publications Limited, London

THE AUTHORS

Joshua Baer
Joshua Baer is the managing partner of Joshua Baer & Company, a fine arts gallery in Santa Fe, New Mexico, that specialises in 19th century Navajo blankets. He is the author of *Twelve Classics* and *Collecting the Navajo Child's Blanket.*

Christopher B. Donnan
Christopher Donnan is a Professor of Anthropology and Director of the Fowler Museum of Cultural History at the University of California, Los Angeles. He has conducted extensive archaeological fieldwork on the North Coast of Peru, and is a leading authority on Moche civilisation.

Kjeld von Folsach
By training a cultural historian, Dr von Folsach has been Director of the David Collection in Copenhagen since 1985, following a short stint as Research Librarian at the Danish Museum of Decorative Arts.

Frances Franklin
For the past eight years Frances Franklin has been a voluntary research assistant to the Indian and Southeast Asian Collection of the Victoria & Albert Museum, London. She has researched, catalogued and photographed the Burmese objects in the collection, recently focusing particularly on textiles.

Roland Gilles & Jim Willams
As well as running their rug gallery, Apamée, in the centre of Paris, Roland Gilles and Jim Williams write and lecture as dye specialists. In 1990 they conducted a carpet dyeing and weaving workshop for UNESCO in the city of Mazar-i-Sharif in Northern Afghanistan.

Donald King
Now retired, Donald King was for many years Keeper of the Department of Textile and Dress at the Victoria & Albert Museum in London. He is a past President of the Centre International d'Étude des Textiles Anciens (CIETA) and of the Textile Conservation Studio. He is a contributing editor of HALI, and author of many publications on carpets and textiles.

Santina Levey
Santina Levey was first employed at the Victoria & Albert Museum, London, in 1967, where she was responsible for the embroidery, lace and vestments collection. She has written and lectured on all three subjects. Between 1980 and 1989 she was Keeper of the V&A's Department of Textile and Dress, and is now a freelance textile historian.

Catherine McLean
Catherine C. McLean has been the Head of Textile Conservation at the Los Angeles County Museum of Art since 1986. She is responsible for the care of an encyclopaedic collection of some 60,000 costumes and textiles, including the museum's famous Ardabil carpet.

John Mills
A chemist by training, John Mills was scientific adviser at London's National Gallery until his recent retirement. His interest in carpets was forged 25 years ago, particularly in carpets in paintings, and he has frequently published on the subject. A HALI contributing editor, he is currently engaged in cataloguing the carpets contained in historic buildings belonging to the National Trust.

Vanessa & Andrés Moraga
San Francisco Bay Area textile art dealers, Vanessa and Andrés Moraga are known for their pioneering interest in new areas such as African (Kuba) and Southeast Asian textiles. Their greatest expertise and involvement, however, is in Andean art, within the context of the Latin American artistic and poetic tradition.

Harriet Sandys
Brought up in England's Lake District, Harriet Sandys became involved with Afghan Refugee aid projects as an indirect result of her work as an oriental rug restorer. In 1990, she was responsible for setting up a UNESCO/UNOCA ikat dyeing and weaving workshop in northern Afghanistan. She is currently involved in Bosnian relief work.

Jacqueline Simcox
Having joined Spink & Son shortly after graduating from Leeds University, Jacqueline Simcox is now a departmental director at the London-based fine art dealers, where she specialises in textiles, Chinese and Japanese ceramics and other works of art.

Deborah Swallow
Deborah Swallow is Curator of the Indian and Southeast Asian Collection at the Victoria & Albert Museum, London. Her research interests include both South and Southeast Asian textiles.

An Volckaert
An art historian, An Volckaert specialises in Flemish tapestries, having studied under Guy Delmarcel at the University of Louvain. She works for the Royal Manufacturers De Wit, Mechelen, and for Bernard Blondeel of Antwerp, and was responsible for the cataloguing of the exhibitions 'Five Centuries of Flemish Tapestries' (1989) and 'Golden Weavings' (1993).

CONTENTS

ASIA

TEXTILES AND SOCIETY

By Kjeld von Folsach

From the earliest centuries of Islam, luxury textiles were imbued with
a formidable value and significance. Highly wrought and crafted with the
finest and most costly materials, garments and furnishings carried messages
of wealth, power and political allegiance. This essay elucidates not the beauty,
style, material, or technique of specific Islamic textiles, but rather their place
in society. In what social, political, and religious contexts were they used?
What did they signal, and how were they viewed and valued in the Islamic
world and in the West?

The rich and complex role played by textiles in Islamic society has attracted the attention of many scholars. A vast body of information is available and many detailed studies have been written on institutions and concepts that will be considered only summarily in this article. But a general survey also has its advantages, and it is hoped that the following kaleidoscopic text will convey the importance and fascination of this aspect of the Islamic world.

NECESSITY TO STATUS SYMBOL

It was the oldest and primary function of textiles in all cultures to protect the human body against heat and cold. A second function was quickly added: to hide certain parts of the body from the gaze of others. It was not long before they began to fulfil a third function: that of expressing social status through the individual's clothing and textile possessions. Within Islamic society a man could radiate wealth, signify his profession and rank, or express his ethnic or religious affiliation. This also held true for women to a certain extent, although it should be noted that since women barely participated in public affairs in Islamic society, female raiment generally functioned less as a symbol of rank than that of a man.

In the earliest period of Islam, the Muslims took a fairly puritanical view of textiles. The Arab nomads clothed themselves largely in domestically woven woollen fabrics, and even if city-dwellers were familiar with the use of silk, fine textiles were not favoured by Muhammad or his immediate successors. The enormous areas that were conquered by Islam in the first century after Muhammad's death in 632, by contrast, had a rich tradition of both weaving and the use of sumptuous textiles; Byzantine and Sasanian silks were admired throughout the civilised world.

The Umayyad dynasty (661-750), which followed the four orthodox caliphs, moved the capital of the new empire to Damascus, which was strongly influenced by Byzantine culture. The Muslim princes and the new Arab upper class learned to appreciate luxury and splendour partly for their own sake, but also because splendour reflected power. This trend was further emphasised when the Abbasid dynasty (749-1258) moved the caliphate to Baghdad, close to the old Sasanian capital of Ctesiphon. Here the remnants of the original Arab puritanism were finally swept away to make room for lavish Persian court practices.

One can sense a mixture of awe and mild indignation in the writings of the Arab historians when they describe the luxury with which the caliphs surrounded themselves. Al Mas'udi (d.956) describes the Umayyad Sulaiman (r.715-717) as follows: "Sulaiman was a large eater and his appetite exceeded all measure. He used to wear fine robes, and robes of variegated silk *(washi* ...Nobody of his household used to enter his presence except in *washi*; thus it was with his friends, governors, and household. He used to wear it while riding, or in the pulpit *(minbar)*. None of his servants, even the cook, entered his presence except in *washi*."[1]

Muhammad's abhorrence of silk as effeminate had most certainly been overcome; wool was now primarily for the religious class and the poor. Al-Maqrizi (1364-1442) relates that the finery-loving Umayyad Hisham (724-743) had chosen so many personal garments for his pilgrimage that seven hundred camels were needed to carry them.[2]

With the stabilisation of the Muslim world empire under the Abbasids, a rich and important middle class emerged that preferred to imitate the culture of the conquered, for example the Persians, instead of holding on to the old, relatively primitive, Arab customs. It was imperative for this new class to express its position, and in this respect clothing was a suitable status symbol. The cities, especially, witnessed the emergence of a fashion-conscious class which, if al-Washsha' (ca. 860-936) is to be believed, must have been exceedingly elegant. He describes the various forms of garb and the exquisite qualities of the fabrics, but simultaneously warns against vulgarity: "The best taste in dress is to wear clothes which suit one another, with a graduated range of colour, and materials which have something in common and do not clash."[3]

Even if the Abbasid realm was soon to be divided into different enclaves, each with its own centre of power, Baghdad seemingly still had precedence in 822 when it came to culture. This is the year the Iraqi singer Ziryab arrived in Cordoba, the capital of the Spanish Umayyads,[4] bringing with him the Persian fashions used in Baghdad. In a short time these were adopted at court, and Ziryab even introduced seasons during which each type of garment could be worn. The capital of the Abbasids evidently enjoyed special prestige in the Spanish-Islamic world for quite some time, as shown by a number of Spanish figurative silks from the 11th and 12th centuries, which have inscriptions stating that they were woven in Baghdad.[5] The silks are of such a high quality that one wonders why the Spanish weavers found it necessary to use a false declaration, especially since at this time Baghdad was hardly more than a shadow of its former splendour and power.

It was the abundant use of luxury fabrics rather than innovative fashion ideas that characterised the highest strata of Islamic society. Certain dynasties, for example the Fatimids in

1. Preceding pages, left: Miniature painting showing Mahmud of Ghazna receiving a robe of honour sent by the Abbasid caliph. Edinburgh University Library, ORMS 20, fol.121 recto.

2. Preceding pages, right: Safavid tomb cover. Iran, dated [1]153 AH, 1740/41 AD 1.18 x 0.91m (3'10" x 3'0"). *Taqueté* technique, with religious and individual inscriptions commemorating the donor and the craftsmen involved in the production of the piece. The David Collection, Copenhagen, inv.no. 30/1971.

Egypt, were known for a sumptuous love of luxury of this kind. The mighty were always able to claim, when challenged by puritanical elements, that they had to surround themselves with a certain measure of pomp in order to impress and rise above the rest of the people. The use of textiles also played an important role in many political contexts in the Islamic world. In prosperous times the middle class did its best to imitate the upper strata. At times this led the authorities to prohibit the excessive use of luxury articles; for textiles, this mainly meant those that contained precious metals, though other costly fabrics were also affected. Restrictions of this kind were, however, often enforced for economic as well as religious reasons.

The ability of garments – and textiles in general – to serve as status symbols is naturally bound up with their aesthetic qualities, but even more with their economic value. In pre-industrial societies, there was an enormous difference in price between the very simple stuffs that were within reach of the poor and the fabrics that were used by the rich. Luxury fabrics were often made of the most costly basic materials, could be worked with gold and silver, and might be dyed with the rarest pigments. No wonder they were objects of great admiration in their day, costing sums that we can hardly comprehend.

It is difficult to give any examples of prices that can be directly translated into present-day terms. A more realistic picture is given by comparing the prices of the day for different goods and, where possible, by comparing them in turn with salaries.[6] Eliyahu Ashtor

3. Silk lampas with Layla visiting Majnun in the wilderness, signed by Ghiyath. Iran, Yazd, or Esfahan, end of 16th-beginning of 17th century. 0.73 x 0.69m (2'5" x 2'3"). The Danish Museum of Decorative Art, Copen-hagen, inv.no. B21/1931.

believes that the price of an elegant costume for a man lay between 5 and 30 dinars, though contemporary sources often mention prices of between 200 and 1000 dinars.[7] If one ignores changing currency rates, 30 dinars converted using the current price of gold would correspond to the sum of about $1,350, which though high, is probably not an exorbitant price for today's fashion-conscious men.[8] It should be mentioned for comparison's sake, however, that Ashtor writes that a carpenter and a post-rider had a monthly salary of two dinars and an artisan slightly less, while the *kadi* (judge) in Cairo received a salary that ranged from 30 up to 200 dinars per month, according to different sources and in different periods.[9] It is worth remembering at the same time that medieval sources abound in references to goods with prices that are much higher than those given here, for example Egyptian turbans from the end of the 10th century which, according to al-Maqrizi, were woven and embroidered with gold thread, the value of the metal thread alone being 500 dinars.[10]

Abu'l-Fazl, grand vizier of the Mughal Emperor Akbar, writes at the end of the 16th century that the prices of woven fabrics had dropped dramatically; a piece made by the renowned Persian weaver Ghiyath (3) cost only 50 gold muhr, whereas it had previously cost twice that much. It is impossible to say how large this piece of fabric was, but calculated along the same lines as before, 50 gold muhr corresponds to approximately $5,827, or 551.65g of pure gold. Even though the Islamic world has had a highly developed monetary economy from the earliest times, there is much evidence that textiles were considered a kind of ready money, or something that could be compared to real estate. But this was naturally not the case for broad segments of the population. True luxury fabrics were barely within the reach even of the wealthy bourgeoisie.

Princes had enormous stores of both apparel and fabrics, partly to satisfy their own needs, but also for use as gifts. In fact, at times raiment was even used as part of courtiers' salaries. Muslim historians wrote at length of the vastness of the rulers' stores. The bulging warehouses of the Fatimids, especially, were legendary.[11] The following story told by the Vizier al-Hasan ibn Makhlad about al-Muwaffaq, brother of the Abbasid al-Mu'tamid (870-892), is one of many that shows that earlier caliphs lacked nothing: " 'Hasan, this stuff pleases me. How much have we in the stores?' Thereupon I brought out of my boot a little roll in which was set forth the total of goods and stuffs in the stores, given in detail. Therein I found 6,000 pieces of this kind of stuff. 'Hasan,' said al-Muwaffak to me, 'we have nothing to wear. Write to the country (of origin) to make 30,000 pieces of this kind of fabric, and to send them with the least possible delay.' " The early Arab historians have often been accused, perhaps rightly so, of exaggeration. Such figures should not be taken too literally, but rather as an indication that a large number was involved.

For the middle class in prosperous times, luxury textiles became more common, and were actually considered suitable investments. Large portions of a family's funds might be put into cloth, which could subsequently be handed down or sold if necessary.[12] People speculated in cloth and stored it as they did objects made of gold and silver, precious stones and so on. High quality textiles had almost the same status as ready money; in the first couple

4. Silk lampas with addorsed lions and double-headed eagles. Eastern Islamic area (?), mid 13th century. 0.53 x 1.02m (1'9" x 2'4"). The David Collection, Copenhagen, inv.no. 32/1989.

5. Kashmir shawl fragment with red flowers on a white ground. India, Kashmir, early 18th century. 0.54 x 0.67m (1'9" x 2'2"). The Danish Museum of Decorative Art, Copenhagen, inv.no. B215/1936.

of centuries after Muhammad's death the caliphs frequently received taxes in the form of textiles.[13] This practice became less common, however, as the princes themselves became increasingly involved in the manufacture of such fabrics, a way of exercising power that was to prove both lucrative and politically useful.

TIRAZ

The designation *tiraz* comes from the Persian word for embroidery, but is normally associated with woven, embroidered, or painted inscriptions on very early and medieval Islamic textiles. The word tiraz can also refer to the textiles or garments upon which the inscriptions are found, and finally it can refer to the workshops where the textiles were produced.[14]

The inscriptions on the *tiraz* textiles were mostly of an official character and, in addition to religious maxims and eulogies, might provide varying amounts of the following information: the name of the ruler, possibly the name of his vizier and of the director *(sahib)* of the *tiraz* workshop where it was made. The status and location of the workshop might also be included, as might the date of manufacture. Even though there are exceptions, it must generally be assumed that this type of *tiraz* was made at workshops that were owned or controlled by the ruling prince or his most trusted top officials. There were also *tiraz* workshops that were not under royal control, where private persons could have inscriptions woven.

Ibn Khaldun (1332-1406) suggests in his informative text on the *tiraz* institution that it probably had its origins in Iran.[15] Many modern scholars, however, seem justified in pointing out that it was in fact Byzantium that served as the model.[16] There were royal manufactories in Constantinople that had a virtual monopoly on producing the coveted, sumptuous Byzantine textiles; similarly, there were Coptic textile workshops in Egypt before the Arab conquest that had imperial privileges, and there is hardly any doubt that they were to become the nucleus of the renowned Egyptian *tiraz* industry. In addition, *tiraz* inscriptions were often placed around the sleeve, at the shoulder, at the neck, or along the border of the garment, locations that are fairly close to what was common for other types of embroideries in the Byzantine world with roots in Roman customs. Finally, *tiraz* was already found under the Umayyads, when the influence of Persian culture was still relatively slight, compared with its later importance under the Abbasids.

Of all the luxury textiles in early Islamic medieval society, *tiraz* textiles were the status symbols that were most easily understood. The wearer of an official *tiraz* inscription showed that he was a prince, or that at least he held the favour of a prince. The woven inscriptions could probably be compared most aptly to our society's orders, distinctions that are bestowed by the grace of those in power but which cannot be purchased. They might take the form of bands that were intended to be sewn on existing garments (**6**), but they might also be woven into larger pieces that in turn comprised a particular item of clothing. They naturally played an essential role in conjunction with the robes of honour (*khil'a*) that the princes bestowed, and as time passed, to some extent they even made up part of the courtiers' salaries.

The caliphs considered the *tiraz* institution highly significant, as evidenced by the exalted position held by the responsible head of the workshops, the *sahib al-tiraz*, especially under the splendour-loving Fatimid dynasty. In order to maintain respect for the *tiraz* institution, it was important that standards be upheld when it came to the excellence of the materials and the skills of the weavers. This control was also the responsibility of the *sahib al-tiraz*. Similarly, it was important that the inscriptions should not be misused. *Tiraz* could naturally be worn only by the person who was entitled to do so. This was undoubtedly the reason why in medieval Malaga, the *muhtasib*, an official who was responsible for ensuring that the markets were properly run, was charged with seeing that no *tiraz* band was transferred from one garment to another unless its owner were present, and that no text was altered.[17]

Since these court manufactories produced many other high-quality fabrics in addition to *tiraz* textiles, they were a major source of income. Al-Maqrizi, for example, writes that around 975 the industrious Egyptian towns of Tinnis, Damietta, and Ushmunayn were paying 220,000 dinar daily into the treasuries of the Fatimid caliph, and that expenditures for gold thread alone totalled 31,000 dinar.[18]

Perhaps more significant for the prince, though less tangible, was the *tiraz* inscription's importance as propaganda, its direct political value. Each *tiraz* inscription that was worn around the vast Islamic empire was a living advertisement for the caliphate's universal power and for the current incumbent (**10**). As soon as a new caliph took office, his name immediately replaced that of his predecessor. This propaganda could only be compared at the time to two other caliphal prerogatives: that of having his name struck on the official coinage and that of being mentioned each week in the Friday prayer (*khutba*) in mosques throughout the realm.

When the Shi'ite Fatimids established themselves in North Africa at the beginning of the 10th century, they claimed that they were descended from the Prophet Muhammad's daughter Fatima. The Fatimids consequently pronounced the Abbasids usurpers and established their own caliphate, with its capital in Cairo. This made them the masters of the rich textile centres in the Nile Delta, where most of the Abbasids' *tiraz* textiles had formerly been woven, and they used this new position to turn their own workshops into active propaganda centres for their rival Shi'ite caliphate.

It is significant that the Fatimid *tiraz* textiles changed character as the dynasty's political and economic power began to wane. By the end of the 11th century, the texts often shrank into expressions of good wishes and similar messages, and various forms of ornamentation – sometimes pseudo-calligraphic – in glowing colours dominated (**8**). The Abbasid caliphate had already been reduced to a formal religious institution without true political significance, and with many local dynasties spread throughout the Islamic world, the universal political message of the *tiraz* inscriptions might have had its day.

The custom of decorating garments with inscriptions persisted into the 14th century, but its significance was no longer the same. The otherwise vital Mamluk dynasty thus maintained the tradition, but instead of the *tiraz* textiles being made in princely workshops, they were simply ordered in the bazaar,[19] and the original concept seems to have been watered down. A few later silks are found outside the lands of the Mamluks with inscriptions that essentially had the same textual content as the classical *tirazes*. An example is a famous piece of silk dated to between 1319 and 1335 bearing the name of the Il-Khanid Khan Abu Sa'id.[20] A later silk bears the name "Sultan Bayazid Khan", which according to Richard Ettinghausen refers to the Ottoman Sultan Bayazid I (1389-1402).[21] While the first silk was undoubtedly made at one of Abu Sa'id's own workshops, the origins of the Bayazid silk are uncertain.[22] In addition, they do not conform to one of the definitions of the classical *tiraz* textiles, which requires that the inscription and fabric itself be made of two different materials and in two different techniques.[23]

In a way it is curious that the proud traditions from the second to the fourth century of Islam were not revived in later empires, for example those of the Timurids, Ottomans, Safavids, or Mughals, but evidently they were not. It is especially strange since *tiraz* was obviously such an excellent political weapon.

In his comments on *tiraz* mentioned above, Ibn Khaldun writes, in Serjeant's translation, "Before Islam, the kings of Persia had placed upon their garments, either the portraits (*suwar*), or likenesses (*ashkal*) of the kings of the country, or certain figures and images designated for this use. The Muslim princes substituted their names for the figures, adding other words considered to be of good augury, which gave the praise of God."[24] What Ibn Khaldun describes harmonises completely with Islam's general reluctance to use figurative presentations, a phenomenon that can be traced in parallel in coinage, where the traditional ruler's portrait also disappeared, to be replaced by inscriptions.

At the same time Ibn Khaldun mentions that earlier kings had their garments decorated not only with portraits, but also with "certain figures and images" that represented royal power. Figurative *tiraz* inscriptions of this kind survived on a more or less conscious level in Islam along with the true *tiraz* textiles. Many of the magnificent Muslim textiles of the

6. Right: Miniature painting showing Badr ad-Din Lu'lu' in a dress with tiraz bands. Iraq, Mosul, 1219 AD. 28 x 21cm (11" x 8"). This frontispiece from the last volume of Kitab al-Aghani *The Book of Songs*, shows a richly dressed rider, who should probably be identified as Badr ad-Din Lu'lu', the ruler who also commissioned this copy of the book. This prince's name is written on the two *tiraz* bands around the rider's arms. The Danish Royal Library, Cod. arab. 168, on loan to the David Collection, Copenhagen.

medieval period were interwoven with lions, griffins, sphinxes, eagles and animal combat motifs, whose content undoubtedly referred to a princely iconography (**4, 9, 11**). But their significance seems to have been quickly watered down, and it is not possible to interpret any specific symbolism in the abundance of heraldic animals and mythical creatures.[25]

ROBES OF HONOUR

Closely related to the Islamic princes' use of *tiraz* textiles was their use of robes of honour. While these often bore inscriptions, with the demise of the *tiraz* institution in the late Middle Ages it became more common for them simply to be made of cloth of a more or less splendid quality, in keeping with the giver's means, the degree to which the recipient was to be honoured, and the recipient's rank. The custom of presenting robes of honour to subjects, servants, or others whom one wished to single out, was an ancient one in the East. The system was also very widespread and carefully regulated in the Byzantine Empire. The emperor had a monopoly on the manufacture of a large range of luxury fabrics, and only those who enjoyed the favour of the ruler had access to them.[26]

In the Islamic world, this practice had an important precedent since the Prophet Muhammad himself had honoured the poet Ka'b bin Zuhayr by bestowing his cloak upon him.[27] The word *khil'a* – 'robe of honour' – implies a piece of clothing that the giver takes from his own body, and one must assume that this is what Muhammad did. It is obvious that it would be a special honour to receive a garment that had in fact been worn by the prince, but once the custom had really taken hold under the Abbasids and Fatimids, this procedure was excep-

7. Kashmir moon shawl of striped twill. India, Kashmir, early 19th century. 1.61 x 1.68m (5'3" x 5'6"). The David Collection, Copenhagen, inv.no. 26/1992.

tional, for practical reasons (1). During this period it became standard practice for robes of honour to be bestowed as an investiture when a high-ranking official was installed, or as he completed his service, or to be given, for instance, to foreign dignitaries. In time, the robes of honour became almost part of the courtiers' regular salary, and the concept consequently lost some of its original meaning.

If wearing a princely robe of honour was not to lose its social and political significance, it was necessary for the prince to consider carefully on whom he would bestow such an honour. It is said that the Caliph al-Amin (r.809-813) had been so enchanted with a singer that he presented him with a silk *jubba* – a kind of coat – worked in gold. He soon regretted his action, however, and saved the day by 'accidentally' dropping a piece of meat on the robe. Because of its metal thread, the textile was much too delicate to be cleaned, and the *jubba* had consequently been rendered worthless.[28]

In certain periods, the robe of honour comprised more than just the garment itself. Al-Qalqashandi (1355-1418) describes the situation under the late Abbasid caliphs: "If the person whom the caliph appointed was one of the kings of the districts far away from the court of the caliph, for example such as the kings of Egypt at that time, and others, the robe of honour was despatched with a messenger to him from the caliph. It was an upper gown of black satin with a golden *tiraz* border, and a necklace of gold to be placed on his neck, and two bracelets of gold, to be placed on his hand...and a sword, the scabbard of which was covered with gold, and a horse with a saddle of gold, and a black standard with the name of the caliph written in white, to be unfurled over his head."[29] A similar display of magnificence was the rule under the Egyptian Mamluks in the heyday of the dynasty. But towards the end, it was in such a sorry state that Sultan Qansauh al-Ghauri in 1507 was only able to present cotton garments worth three dinars apiece to officials who were entitled to receive robes of honour.[30]

Concerning ranks under the same dynasty, al-Maqrizi notes that there were different robes of honour for the sultan's officials, depending on whether they were members of the military class, served in the civil administration, or were scholars of the religious class.[31] He describes the robes in great detail and also notes that if a person rose in rank, his promotion could be shown by having a *tiraz* band sewn onto his robe. Otherwise, it was customary for every new appointment to be followed by a new robe of honour.

As noted above, the use of robes of honour survived the *tiraz* institution by many centuries, and the custom was carried on by all the great dynasties, continuing into the 18th and 19th centuries. Alfred Leix writes that it became common at this late date for the recipient of a robe of honour to present a gift in return. Under the last Mughals, this practice became pure blackmail since the Mughal emperor, in return for a worthless robe of honour, expected a sizeable monetary present.[32]

OTHER POLITICAL ASPECTS

There were many other ways in which textiles carried political messages. The use of colour could signify party allegiance; sumptuous textiles spoke of political power; individual objects such as the turban and the Kaaba cover had special significance; control of the use of textiles brought political advantages, while the waging of trade wars showed them to be of considerable economic importance.

The use of colours to signal that one belonged to a specific party or a specific group in society is known in most cultures. In Byzantium, for example, the use of the colour purple was the prerogative of the imperial family, and private persons were prohibited, under penalty of death, from selling – to say nothing of manufacturing – purple-coloured textiles.[33] The use

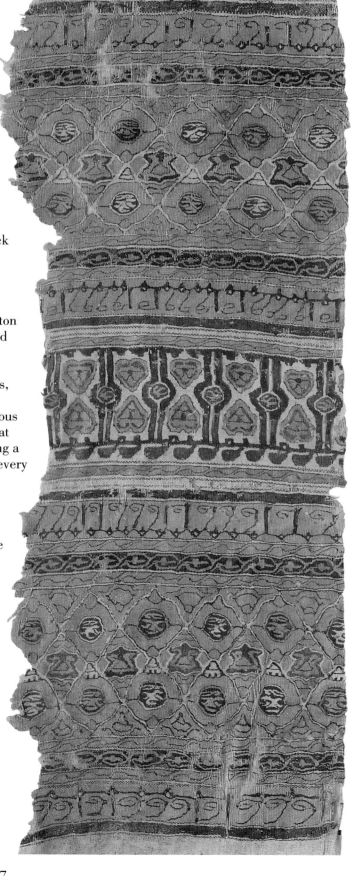

8. *Tiraz* tabby-woven fragment (detail), in which text becomes ornament. Egypt, late 11th/early 12th century. 56 x 13m (1'10" x 5"). The Danish Museum of Decorative Art, Copenhagen, inv.no. B29/1938.

of black as the colour of the Abbasid dynasty was introduced under the Caliph al-Mansur (754-775), and from then on, the Abbasid caliphs wore black on official occasions.[34] The robes of honour and standards that the Abbasids sent out to their provincial governors were black; even the mighty Egyptian Mamluk sultans, who served as the protectors of the enfeebled Abbasid caliphs following their expulsion from Baghdad by the Mongols in the middle of the 13th century, clad themselves in black on important festivals in order to show their political and religious allegiance.[35] The political importance of this symbolism of colours can be seen from an incident in 1051. When the Zirid al-Mu'izz ibn Badis assumed power in the Maghrib, he shifted his alliance from the Fatimids to the Abbasids. He summoned dyers and gave them white cloth from his textile stores to dye black. At times, specific colours were also used to separate those of different faiths from the Muslim majority.

Certain articles of clothing, such as the turban, might also possess a high degree of religious, social, or political significance. The turban had already been used by the Arabs in pre-Islamic times, but became almost a symbol of the devout Muslim, for whom Muhammad was *Sahib al'imama* – the Bearer of the Turban.[36] It should be remembered in this connection that it was natural for both Jews and Muslims to cover their heads out of respect for both God and man. The turban was an important symbol of power to the princes, one that at times could assume almost ludicrous dimensions and cost ridiculous sums. The Fatimid Sultan al-'Aziz (975-996) reputedly owned a turban about 50 metres long, worked with gold and woven of silk and the finest linen in the Delta town of Dabiq. It was valued at the tidy sum of 4,000 dinars,[37] possibly an exaggeration, but nevertheless an indication of its perceived value.

Anyone who is familiar with 16th century Persian miniature painting will remember the characteristic white turbans wound around a hat so that a long red 'pole' sticks up in the centre of the turban. This distinctive turban, which was used by the Shi'ite Safavids and their followers, was the reason why the Sunni Ottomans derisively called them *kizil bash* – red caps.[38] The famous copy of the *Shah-nameh* (Book of Kings) of Shah Isma'il and Shah Tahmasp shows not only all the Persian heroes outfitted in this way, but also the Prophet Muhammad, the Caliph 'Ali, and his sons Hasan and Husayn wearing this Shi'ite turban. It was a subtle religious manifestation that was simultaneously a challenge to the Sunni, Ottoman sultans, who had taken over the caliphate after the last Abbasid.

The textile that was perhaps linked with the greatest political prestige in the Islamic world was the one that covered the Kaaba in Mecca, the foremost Muslim shrine. The custom of covering the Kaaba with a special cloth (*kiswa*) was older than Islam, but was continued after Muhammad had cleansed the shrine of idols. The right to drape the Kaaba was bestowed on the Caliph at an early date: 'Umar (r.634-644) is said to have done so with an imported Coptic cloth.[39] The *kiswa* generally seems to have been black, but other colours, such as red, yellow, and white, could also be used.[40]

The cover was worked with quotations from the Qur'an and in addition had *tiraz*-like inscriptions that made clear the donor's identity. And this is precisely where its political significance lay; for the thousands of pilgrims who came to Mecca each year, the inscription on the *kiswa* bore testimony to the one invested with the formal, and at times real, authority in Islam – the protector of the holy cities of Mecca and Medina. Until around 1260, it was mostly the Abbasids who donated the *kiswa*, though members of other dynasties also seem to have sent covers of this kind to Mecca. After the Mongols destroyed Baghdad the right was assumed by the Mamluks, and finally, after 1517, by the Ottomans.

In 917, the Abbasid Caliph al-Muqtadir received an ambassador from one of the caliphate's most powerful neighbours – the Byzantine emperor: "The number of gold curtains of brocade with magnificent gold embroideries (*tiraz*), with figures of cups, elephants, horses, camels, wild beasts, and birds, and large Bassina, Armenian, Wasit, and Bahnasa curtains, plain or with drawings, and Dabiki with the tiraz which were suspended in the castles of the Commander of the Faithful al-Muktadir bi'llah, consisted of 38,000 curtains, of which the aforementioned gold curtains of brocade made up the number of 12,000. The number of carpets, and strips of Djahram and Darabdjird and Dawrak in the passages and in the courts, on which the generals and envoys of the emperor of Rum trod, from the New Public Gate to the presence of al-Muktadir bi'llah, not counting the Tabari and Dabiki carpets which were under them, in the private rooms and in the assembly rooms, for display, and not to be trodden upon, came to 22,000 pieces."[41]

It is impossible to know whether the curtains with elephants, horses, camels, and other figurative motifs were hung especially to impress a non-Muslim envoy, but it is obvious that textiles were a far more flexible form of decoration than murals; they could be taken down and others hung, to suit the occasion. If one adds the costumes of the court and of the caliph's guards, then a reception of this kind must have made a impression on anyone, even on an envoy from Imperial Byzantium, which at the time was capable of far greater magnificence than anything Europe could otherwise muster. It is not known exactly how the

9. Right: Silk lampas fragment with confronting lions and *makaras* in ovals. Western (?) India, 15th century (?). 0.48 x 0.58m (1'7" x 1'11"). This textile provides evidence that the iconography of the 'royal' heraldic style, with its message of power, reached the Indian subcontinent. The David Collection, Copenhagen, inv.no. 34/1992.

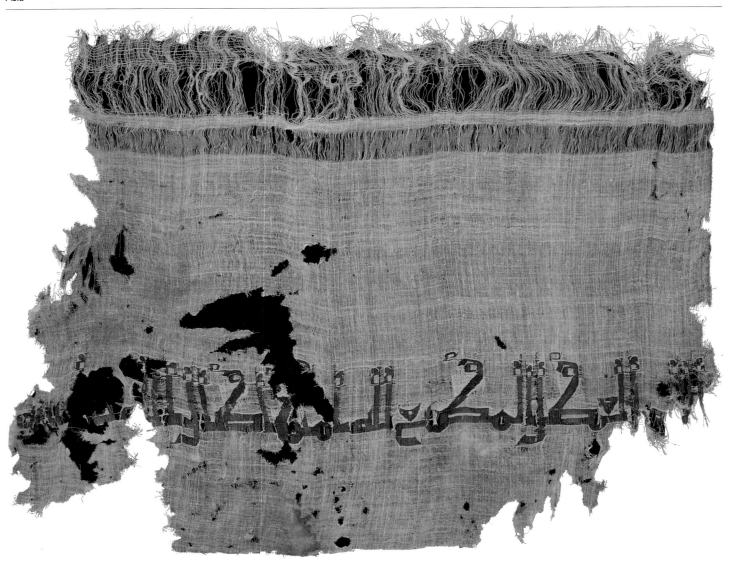

caliph's guard were dressed, but the Abbasids' partly independent governor in Egypt, the Tulunid Khumarawayh (884-896), had a personal guard of one thousand Nubians, dressed in silk brocade and in turbans, all black.[42]

Textiles were also used to shield the prince from the gaze of his subjects. Perhaps following a Sasanian or Byzantine tradition, a curtain of this kind (*hidjab*) was first used by the Umayyads. The Fatimids, in particular, exploited this custom effectively at audiences, where the caliph, unnoticed by those seeking his presence, made his way behind the *hidjab* after they had waited a substantial time. At a signal from a high-ranking official the curtain was raised, and the richly clad caliph was revealed in all his glory.[43]

It is obvious that this kind of demonstration of magnificence could be used as a political weapon. It is almost as obvious that political power could also be wielded to prevent others challenging the glory and exclusivity of the prince by similar displays of magnificence. The textile trade was very strictly regulated, especially in Byzantium, whose laws were in many respects more rigorous than those of Islam. As well as restricting the use of purple to the imperial family, the emperor permitted only the top stratum of society to acquire the ex-quisite silks that were produced in the imperial workshops, which can incidentally be seen as pendants to the *tiraz* workshops of the Islamic princes. The middle class of Constantinople had unlimited access to second-quality silks, enabling the inhabitants of the capital to help reflect the glory of the emperor, but these textiles were never under any circumstances to be exported to the surrounding barbarian peoples. An effort was made by the central authorities to bring about what has been called 'hierarchy through clothing'. This system stratified one's own society, while aiming to ensure that people outside found themselves at the lowest level.

The use of textiles as a social and political weapon was evidently not consistent throughout the Islamic world. The Abbasid caliphs' black, for example, was not reserved for this dynasty in the same way as purple was reserved for the emperors. However the Muslim princes wielded similar political power; nothing from the *tiraz* workshops could be sold without the ruler's permission. In his description of the Egyptian textile workshops from 1047, the Persian poet Nasir-i Khusrau notes that one of the Buyid rulers of Fars had sent

10. *Tiraz* tabbyweave fragment with the inwoven name of the Abbasid Caliph al-Muti'. Egypt, 946-974 AD. 0.41 x 0.52m (1'4" x 1'8"). This textile must have been woven just before the Abbasids were driven out of Egypt by the Fatimids in 969 AD. The David Collection, Copenhagen, inv.no. 18/1971.

agents with 20,000 dinars to Tinnis to buy a complete set of princely raiment. But even though his agents remained in the city for several years, they were unable to purchase what he wished.[44]

TEXTILES AND RELIGION

As was mentioned earlier, the earliest Muslims took a rather puritanical attitude to the use of luxury textiles, especially silk. While the Qur'an makes no specific mention of textiles other than to state that those who enter Paradise will be clad in silk (*harir*), Muhammad seems to have considered it decadent for men to wear silk. All schools of religious law were against men using raiment made only of silk – at least next to the skin.[45] This dictate was also open to interpretation, however, and history has demonstrated that most of the mighty of this world took the prohibition fairly lightly.

The custom of wearing a veil outside the home seems already to have existed in pre-Islamic Arabia.[46] In the Qur'an the veil (*hijab*) was first made obligatory for the Prophet's own wives and adult daughters, and then for all orthodox women (*sura* 33 verse 59, and *sura* 24 verse 31). Depending on time and place, the veil was designed in different ways, and covered varying amounts of the face. It was generally more widespread in the upper and middle strata of urban society than in the lower classes and among the rural population. There can be no doubt that the veil played a part in making the home the natural domain of the Muslim woman, and that it sequestered her from the surrounding world.

There were naturally numerous inhabitants in the Islamic world who were not Muslims.

11. Tapestry-woven roundel with lions and sphinxes around a stylised tree-of-life. Egypt, 9th-10th century. 0.56 x 0.43m (1'10" x 1'5"). Warp of wool, pattern weft of wool and linen. The David Collection, Copenhagen, inv.no. 1/1989.

Among them, the Jews, Samaritans, Christians and certain other groups had a special status: like the Muslims, they were 'People of the Book', and like them, they were monotheists. In the great majority of cases, these *dhimmis* (privileged infidels) were given permission to live peacefully side by side with the Muslim inhabitants. One of the conditions imposed was that they were forbidden in the reign of 'Umar b. 'Abd-al-'Aziz (717-720) to imitate Muslim fashions. Harun al-Rashid (786-809) decided that they were to look different from Muslims, and al-Mutawakkil (847-861) finally enforced a separate law that specified how *dhimmis* were to clothe themselves.[47] These laws or regulations were called *ghiyar*, which can most accurately be translated as 'cognizance' or 'distinction', and the concept *ghiyar* covers in a broad sense the special symbols that non-Muslim citizens were forced to wear in certain periods of history,[48] which could cover everything from a ban on wearing specific types of raiment to an order to wear different coloured badges on clothing, designating whether one was a Christian, Jew, or Samaritan. Baghdad's *dhimmis* paid 20,000 dinars to the Seljuk Sultan Mahmud II (1118-1131) and 4,000 dinars to the caliph in order to avoid the stigma. In other periods, the *ghiyar* was used specifically to humiliate the *dhimmis*. For example, the mad Fatimid Caliph al-Hakim decreed that Christians and Jews should wear heavy wooden crosses and bells around their necks when they showed themselves in public.[49]

ISLAMIC TEXTILES AND THE WEST
It is important to emphasise that throughout most of the Middle Ages, both Byzantine and Islamic textiles surpassed by far what was made in Christian Europe, and even if complex high-quality textiles were woven in Italy, France, and Germany from the 13th century, these products were unable either to measure up to or replace those that were brought in from the Orient in different ways.[50] The situation gradually changed from the 14th to the 16th century, but Islamic textiles nonetheless generally reigned supreme for several centuries, and Europeans never achieved a quality that could be compared to the velvets of the Safavids, for example, or the northern Indian Kashmir shawls of later periods (**7**).

When one remembers that, for long periods, the Islamic Middle East was almost *a priori* an enemy of Christian Europe for religious reasons, and that the relationship between the two cultural spheres was often highly strained, there is good reason to wonder why Christian princes of both Church and State let themselves be clad, both in life and in death, in sumptuous fabrics that had been woven by heathens. They even went so far as to use these textiles for vestments and altar cloths, and to wrap around reliquaries of the most revered saints. In Spain, the Christian Castilian kings, who had slowly reconquered their land piece by piece in the course of the Middle Ages in a hard and bitter struggle, were largely buried in Moorish textiles, as shown by finds in Las Huelgas de Burgos.[51] And if Christian princes were buried in Islamic fabrics, why should they not also wear them in life?

Naturally this appreciation was linked with the high quality of Islamic textiles, their costliness and rarity, but at the same time, like many other Islamic art forms, they had the advantage of not being 'tainted' by a specific Islamic iconography that would have made them unacceptable to Christian users. While Christian textiles with depictions of the Virgin Mary, Jesus crucified, or simply stylised crosses would have seemed offensive in Islamic contexts, the arabesques, geometric patterns, heraldic animals and mythical creatures of the Islamic world fitted well into the Christian medieval universe. The only elements that conveyed clear Islamic messages were the inscriptions, but this evidently did not bother Christian users, who only in exceptional cases were able to decipher the Arabic texts. In any case, there are innumerable inscriptions on ecclesiastical textiles. Paintings show the Virgin Mary and other holy persons wearing raiment bordered with Islamic inscriptions, and 14th century Italian silk manufacturers even wove pseudo-Arabic calligraphy into their textiles.[52]

Even when, from the late Middle Ages onwards, Europe was able to match the achievements of its mentor, Islamic textiles continued to be treasured and preserved with great veneration. Many thousands of oriental carpets graced the palaces, middle-class homes, and churches of the West. The banners, tents, and garments that were captured in the Turkish wars, for example, were kept as booty not simply because they were trophies of conquered enemies, but also because they were often of a quality that could not be produced locally.

The European states competed among themselves on opening trade routes to Iran and India, partly in order to import textiles for the growing and prosperous home market (**9**). This development began to change in earnest in the 18th century, when Europeans took the lead both economically and industrially. The English textile industry, in particular, was now able to manufacture fabrics by machine that gradually made oriental craftsmanship completely obsolete. What had been flourishing textile centres shrank to provincial status, and finally almost died out. The curtain fell, at least for the time being, on one of the world's great textile traditions.

Notes see Appendix

11. Right: *Tayang Khan is Presented with the Head of Ong-Khan,* **miniature from Rashid al-Din's** *Jami al-Tawarikh (World History).* **India, Mughal period, ca.1595. 0.35 x 0.21m (1'2" x 0'8"). The David Collection, Copenhagen, inv.no. 39/1980.**

LOVE AND UNDERSTANDING

A Personal Choice from the Orient Stars Collection

By John Mills

Heinrich and Waltraut Kirchheim's Orient Stars Collection of Eastern carpets, kilims and embroideries, which was exhibited in Hamburg and published during 1993, has been hailed as a significant milestone in the evolution of 'love and understanding' of certain types of oriental carpets, especially early material from Anatolia. Here, one of the most widely respected of current writers on the subject discusses aspects of the collection and the multi-author catalogue, and their longer-term relevance to carpet studies.

1. Preceding pages, left:
'Early Animal' carpet
(detail). Anatolia, Seljuk
period, 12th-14th century.
Carbon-14 dated to 1190-
1300 AD with 95% prob-
ability. 1.73 x 3.10m
(5'8" x 10'2"). Kirchheim
Collection, Stuttgart,
Orient Stars, p.15.

2. Preceding pages, right:
The Marriage of the Virgin.
Sienese School, early
15th century.
The National Gallery,
London, inv.no. 1317.

Orient Stars[1] touches different aspects of one's love affair with carpets in ways which are both engaging and maddening. One needs to be able to go into different modes, to adopt different 'mindsets', to appreciate fully the different sections of this work.

Nearly every carpet lover has at some time, very often at the onset of his enthusiasm, been captivated by the bold designs and pure, bright colours of 19th century Caucasian rugs, and has sought to acquire some. So it was with this collector, who, possessed of ample means, was able to assemble a group of fine examples of many of the different and easily recognisable types. To appreciate the 'later' Caucasian part of the book it is best to fall back into the old collecting mood; recall the days of poring over books and catalogues and of dreaming of filling in gaps, perhaps by coming across old pieces, albeit damaged and dirty, lying unregarded on the floors of provincial antique shops, as could, twenty years ago, still happen.

One can dwell with these straightforwardly beautiful things in a state of innocence, as in some flowery Garden of Eden, but, eventually, voices whisper suggestions and questions. Should one not be making a *study* of them? Worrying about their real age and provenance, the meanings of their designs, their structure, their materials and dyes? And thus one sets foot on the *via dolorosa* of carpet studies. Soon one finds that there is not all that much to be discovered about 19th century Caucasians. Older and more elusive types beckon, among which many find that Turkish rugs have the most fascination.

It is indeed the early Turkish rugs which are the major and most beautiful element in the Kirchheim Collection. In the past fifteen or twenty years our understanding of the range and variety of the rugs produced by town, village and nomad weavers in Anatolia from the 15th to 19th centuries has been enormously enlarged. This is for several reasons: the publication and exhibition of many of the pieces from the stores of the Vakıflar Foundation and the Turkish and Islamic Arts Museum, both in Istanbul; the greater attention paid to unfamiliar pieces in Western museum collections, whose age and importance had been overlooked or underestimated; and the appearance in the international carpet trade of many largely fragmentary rugs which must have come out of Turkey.

Before this, the study of Turkish carpets had, from its beginnings in the late 19th century, been almost entirely concerned with what have become known as 'classical' carpets, that is to say the fairly limited range of design types which were exported to western Europe from the 15th century onwards and which survived there in some numbers. These types must have been largely selected from the west Anatolian production, made in areas accessible from seaports such as Izmir. Many are indeed now attributed to the town of Ushak and its surrounding villages. The appearances of these types in European – mainly Italian – paintings made it possible to construct a very plausible chronology for them and for their changing design modifications.

With the many and varied rugs which we now have to assess, there is very much less in the way of evidence to go on, especially in the matter of dating. There is carbon dating, and this has proved well worthwhile, but the method is very expensive and does not work well for materials later than the 16th century. Moreover the results are rather imprecise and usually expressed in some such terms as '1250-1400 with 95% probability'. Nonetheless, the technique very much needs to be applied to some key groups of carpets, since much carpet scholarship depends precisely on comparisons with these groups.

Only a small proportion of the early Turkish pieces in the Kirchheim Collection can be related to, and dated by comparison with, so-called 'classical' rugs. Even when they can,

3. 'Early Animal' carpet.
Probably central Anatolia,
Seljuk period, 12th-14th
century. 1.26 x 1.53m
(4'2" x 5'0"). Metropolitan
Museum of Art, New
York, inv.no. 1990.61.

it has always to be remembered that some designs continued in use, more or less modified, until modern times. And this brings us to a core problem of all dating methods based on design, namely what one believes concerning the origins of designs and the ways in which they change. Different people hold widely differing views on this. The most fundamental difference is as to whether designs, such as those of the 'classical' rugs, are the creations of urban or court designers, which were subsequently copied with varying degrees of misunderstanding and modification by village or nomad weavers, or whether these latter were the bearers of the flame of meaningful, if unconscious, imagery, which was poached by the urban workshops, and formalised and standardised for commercial purposes. The likelihood is that both these views reflect the truth at times: the difficulty is to distinguish which applies in

4. *Madonna and Child* *with St John.* Domenico Ghirlandaio or follower, late 15th century. The National Gallery, London, inv.no. 2502.

any particular case, for they lead to very different assessments of merit and date.

Contributors to the *Orient Stars* catalogue show these widely varying approaches even when they are all discussing early Turkish rugs, which might be thought to call for some consistency of scholarly method. Moreover their enthusiasm for the rugs they discuss (with which they have often, though not always, been associated as dealers) and, indeed, their conception of what is beautiful, are necessarily influenced by their personal preoccupations, whether these involve studies of particular design or regional groups, or a dedication to the 'sacred flame' idea to which I have alluded.

We are all, as we advance in knowledge of and familiarity with the ever increasing range of published rugs, influenced in our likes and dislikes (and our judgement of what is a 'great'

6. Re-entrant rug. Central Anatolia (?), 16th century. 1.30 x 1.88m (4'3" x 6'2"). Turkish and Islamic Arts Museum, Istanbul, inv.no. 725.

7. 'Lotto' arabesque rug. Central Anatolia (?), 16th or 17th century. Turkish and Islamic Arts Museum, Istanbul.

rug) by different factors which can be far more compelling than simply that of the bold design and play of bright colours which first struck the innocent eye and awakened our delight. These influences are subtle, often unconscious, and not always easy to uncover even if one wants to. But they certainly have to do with what one has already learned and what questions are yet unanswered; what one dimly recalls and what 'rings a bell'; what seems to fit in and helps to complete the larger picture. How these operate is perhaps illuminated by my response to the first of the rugs I have chosen as some of my favourites from the collection.

The carpet illustrated in (1) belongs to a small group known as the 'Early Animal' carpets, generally believed to have been woven in Anatolia. Two small rugs, and a few small fragments, of different designs, have been known for about a century, while representations of these, and other designs which apparently had not survived in actual examples, were known from Italian paintings of the 14th and 15th centuries. Among these paintings is one of *The Marriage of the Virgin* (2) by an anonymous Sienese painter of the early 15th century, in The National Gallery, London. This shows the wedding group standing on a carpet with part of a puzzling design which did not correspond to anything known and was impossible to reconstruct.

About four years ago a rug appeared on the market (and was acquired by the Metropolitan Museum of Art, New York) with a design of animals within animals which immediately made sense of the formerly inexplicable design in the painting (3). Subsequently, two other pieces with the same field design emerged (like the first apparently from Tibet), one of them being the carpet under discussion (1). This example is the largest of the three and the one with the greatest 'presence'. My first view of it, when exhibited in Hamburg in June 1993, was indeed thrilling, but I doubt whether I should have enjoyed such a response if it had not been for my awareness of the long scholarly debate as to where and by whom exactly the group was made, a debate in which I had myself played some role eighteen or so years ago.[2]

No one, I think, had ever seriously expected that after so many years – during which all the old hiding places such as European churches and houses, the floors of mosques, and the rubbish heaps of Old Cairo, had (we supposed) long since yielded up their treasures – any new example, let alone new type, would turn up. Yet here was one, and in an edition of three! To look at this rug was greatly suggestive of relationships as well as novelties. The Kufic-style border is similar to those shown not only on an animal rug in a 14th century Persian miniature, but also (though less exactly) to those on some of the so-called Seljuk carpets from the Alâeddin mosque in Konya.[3] But I need not dwell on these points, which are admirably made by Michael Franses in his account of the carpet in the catalogue.

We also have a carbon-14 dating (1190-1300 with 95% probability), and if the rug was indeed made between these dates one wonders when exactly, and by whom in that extraordinary and turbulent 13th century. This not only saw the apogee of the Seljuk state but also its overthrow by the Mongols, the ultimate break-up of central authority and the resurgence of the various Turkoman emirates, none of which appeared to stem the tide of commerce or the travels of Westerners such as Marco Polo or William of Ruysbruck. Then there is the extraordinary fact of the finding of all three of these rugs in Tibet. Pure chance or significant? We cannot be sure, but it must be said that there are also remarkable parallels in the 'Kufic' border design to such borders in certain early Mongolian rugs.[4] The last word on these animal rugs has certainly not yet been spoken.

My other choices are of rugs which have links one with another, not in their field designs but in the borders and minor details. They are also rugs which seem to me to be exceptionally beautiful, even when severely damaged. The first of these (5) shows the major part of a rug in a directional design, usually thought of as a prayer rug, called variously the 'Bellini', 'keyhole' or 're-entrant' design. A considerable number of rugs of this type appear in Italian paintings of the late 15th and early 16th centuries, for example the lovely *Madonna and Child with Saint John* by Domenico Ghirlandaio (4).

I do not want to discuss here the design as such or the group of rugs of this kind, which

LONGEVITY

5. 'Bellini', 'keyhole' or 're-entrant' rug fragment. Anatolia, 14th or 16th century. 1.62 x 1.32 m (5'4" x 4'4"). Kirchheim Collection, Stuttgart, *Orient Stars* pl.189.

receives very full treatment in the catalogue in a section by Michael Franses. It suffices to say that this particular rug is the only one of the group which carries this wide and complex border, which is also quite rare on other rugs. Otherwise the rug seems to relate most closely to a piece (**6**), now in the Turkish and Islamic Arts Museum in Istanbul, which came from the Seljuk *türbe* (mausoleum) in Konya and was perhaps made in that region.[5] Both rugs are rather different in most of their characteristics from other pieces of the Bellini group.

The broad border is, as I say, uncommon, with no obvious relations but seeming rather to have sprung, fully formed, out of nowhere. It is to be found, however, on a small rug (**7**) with the so-called 'Lotto' design, in the Turkish and Islamic Arts Museum, which might seem to relate it to this well-known 'classical' type from western Anatolia of the 16th and

8. 'Red Monolith' carpet. Anatolia, 15th century. 1.71 x 3.43m (5'7" x 11'3"). Kirchheim Collection, Stuttgart, *Orient Stars*, pl.197.

9. 'Anchor' design carpet. Anatolia, 16th century. 1.64 x 3.33m (5'5" x 10'11"). Kirchheim Collection, Stuttgart, *Orient Stars*, pl.198.

LONGEVITY

17th centuries. In fact, I think it more likely that in this case the 'Lotto' design had found its way to, and been used in, Central Anatolia.

We find the border again in my third selection from the collection (**8**), there given the soubriquet 'Red Monolith' carpet. There are so many points of similarity, other than the field design, between this carpet and the Bellini rug (**5**), that I feel they must have been made in the same locality. And here I must lament the absence of any provenance for most of the early Turkish rugs in this collection. So much potentially helpful information is denied us. Had it been known, for instance, that these two rugs had been found together in the same location, would not this have been highly suggestive (given their similarities) of their having the same origin? In addition to the main border, two other points of similarity are the triangular 'bat-wing' corner pieces around the centre medallion on both rugs, and in the corner of the outer field in the second, as well as the trailing vine minor borders. The single dependent motif in the niche of the Bellini rug, often thought of as representing a hanging lamp since it sometimes seems to be attached with a 'chain', appears twice at either end of the central medallion on the 'Monolith' rug, where presumably it can have no such implication.

And what of dating? The two rugs are dated 15th-16th century and 15th century respectively by the authors of the book, and I would tend to agree with this, at least as far as their relative ages are concerned. But objectively there is almost nothing to go on.

The same border occurs yet again on my fourth choice, the so-called 'Anchor' carpet (**9**) which, whether by pure coincidence or not, has almost exactly the same dimensions as the 'Monolith' carpet. Initially it did not appeal to me, probably because of its overall darker tonality, but I have succumbed to its grandeur. This is not enhanced by fanciful speculations in its catalogue caption, best left unread. A particular charm for me is the design of the two minor borders, which I have elsewhere given the convenience name of the 'skewed dumb-bell' design.[6] This is known only on very few surviving carpets, but is often seen on rugs in 15th and early 16th century Italian paintings (**4**). One cannot be sure whether its presence denotes such an early dating, but it is certainly a point in favour of it.

The last rug I have chosen (**10**) confronts us squarely with the problem I have touched on above: do designs develop by progressive elaboration or by simplification? Or are the elaborate and the simple versions concurrent and dependent on the weavers' milieu? The design of this rug is sometimes thought of as a variant of the Bellini type (of which symmetrical versions with two 'keyholes' are also well known) with the 'keyholes' turned through 180° instead of facing inward to form the re-entrant. It persists into modern times and is found on several types of 19th century Caucasian rugs. Undoubtedly old rugs in this design exist – there are three in the Vakıflar Museum in Istanbul which came from the mosque at Divriği (east central Anatolia)[7] – but the present example shows marked simplification in many of its elements in comparison with these. This, indeed, contributes to its charm, produced primarily by the wonderfully assured concentric placing of its three main colours, yellow, red and blue-green, enlivened by the white outlining of the motif within the three octagons.

The border is a version of one which appears, in more sophisticated form, on a small group of rugs in the 'Lotto' design but with an abnormal blue ground colour.[8] These seem to date from the early 17th century, as they are to be seen in Dutch paintings of that time, particularly those of Cornelis de Vos.[9] Another example of the border even closer to that seen here is on a 'Lotto' rug of the normal red and yellow colouring, which was found at Divriği and is now in the Vakıflar Museum.[10] This quite clumsily woven piece must have been a provincial version made, presumably, somewhere near Divriği. Friedrich Spuhler suggests tentatively that the rug under discussion could have been 'a red-ground precursor' of the so-called 'yellow-ground' carpets of the Konya region, of which the Orient Stars Collection has a large number. However this may be, it is a noble rug. Perhaps we should not fuss too much concerning its age, but the desire to know does nag. I would be inclined, from its details, to assign to it a rather later date than the 16th century to which it is ascribed in the catalogue.

I have tried to indicate some of the weak and uncertain tools at our disposal in assessing age and relationships of the unprovenanced pieces which appear, as it were, out of nowhere; survivors of a vast production now largely disappeared. It is like trying to place individual pieces into a jigsaw puzzle of which more than ninety-five per cent of the pieces are lost. We can never be sure we have placed our pieces correctly since the complete picture will never appear. But there is no reason to despair. Much can be known and certainly very much more *is* now known than was the case only twenty years ago. A logical and scientific approach to the subject, even one utilising modern scientific methods for the analysis of dyes and other materials, means that carpet studies are verging on respectability as an academic discipline even if, curiously, wild flights of fancy have burgeoned in parallel, drawing on realms of myth and imagery. I have not dwelt on this here but if these are your preferred dream playgrounds, well, no special qualifications are required and anyone can play!

Notes see Appendix

10. Left: So-called 'Bellini' carpet. Central Anatolia, 16th or 17th century. 1.49 x 2.24m (4'11" x 7'6"). Kirchheim Collection, Stuttgart, *Orient Stars*, pl.159.

TRACING THE DRAGON

The Stylistic Development of Designs in Early Chinese Textiles

By Jacqueline Simcox

While still extremely rare, early Chinese textiles have begun to appear more frequently on the international market in recent years, many emerging from centuries of storage in Tibetan monasteries. The small corpus of surviving silk embroideries, brocades and tapestries represents a mere fraction of the products of one of the most important of Chinese industries, but it nonetheless provides enough information to trace the development of particular motifs, and thus to establish a chronology of style and technique.

3. Left: *Dragons*. Silk *kesi* hanging, China, Ming dynasty, Wanli period, 1573-1619 AD. 1.75 x 2.30m (5'9" x 7'7"). This slit-tapestry hanging incorporates gold-wrapped thread for the background and peacock feathers for the central dragon. Above the dragon's head the spray of *lingxi* fungus, the *shou* character and the four swastikas form a rebus meaning 'may you live for ten thousand years', which was reserved for the use of the emperor and can be seen on textiles excavated from the tomb of Wanli. The dragons have the typical late Ming face – long snout with flowery nostrils, upstanding eyebrows, pointed mane crest and long curving horns. The large flowers with drooping leaves, and the curious central pierced rock, are also indicative of the late Ming period. Courtesy Spink & Son, London.

1. Preceding pages, left: *Long-Snouted Dragons among Flowers*. Silk *kesi* fragment from a robe, China, Song dynasty, 960-1279 AD. 0.33 x 0.54m (1'1" x 1'10"). The dragons have long curved snouts extending over the teeth, open mouths and protruding tongues, as well as tails wrapped around one hind leg, characteristic features of Song and Yuan dragons. The background leaves are not outlined in contrasting colours, as seen on (5), but their simple pointed form is typical of the period. Metropolitan Museum of Art, New York, Fletcher Fund, inv.no. 1987.275. Courtesy Lisbet Holmes, London.

The development of Chinese textile design is closely related to that of other Chinese arts such as ceramics, lacquer and enamels. Indeed, in many cases it is believed that textile designs were precursors of those in other media, partly because the finest silk costumes and hangings were made for the emperor and the aristocracy, and thus provided a strong institutionalised focus for artistic endeavour. Certainly the extravagant consumption of magnificent textiles is well documented from Han times (206 BC-220 AD) onwards.[1]

The constant influx of foreign ideas over the centuries led to the absorption of new designs into the Chinese decorative repertoire. During the Tang era (618-906) new patterns were introduced as a consequence of the country's wealth, which attracted foreigners, while the growing export trade meant that certain designs were developed for foreign markets.

Additionally, battles such as that against the Arabs, Western Turks and Tibetans in 751 (provoked by the execution of the King of Tashkent by a Chinese general), resulted in defeat for the Chinese and the capture of thousands of artisans, many of whom were taken to Samarkand. Amongst those whose skills were taken westwards were papermakers and weavers, who introduced paper to the West and Chinese silk weaving skills to the Muslim countries.[2] The reverse process took place in the 13th century when the Mongols brought Middle Eastern weavers back to the Far East after their conquest of Khorasan and Transoxiana.[3]

The quantity of silk produced in China must not be underestimated. Its importance to the economy, both for consumption at home and for trade, was immense. In the mid 8th century the annual budget of the Tang state, with a population of some fifty million, included 27 million pieces of textile, some of which some were used as currency for the purchase of grain.

4. Right: *Phoenixes in Flight.* Embroidered gauze canopy, China, Yuan dynasty, 13th/14th century. 1.35 x 1.43m (4'5" x 4'8"). This silk and gold embroidery, which echoes the design of a Yuan stone plaque at Dadu (Beijing), shows two phoenixes with different tails: one with serrated edges to the five plumes and the other with curling plumes. The leaves are naturalistically rendered and have not yet developed the exaggerated pointed and turned back forms seen in the some Yuan and Ming textiles. Metropolitan Museum of Art, New York, purchase in honour of Ambassador Walter H. Annenberg, inv.no. 1988.82.

SPINK & SON

2. Preceding pages, right: *Dragons and Phoenixes.* Silk hanging (detail), China, 13th century. 1.35 x 1.47m (4'5" x 4'10"). The confronting dragons are set within octagonal panels and the paired phoenix within cruciform panels. The dragons retain the long snout and open jaw of the Song period, but the tail is no longer wrapped round the hind leg, which still has only four claws. The triple pearl can be seen within the claw. A century later the snout shortens and the claws normally increase to five in number. The complete hanging shows just over five repeats of the dragon roundel. Courtesy Spink & Son, London.

Silk textiles were also used as a tribute to placate hostile neighbours: in the 8th century, after the Uighurs captured Loyang, the Tang rulers gave them 10,000 rolls of silk each year, with a promise to increase the tribute to 20,000 rolls. A hundred years later, in 960, the Song were paying two per cent of their revenues – an annual gift of 200,000 bales of silk – to the Liao state in the north in order to maintain peace.[4]

The body of material that survives today is therefore only a minute fraction of what was produced, but from this it is nevertheless possible to trace the development of certain styles and ornaments. Of the motifs used, the dragon is probably the most familiar, and the way in which it is interpreted changes markedly over the centuries, thereby offering an excellent guide to stylistic dating.

THE EVOLUTION OF DRAGON DESIGNS

During the Tang period the dragon is frequently depicted on bronze mirrors and other works of art in a coiled position, with open mouth, extended upturned snout, long upswept curving horns and three or four claws. The body is thin but muscular, and the most distinctive feature is the manner in which the tail is wrapped around one hind leg. This style continued into the Song (960-1279) and Yuan (1279-1368) dynasties, but died out after the end of Mongol rule in China during the late 14th century, when a new style was introduced under the Ming emperors (1368-1644). The equally distinctive feature of the elongated and upturned snout runs a parallel course, although it is still occasionally used during the Ming dynasty on Xuande (1426-1435) ceramics. On textiles this variety of dragon occurs in Northern Song *kesi* (silk slit-tapestry) fragments, where they are depicted amongst clouds on a purple silk ground (**1**), and also on Yuan embroidered or brocaded silks.

With the Ming dynasty the style of the dragon changed. In many early 15th century depictions the squared jaws have snapped shut, leaving only a couple of teeth protruding; the eyes have become circular and bulbous and the mane stands upright behind the head. The snout is still evident in a few instances, but often is shorter, with the nostrils more prominently displayed. As a result of stricter regulations restricting the use of dragon imagery to the imperial court, dragons are usually shown with five claws. The three pearls, one of the 'Eight Treasures' of Taoist belief, are evident on the sole of the foot – a feature which was only to die out during the Kangxi reign (1662-1722).

Dragons on late Ming (16th and 17th century) textiles from the reigns of Jiajing (1522-

5. *Phoenixes in Flight*.
Silk *kesi* robe fragment
(detail), China, Song
dynasty, 960-1279 AD
(Carbon-14 dated to
1014-1227 AD with 95%
probability). 0.33 x 0.56m
(1'1" x 1'10"). The birds
are seen against a back-
ground of flowers. No
attempt has been made
to show the five different
colours in the tail of the
phoenix, although the
beginning of another
phoenix can be seen, with
its curved tail feathers.
The background leaves
are typical of the Song
period, being pointed in
form and outlined in a
contrasting orange colour.
Courtesy Spink & Son,
London.

6. Right: *Phoenixes.* Emb-roidered gauze festival badge (detail), China, Ming dynasty, Wanli period, 1573-1619 AD. 24 x 25cm (10" x 10½"). Made for wear at the winter solstice festival in the eleventh month. The phoenixes are work-ed in gold thread which adds a sumptuous appear-ance to the badge. The use of the phoenix on a badge was restricted to higher-ranking imperial princesses. The symbol-ism here is particularly complex. The evergreen pine, prunus and bamboo decoration is particularly associated with the winter solstice, as is the green background of the badge. The *yang* or male princi-ple is dominant at this time of year, and as 'yang' is also the Chinese char-acter for goat, it is used here as a visual pun. This badge, together with the one for the front of the robe, shows three rams which, together with the red sun disc on which each ram sits, form a rebus, *'san yang kai tai'* (three rams heralding spring). In addition, there are nine phoenixes on the two badges. Nine was con-sidered a perfect numeral: squared it gives 81, the number of days between the winter solstice and the official start of spring. Though the flowers are subordinate to the main decoration, their use is also dictated by the mean-ing conveyed in the tex-tile. **Courtesy Chris Hall Collection Trust, Hong Kong.**

1566) and Wanli (1573-1619) echo those seen on cloisonné enamels, lacquerware and ceramics. The bulbous eyes are still present, but now with bushy, surprised-looking, upstanding eyebrows. The mouth is open and the upper jaw is elongated with prominent 'flowery' nostrils, shaped like a *ruyi*-head, the sacred fungus used, according to Chinese tradition, to make an elixir of immortality. The mane still stands behind the head, but the hair is less wildly represented and is often gathered into a point (**3**). On Chinese ceramics and other works of art it is only from the reign of Jiajing onwards that dragons are depicted face on. Before that time, they are invariably drawn in profile or three-quarter view. This rule also seems to hold true for textiles, although the available body of Ming textiles is not as extensive as that of ceramics, and, as noted above, innovative designs were often seen on textiles somewhat earlier than on ceramics.

The dragon is most usually represented in gold-wrapped thread – a process which is as time-consuming as that needed to produce silk. The use of gilded paper (or leather), either wrapped around a silk core, or woven flat into a textile, has remained consistently popular throughout China's history from Tang times onwards. Its popularity reached a peak during the Yuan period, when the Mongols were reputed to love the richness of gold cloth, and again in the late Ming dynasty when the demand for gold for weaving increased dramatically. This was associated with a shortage of silk, caused by declining cultivation of mulberry trees dur-ing a period of turmoil in the country.

Even gold thread shows technical changes over the centuries. Between the 10th and 14th centuries some weaving centres used gilded leather or gut rather than gilded paper – espe-cially in western and northern China during the Liao (907-1125) and Jin (1115-1234) dynas-ties – a shift reflecting the nationality and weaving tradition of the craftsmen active in those centres. During the Ming dynasty, paper was the normal base for gold, and at this time a red layer is seen between the gold and the paper, which gives it an added richness and depth of colour. In the following Qing period (1644-1912) the red base is discarded and the gilded paper itself becomes thinner and less tightly woven. Finally, in the 19th century, gilded wire is introduced and used alongside paper.

Occasionally on early silks both sides of the paper were gilded,[5] but this was a rare feature and wasteful of gold. An interesting use of gold is seen on a pair of silk boots in Cleveland,

SPINK & SON

7. Left: *Buddhist Lion*. Silk *kesi* military rank badge, China, Ming dynasty, 15th/16th century. 25cm (10") square. The large lion has the bushy tail and mane and the large eyes of the early to mid-Ming dynasty. The background of swirling clouds and the peony flowers with drooping leaves are all indicators of date. Qing dynasty badges are small in overall size and the size of the animal is considerably reduced. Private collection.

reputed to have come from a Liao or Jin tomb. Their uppers consist of a woven brocade with a charming design of large confronting ducks with a vase of flowers between them. The legs of the boots are of a finely woven *kesi* with a gold pattern woven into it. The gold leaf has been pressed onto the warps and clings round each warp. Given the extremely fine quality of the *kesi* weave it is astonishing that the gold was not attached to a paper or leather base.[6]

BIRD IMAGERY

Bird images were commonly used to decorate textiles. The pairing of birds was particularly favoured for symmetrical designs: confronting birds were popularly used in the Middle East and at the same time on Tang and Song textiles in China. Later they were paired in flight in circular formation, and in the Ming period were shown either in this form or individually. On Song *kesi* panels individual birds are seen grasping foliage in their beaks, clearly following the traditional Tang ceramic designs of previous centuries. Generally birds are rendered in a naturalistic way. The influence of paintings on the Southern Song (1127-1279) and Yuan tapestry weavers, who faithfully copied their pictures, is seen to full effect in the various superb *kesi* of birds in the National Palace Museum, Taiwan, and naturalism was the hallmark of succeeding centuries.

It is only with the mythical bird, the phoenix, that textile designers could allow their imaginations free reign. A commentary to the *Spring and Autumn Annals* in the 4th century BC mentions that the male phoenix, along with the 'five magic beings', signifies the rule of a just king in the land. The phoenix was considered the ruler of all feathered creatures and only later came to represent the empress, as the dragon represented the emperor. In Tang times the paired phoenixes are depicted as identical birds, but in the Yuan era they develop individual tails: one with five serrated-edged streamers with colours corresponding to the five colours; the other with long curling feathers which frequently resemble those of a peacock. Thus the types of the male and female bird become fully established. An embroidered purple gauze canopy (4) in the Metropolitan Museum, New York (its design echoing a stone relief at Dadu, Beijing, site of the Yuan capital), clearly shows the new style.[7]

The popularity of phoenix imagery increased greatly during the Ming dynasty, especially throughout the 16th and 17th centuries, when the birds are frequently seen paired in flight

8. Left: *Birds in Flight*. **Silk brocade fragment, China, late Tang (?) dynasty (Carbon-14 dated with 95% probability to 711-983 AD). Height 20cm (8"). The repeat pattern shows a pair of birds in flight around a complex floral medallion, as well as rounded clouds with long pointed ends. The cloud forms become more rounded in later centuries. This textile is of the same design as an incomplete robe in The Cleveland Museum of Art, which is reputed to have come from a Liao or Jin tomb. Courtesy Spink & Son, London.**

9. Silk damask (detail), China, Yuan dynasty, first half 14th century. Height 1.65m (5'5"). The decorative ground of the 'Eagle' dalmatic in the Vienna Treasury shows rounded clouds in the shape of *ruyi* (fungus) heads joined together with long wisps of cloud. The robe may have been used in 1338 by Ludwig of Bavaria when he met Edward III of England. Hofburg Schatzkammer, Vienna. inv.no. XIII.X.III.15.

among large flowers, with rocks beneath and large clouds above. The designs can be found on large wall hangings, perhaps made as wedding gifts, where the paired phoenixes (representing the *yin-yang* duality present in every human), symbolise the lover, and the peony flowers the beloved. Other flowers used on these large tapestries include the lotus, chrysanthemum and plum blossom, emblematic not only of the four seasons but of wealth, distinction, purity and other virtues (**6**).

OTHER CREATURES

Other mythical creatures show similarities to Ming dragons and the phoenixes. The Buddhist lion, used for the second grade military rank badge during the Ming era, has the same protuberant eyes of the early Ming dragon and also has a boldly worked bushy mane and tail (**7**). Later in the dynasty this animal appears less awesome, and by the Qing period is merely a charming friendly beast. Similar characteristics are seen on the *xiazhai* – the mythical beast with a white coat, striped chest and single horn, used for the censor's badge. This animal did not harm virtuous men, but could smell immorality and would tear the offender apart.

In late Ming times, during the reigns of Chengde (1506-1521) and Wanli (1573-1619) other creatures appeared on rank badges. The order of the python and of the flying fish were both within the personal gift of the emperor and elevated the wearer above all civil and military ranks. In the 16th century these awards were restricted to a few officials, military officers and chief eunuchs. No examples of these badges appear to be known (though I have seen a late Ming ancestor portrait with a rank badge showing a fish emerging from water) but they would certainly share the characteristics of other Ming badges.[9] Birds were also used on badges, and like the phoenixes were usually shown in pairs, although the postures become more naturalistic toward the end of the dynasty.

NATURAL ORNAMENT

In conjunction with the main decorative elements, the background ornamentation of a composition often provides additional clear evidence of stylistic developments which help to place a textile within a given century or reign.

The characteristic cloud formations on Tang textiles, as on Tang ceramics, show rounded

SPINK & SON

10. *Boys and Lotus Blossoms*. Silk brocade fragment (detail), China, Song dynasty, 960-1279 AD (Carbon-14 dated to 1018-1226 AD with 95% probability). 21.5 x 20cm (8¹/₂" x 8"). The design shows small boys wearing bibs and holding the stems of lotus flowers. The style of the boys seen here hardly alters over a millennium, but the leaves show the typical pointed arrow-head form and outlining in a contrasting colour which was so popular in the Song period. Private collection.

clouds with one side elongated to a point, as though a strong wind is driving them across the sky (**8**), whereas in the 14th century, clouds are frequently used as a background motif (**9**) on which other designs can be overlaid: thus they are rounded or elongated to form repeat pattern backgrounds. Where individual clouds are required, the elongated points are abandoned in favour of clouds that are rounded and massed on top of each other.

This contrasts with early and mid Ming examples where a central formation of four distinct rounded lobes is bordered by four wisps of cloud – giving the appearance of a catherine wheel with exterior spokes. A few late Ming hangings show soft clouds draped over horizontal bars of clouds, as if they were about to melt, but this style does not continue into the Qing period.

The Tang era practice of decorating Chinese Buddhist cave temples with figures and leaf scrolls was an inheritance from provincial Hellenistic architecture in Central Asia. This type of decoration, together with the acanthus leaves, vines and designs of small boys holding lotus flowers and stems, passed into textile design. The rendition of small boys (**10**) wearing decorative bibs, or baggy trousers with jackets, hardly varies from the Tang era to the 19th century, but the associated leaves and flowers show great changes.

On Northern Song *kesi* and some Song brocades the leaves are shaped like pointed arrow heads, woven in very simple forms, and have an edging of a contrasting colour to emphasise the pattern. However, during the same era, leaves copied from paintings onto textiles show great attention to natural forms. Leaves of the 13th to 15th centuries become more elaborate and have exaggerated points with the body of the leaf widening and curving in a rounded form to make a double lobe before it joins the leaf stem. The stems themselves are usually drawn to encircle a flower which grows from the same stem, and where the stems touch a bud conceals the join. Thus a pattern of flower stems and leaves gives the appearance of linked circles with central flowerheads (**11**). From the late 15th century onwards this feature changes, the stems take on an individual life of their own, and the circular pattern motif is discarded in favour of naturalism.

From the 15th century to the late Ming period, leaves are large, naturalistic and slightly down-turned, as if too heavy for their stalks, although in these textile designs the leaves are subordinate to the flowers. In general, the relative size of the flowers increased during Ming times. This is particularly apparent on some 15th and 16th century rank badges, where large flowers form the background to bird or animal motifs, and on the large bed and wall hangings from the late Ming era, where flowers become a major part of the ornamentation.

A wide variety of different flowers is used on textiles. For dramatic effect the peony is favoured, its petals worked in silk shading from rich pinkish-red to white. The lotus blossom, which is especially associated with Buddhism and is an emblem of purity, is not confined solely to religious textiles, but is used in conjunction with other flowers on textiles intended

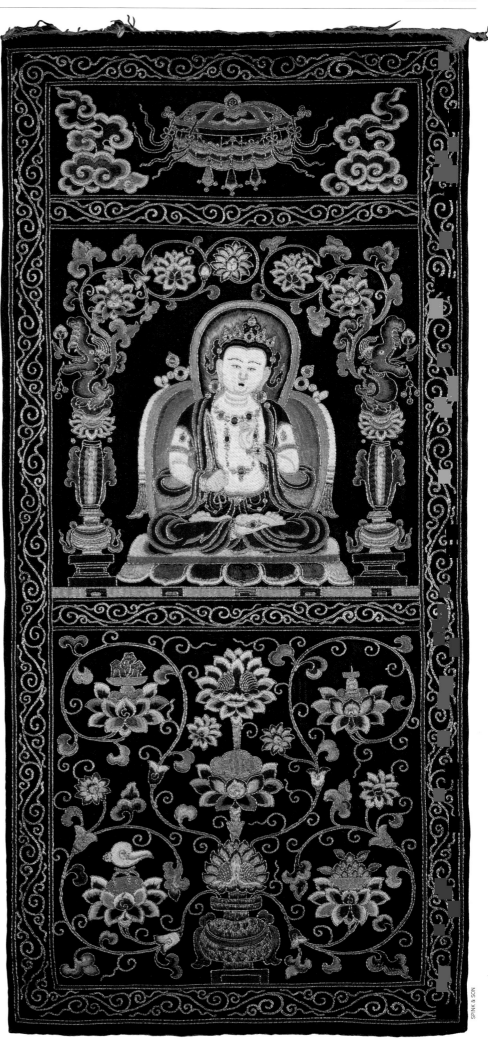

11. *Manjusri*. Silk embroidered votive hanging, China, Yuan dynasty, 13th/14th century. 19.4 x 44cm (7¹/₂" x 1'5"). The leaves and flower stems show the characteristic rounded and turned back leaves associated with the Yuan and early Ming periods, while the stems encircling the lotus blossoms are joined by flower buds, also a feature of this period. The back of the hanging is inscribed 'The Tenth Bodhisattva'. The Indianapolis Museum of Art, Martha Delzell Fund, inv.no. 1992.66.

SPINK & SON

13. Right: *Vighnantaka.* Silk *kesi* thanka, Xi Xia Kingdom, Kara Khoto, eastern Central Asia, before 1227 AD. 0.74 x 1.05m (2'5" x 3'5"). This thanka, of silk slit-tapestry with pearls, depicts the Buddhist guardian figure surrounded by his retinue, with the Hindu gods Shiva and Ganesha beneath his feet. It is related to the Hermitage Museum's *Green Tara* (14), and shows the influence of the arts of the Tangut kingdom combining the designs of the Tibetan Khampa style with that of Kara Khoto. Note the leaves above the five Dhyani Buddhas, which are also seen in the *kesi* weaving *Immortals in a Mountain Palace*, and the curving flower stems at the top and bottom, which were to be much simplified by the 14th and 15th centuries. Cleveland Museum of Art, J.H. Wade Fund, inv.no. 92.72.

12. Left: *Manchurian Crane, Pheasant and other Small Birds in Flight.* Silk *kesi* fragment from a large wall hanging (detail). China, Ming dynasty, 17th century. 0.68 x 1.20m (2'3" x 3'11"). The rocks are dramatic and bizarre and show the strong contrast of exotic pattern-making with the naturalism of the birds and the peony, prunus, magnolia and peach blossoms. Courtesy the Neutrogena Corporation, Los Angeles.

for domestic use. More delicate flowers, such as the narcissus, often appear in textiles with restrained designs, for instance on small album leaves, which have a more delicate composition in the style of paintings. These textiles, mounted as pictures, are to be found in the collections of various museums. They survived more readily than other textiles because they were rolled and stored or shut inside their albums and thus protected from light. The decorative use of flowers was not confined to the Ming period, but continued in the following Qing dynasty and into Chinese textiles of the 20th century.

While clouds fill the backgrounds of textiles, and leaves and flowers the middle range, the lower part is usually decorated with water and rocks. Water is normally depicted as rounded, rolling waves with a few splashes. In contrast, the rocks are more dominant, rising boldly from the water. Some are divided to form a group of three with a tall central summit and lower peaks on either side, symbolising Mount Meru, the Taoist sacred mountain. These rocks are characteristically seen forming the lower borders of Ming and Qing dynasty robes. Depending on the requirements of the design, other rocks merely form the base from which trees or flowers grow, or provide a perch for a bird. Early Ming rocks are more concave in form than later examples, where their outlines become rounded and convex. On some late Ming textiles the rocks themselves take on a dramatic 'modernist' appearance. Pierced with holes and rendered in different colours, they produce a strange geometric pattern in an otherwise naturalistic design (**12**).

JOHN BIGELOW TAYLOR

14. *Green Tara.* Silk *kesi* thanka, Kara Khoto, eastern Central Asia, before 1227 AD. 0.52 x 1.01m (1'8¹/₂" x 3'4"). The *Green Tara* is shown with the five transcendent (*Dhyani*) Buddhas above and the *Yellow Marichi* (the goddess of the dawn) and the *Blue Ekajata* below. The central figure is elegantly woven with great naturalism, while the edges of the thanka are more formalised and simple. The staves at either side of the central figure are indicative of Pala influence. The leaves on the palm trees are also seen on the Cleveland Museum's *Vighnantaka* thanka (13). As with the Cleveland piece, this tapestry exhibits a fusion of styles. It was excavated from a ruined stupa at Kara Khoto and brought to Russia by Colonel Kozlov. Hermitage Museum, St. Petersburg.

15. *Immortals in a Mountain Palace*. Silk *kesi* album leaf, China, Song dynasty, 960-1279 AD. 36 x 28cm (1'2½" x 11"). This superb album leaf shows the style of clouds with pointed ends more prevalent during the Tang dynasty (686-906 AD). The leaves on the trees and the decoration on the pavilion roof are similar to leaves on the *kesi* thankas (13, 14) with their small regular forms outlined in a contrasting colour. The bold concave rocks also bear close similarities to the staves in the same thankas. National Palace Museum, Taiwan.

RELIGIOUS THEMES

Buddhism was the source of several other themes which came to China. The Pala style of Indian art can be seen in the painted Tibetan thankas of the 11th to 13th centuries.[9] In particular a 12th century thanka in the Gilmore Ford collection shows an elegant and sophisticated central figure with deities to the sides and a background of rocks which look like pointed fences or staves. Where leaves are shown they are small and pointed and often attached to palm trees. This same design can be seen in the famous *kesi* thanka of the *Green Tara* in the Hermitage, St Petersburg (**14**), which was discovered at Kara Khoto and must predate the Mongol destruction of the city in 1227. The splendid silk slit-tapestry and pearl depiction of the Buddhist guardian figure *Vighnantaka* (**13**), now in Cleveland, also came from Kara Khoto. Heather Karmay believes that this Pala style may have spread through the Kagyupa order in Tibet from Lhasa and other centres to Kara Khoto. It is also seen at Dunhuang during the reign of Kublai Khan in the 13th century.

The same rendition of leaves is seen in the *kesi* thanka of *Pamadunyuezhuba* in the Potala Palace, Lhasa. Dated to the Southern Song period, and with a Sanskrit and Tibetan language script, it bears tantalising inscriptions saying that it was "done by Jiangzunzhuicha, who sent it to his priest Zhabajianzan" and that it was "made to order in the hinterland of China during the late Southern Song dynasty" (1127-1368).

Identical leaf groupings appear in the *kesi* picture of *Immortals in a Mountain Palace* now in the National Palace Museum, Taiwan (**15**). This is the last page from *Genuine Works of Famous Paintings* and its content is similar to a painting collected in the book entitled *Lu Hui Ji Jin*. Attributed to Shen Tzu-fan, this tapestry also has pointed clouds more reminiscent of the Tang clouds described above. The close similarities of these *kesi* pieces lead one to the conclusion that there was a professional weaving centre working not only for religious commissions, but also for the aristocracy and the court. Obviously religious textiles would take their designs from religious paintings, but some decorative elements would pass into other types of commissions and so into the general repertory of fabric designs that were handed down in the weaving and embroidery tradition and adapted to suit the demands of a discerning population.

From the small body of early Chinese textiles that still survive, it is possible to trace the development of many varieties of ornamentation over the centuries. This helps to establish a relative chronology, and the examples illustrated here provide us with some helpful pointers towards a more comprehensive study. Additionally, the translation of various Chinese texts has given us greater insights into the emphasis on certain ornamentation in different periods, and has not only increased our awareness of the various combinations of decorative elements, but also of the meaning behind them.

Notes see Appendix

IDENTIFYING WITH THE GODS

By Frances Franklin & Deborah Swallow

The Indian Department of the Victoria & Albert Museum in London holds a well-documented group of richly decorated formal court costumes and simple everyday textiles from Burma which were acquired during the 19th and early 20th centuries. With reference to contemporaneous Burmese books and paintings, as well as to the accounts written by British soldiers, diplomats, traders, missionaries and travellers who visited the Burmese court during the last century, it is possible to reconstruct with a high degree of accuracy the costume conventions that applied both at the royal court in Mandalay and in all strata of 18th and 19th century Burmese society.

1. Preceding pages, left: The robe of state formerly worn by one of the chief queens of King Mindon: a green velvet *du-yin thindaing* (short fitted jacket) with bell-shaped sleeves, finished in a double row of tail pieces, lined with pink silk satin; a green velvet *dwadaya* (bandolette) terminating in flamboyant tailpieces of green velvet; a collar or belt of green velvet; a *sulyar* (long shawl) with attached 'fish-tail' pieces of green velvet formed by stretching the embroidered fabric onto a shaped bamboo frame; a highly elaborate "cover for the front"; a cloud collar, wings and three overlapping winging panels hanging from waist to hem, in embroidered green velvet fabric stretched on to shaped bamboo frames. Victoria & Albert Museum, London, inv.nos. IM 45 to E-1912.

2. Preceding pages, right: The Burmese *Kinwun Mingyi* (Prime Minister) proceeding to a meeting with the British near Prome on 2 October 1825. Watercolour attributed to T.A. Trant. India Office Library, London, inv.no. WD 4167.

3. Left: The three elements of a Burmese woman's dress, as worn – the lower garment *(hta-mein)*, the breast cloth *(tabet)* and the jacket *(ein-gyi)*. Victoria & Albert Museum, London, inv.nos. 9756 (IS), IM 10-1909, 5623 (IS).

4. Right: Detail of a breast cloth *(tabet)* of *acheik-luntaya* from Mandalay Palace. Victoria & Albert Museum, London, inv.no. IM 8-1909.

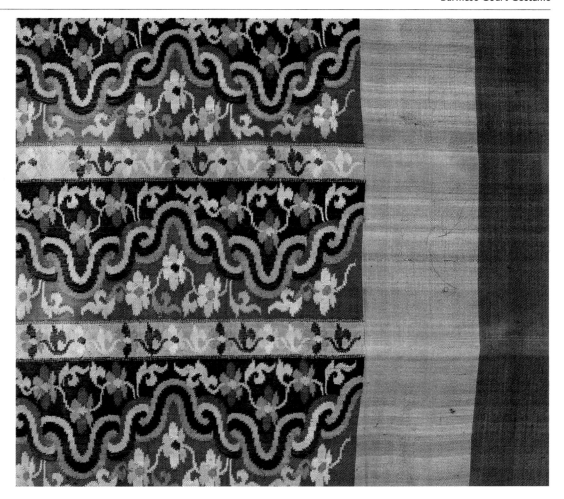

I ts first appearance was splendid; it seemed like a moving mass of gold; which, by reflecting the rays of the sun, prevented us at first from distinctly seeing of what it was composed; but as it slowly advanced, we gradually could perceive, under a canopy of gilt umbrellas...two figures dressed in the most gorgeous and extraordinary manner: they were covered with golden ornaments and embroidery, and behind them were fourteen others habited in a similar mode...there was something so unexpected in the sudden appearance of this brilliant procession in the midst of these wilds, that...my mind involuntarily recurred to those tales of fiction related of the East, and I could almost have fancied myself an inhabitant of Faery-land..."[1]

Major Trant, witnessing the peace negotiations between the British, represented by Sir Archibald Campbell, and the Burmese, represented by a delegation of King Bagyidaw's ministers, at Nyannbinzeik near Prome in October 1825, was not alone in his wonder at the magnificence of Burmese ministerial deputations and royal appearances. A year later, John Crawfurd, leading a commercial mission to Bagyidaw's (r.1819-1837) capital at Ava, was impressed by the pomp and circumstance of the court, by the brilliance and richness of the palace and by the costumes of the King and Queen.[2]

Later still, Captain Henry Yule, accompanying Major Arthur Phayre, the Governor General of India's envoy, on his embassy to Amarapura in 1855, records the appearance of King Mindon (r.1853-1878).[3] The accuracy of the descriptions of 19th century emissaries can be tested against both contemporary court paintings and actual examples of royal dress that survive in the national collection in Burma and in other public collections. Although everyday garments of the court and the people were similar in overall appearance, varying only in the degree of costliness of the fabric, elaborate sumptuary laws regulated official court dress and the textiles that could be used with it. Overseeing the royal wardrobe and protocol was a key part of the work of the *akyok-won* (court chamberlain), and appropriate forms of dress were recorded in court *parabaiks* (folding books).

Women's everyday dress consisted of three main elements (**3**). The *hta-mein*, a wraparound skirt, was a long rectangle of cotton or silk cloth constructed from three panels, lined in a lightweight Indian cotton. The *hta-mein* overlapped slightly in the front, revealing a portion of the woman's leg as she walked. The top panel, made from a soft, dark-coloured piece of cotton or velvet, provided a band which was either tucked in at the waist or over the bosom. The central panel was the focus of decorative interest and was woven in cotton or silk

5. Above: Detail of a lower garment *(hta-mein)* of *acheik-luntaya*. Victoria & Albert Museum, London, inv.no. 9757 (IS).

6. Left: A long sleeved, front opening, man's jacket (*ein-gyi*) and a handwoven red cotton man's lower garment (*pah-soe*) embroidered with yellow floss silk. Victoria & Albert Museum, London, inv.nos. IM 43B-1912, IM 43A-1912.

8. Right: A man's turban (*gaung-baung*) of fine white muslin. Victoria & Albert Museum, London, inv.no. IM 43C-1912.

7. Right: Detail of a man's lower garment (*pah-soe*) of *acheik-luntaya* weave, described as coming "from the Royal loom in King Theebaw's Palace at Mandalay....". Victoria & Albert Museum, London, inv.no. IS 2-1888.

in a variety of patterns including the intricate *acheik-luntaya* weave discussed below (**4, 7**). The bottom section consisted of two lengths of silk or cotton, hand-sewn together along their weft edges, the upper part typically being patterned into horizontal stripes. Observers differ in their views, but judging from photographs of the period the mode of wearing the *hta-mein* was determined by the activity and probably the class of the wearer.[4] For the working day it was shortened by wrapping it over the bosom. For special occasions it was brought down to the waist creating a train with the lower section, "and its graceful management, in either walking or dancing, is one of the accomplishments of a Burmese belle".[5] The *hta-mein* was worn with a long breast cloth *(tabet)* and the ensemble was completed with a tight-fitting jacket *(ein-gyi)* of quilted cotton, lace or muslin, and open red sandals.[6] Flowers and jewels decorated a woman's hair which was dressed with perfumed coconut oil and twisted into a cylindrical coil on the top of her head.[7]

The man's lower garment *(pah-soe)* was made from a woven cloth of about 50cm (20") wide and 660cm (260") long, which was generally checked or striped, sometimes with elaborate patterns.[8] The method of wrapping the cloth could be varied. For formal wear it was wrapped around the waist to form a sarong reaching to the ankles, with a large piece of spare cloth draped in folds down the front. For work and exercise the spare cloth would be passed through the legs and tucked into the waist at the back to form breeches. With this was also worn an *ein-gyi* (jacket) of muslin or quilted cotton (**9**). Elders or richer persons wore the *pah-soe* with a long white jacket open in front and reaching to the knees (**6**) when they paid a formal visit or went to a pagoda or monastery.[9] Men wore their straight black hair long, tied in a knot on one side. A strip of silk or muslin (**8**) wound round the head *(gaung-baung)*, completed the costume. Foot-gear was a luxury at the end of the 19th century. In houses and boats people went barefoot. On rough or thorny ground slip-on sandals or Indian type wooden pattens would be worn. The soles and thongs of the common sandal were fashioned from buffalo hide and woollen cloth.

These items of dress were worn by all classes of society. At an informal meeting with Arthur Phayre in 1855, King Mindon reclined on a sofa dressed in "the ordinary garb of the country, a silk putsho [*sic*], or waist-cloth of gay colours, a white cotton jacket reaching a little below the hips, and a single fillet of book-muslin round his head".[10] In 1879 King Thibaw, Mindon's son (r.1878-1885), was seen wearing a "white short coat and a plain check pattern, yellow silk *pah-soe* such as any ordinary townsman might wear".[11]

9. Left: The elements of man's dress, as worn, the lower garment (pah-soe) and the jacket (ein-gyi). Victoria & Albert Museum, London, inv.nos. 0798 (IS), 5631 (IS).

11. Right: A hat (mauk-yu), fashioned like a head-band fitted with ear- and neck- pieces of green and crimson velvet, decorated with silver gilt sequinned embroidery, was worn under a gilt cardboard hat/helmet. Victoria & Albert Museum, London, inv.no. IM 44E-1912.

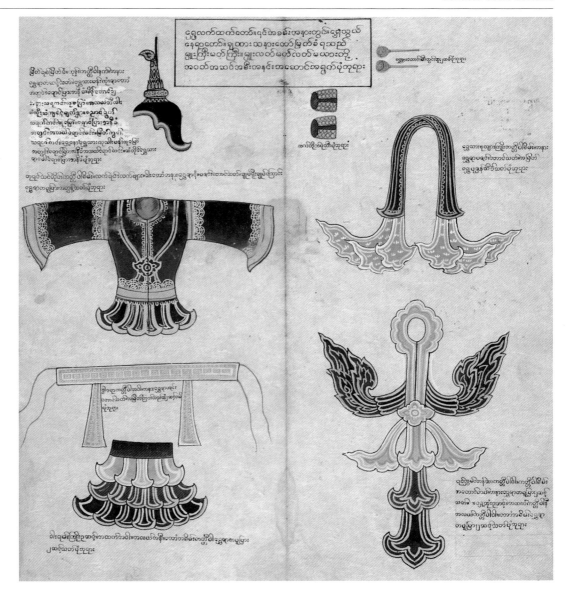

10. Right: A double page from a court *parabaik* (folding book) sets out the lavishly ornamented dress and articles worn by the wife of a Governor of Legaing at the ceremony of a wedding in 1888 at the West Palace at King Thibaw's court at Mandalay.
Victoria & Albert Museum, London, inv.no. IM 320-1924; pp. 47 & 48.

The most prized of the textiles used for ceremonial or 'dress' *hta-mein* and *pah-soe*, however, was a silk cloth in interlocking tapestry weave in which patterns of many colours were woven into the warp with 100-200 small shuttles. The cloth was known as luntaya, the '100 spool' design, or *acheik*, referring to its horizontal weft pattern.[12]

The history of the development of the *acheik* design and *luntaya* cloth is both fascinating and controversial. It has frequently been claimed that *acheik-luntaya* cloth manufacture was introduced to Burma by Manipuri weavers in the second half of the 18th century. Yule's account of Phayre's mission to the court at Ava in 1855, possibly the source of this belief, describes the Manipuri community in Mandalay and confirms that they were responsible for *acheik-luntaya* production.[13] A recent pamphlet published in Rangoon suggests that the *acheik* patterns were originally created by appliqué work, and that subsequently the Manipuri weavers introduced a means of weaving these patterns.[14] Yule's account does not, however, suggest that the Manipuris brought the weave or pattern with them, and nowhere does the literature on Manipur indicate a cloth tradition of this kind within Manipur.[15]

In fact the *acheik* (S-shaped hooking or interlocking) pattern pre-dates both the Burmese and Manipuri traditions of the 18th century, and must be a survival and development of designs evolved hundreds of years earlier as part of a common Chinese and Southeast Asian heritage. Running wave patterns are found on the pottery and jewellery excavated at Ban Chiang in northeast Thailand (ca. 1600 BC -400 AD), and excavations of tombs of the Han dynasty at Niya in China (206 BC-220 AD) have produced textiles with vertical rows of cloud-scroll patterns similar to the later Burmese weft patterns.[16] Moving on in time, an 8th century Yunnanese bronze Avalokitesvara, in the Musée Guimet in Paris, has a pedestal decorated with a pattern similar to those found on Burmese *acheik-luntaya*.

Certainly the striped pattern of several wrap-around skirts painted at the Taungbi Monastic Library, Pagan, in 1704 under the patronage of King Sane[17] may be evidence of the

acheik-luntaya silk cloth being in production as early as the turn of the 18th century.[18] By the late 18th century there is more visual evidence. Wall paintings from the Upali Thein and Ananda monasteries at Pagan show ladies wearing long skirts of a pattern of broken stripes of wavy lines. Paintings in the Kamma Kyaung-U Pagoda, Pagan (attributed to the 1790s), show Prince Siddhartha in a *pah-soe*, apparently made of the *acheik-luntaya* weave.[19]

The earliest extant examples of *acheik-luntaya* weave date to the first half of the 19th century, by which time Amarapura was the main centre for *acheik-luntaya* weaving, and production was dominated by Manipuri weavers who were described as excelling in the work. The real history of the introduction of the design and technique is still to be solved, but the origins of this particular tapestry weave are most likely to be found in the Chinese tradition.[20]

In the 19th century strict sumptuary rules pertained to the use of *acheik-luntaya*. The best of this cloth and particularly certain patterns were restricted to the use of the royal family (**4**, **7**). Green and red were reserved for royal *luntaya*, and pink specifically for royal ladies. *Luntaya* of other colours were permitted to ministers and wealthy Burmese, but the weaving would be of an inferior quality.[21] The rules pertaining to *acheik-luntaya* cloth

12. Above: A robe of state (*watlum*), possibly King Thibaw's, embroidered with spangles and beetles' wings and bejewelled with diamonds, rubies and emeralds. An item from the Mandalay regalia deposited with the Victoria & Albert Museum for safe keeping in 1890 and returned to Burma in 1964. Photograph courtesy the trustees of the Victoria & Albert Museum, London.

13. Right: Double page of a court folding book (*parabaik*) showing civil and military court dress and accoutrements awarded to Maha Minhtin Sithu, Governor of Sagu and Lord Chamberlain to King Thibaw. There was no distinction between civil and military services in Burma. Treasurers and judges were expected to take command of armies. The army comprised the whole adult male population and, when necessary, levies were made of the whole population, and civil officials became generals (see A. Fytche, *Burma Past and Present*, p.245). Victoria & Albert Museum, London, inv.no. IM 320-1924; pages 1 & 2).

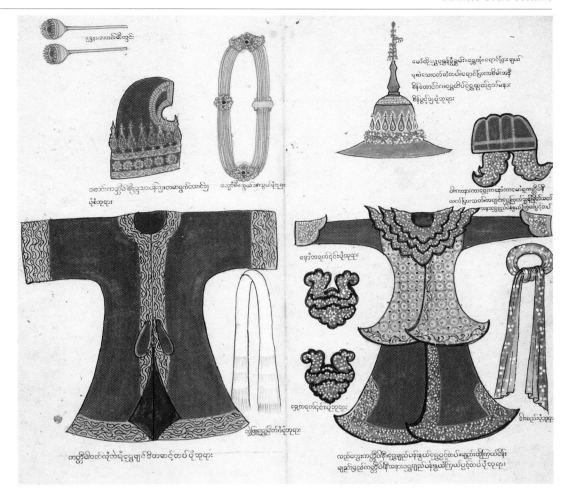

14. Above: A black velvet headdress decorated with tinsel and surmounted by a gilt openwork finial, identical to the type worn by senior ladies at the court. Victoria & Albert Museum, London, inv.no. IPN 2633.

were part of a more elaborate set of sumptuary laws relating to costume at the court of the Konbaung kings.

Sumptuary laws were common throughout Southeast Asia, and the court of the Konbaung kings was no exception. Almost every article of use and ornament, particularly dress, indicated the rank of a person at the court, and there were grave penalties for "him that assumes the insignia of a degree which is not his legitimate right".[22] Court manuals documented and prescribed the appropriate dress and ornament of different ranks for particular ceremonies. For example, the consecration ceremonies for the various stages of building the nine throne rooms of Bodawpaya's new palace at Amarapura had to be attended by princes and ministers of state in their *bon watlum* (court robes) which defined the rank they had been awarded by the king.[23]

It was in the Great Audience Hall of the Palace, which held the Lion Throne (*sinhasana*), that the greatest and most solemn ceremonies were regularly performed. In the west room of the *baungdaw-zaung* (Royal Crown Room) behind a partition, the King vested himself in his state court dress and ornaments and put on his crown, before proceeding to the Audience Hall. It was there that King Thibaw and his Chief Queen, seated on the Lion Throne, received all the presents brought them on the occasion of their coronation, which were piled on the floor before them. Three great ceremonies, called *kadaw* (paying homage), were held annually, when the oath of fealty to the king was taken. Princes, ministers and officials of the city had to attend the first at the beginning of the Burmese New Year (April) and the second at the beginning of the Buddhist Lent (about June or July). Governors of the provinces of the empire and tributary Shan chiefs also had to attend the third ceremony at the end of the Buddhist Lent (October).[24]

The King's court dress on such occasions was extremely elaborate (**12**). King Bodawpaya (r.1782-1819) "bore the appearance of a man, cased in golden armour, whilst a gilded, or probably a golden wing on each shoulder did not add much lightness to his figure. His crown was a high conical cap, richly studded with precious stones" (**18**).[25] In 1826 the king mounted the steps to the throne with difficulty, "as if tottering under the load of dress and ornaments. His dress consisted of a tunic of gold tissue, ornamented with jewels. The crown was a helmet with a high peak, in form not unlike the spire of a Burman Pagoda, which it was probably intended to resemble."[26]

Yule, in 1855, was equally transfixed by King Mindon's "sort of long tunic or surcoat, of a light-coloured silk apparently, but so thickly set with jewels that the fundamental material

15. Left: The court dress of the *Kin Wun Mingyi* (Chief Minister) who served both King Mindon and King Thibaw in the period ca. 1850-1880 consists of a *watlum* (long robe) of crimson velvet lined with apricot silk with a deep border of gold brocade. It is worn with a *pah-soe* embroidered with yellow floss silk on a red cotton ground. Victoria & Albert Museum, London, inv.nos. IM 43-1912, IM 43A-1912.

18. Right: Royal Head-dress which possibly belonged to King Thibaw, of thin gold open-work, ornamented with beetle-wings and pearls. An item from the Mandalay Regalia which was deposited with the Victoria & Albert Museum for safe keeping in 1890 and returned to Burma in 1964. Photograph courtesy the Trustees of the Victoria & Albert Museum, London.

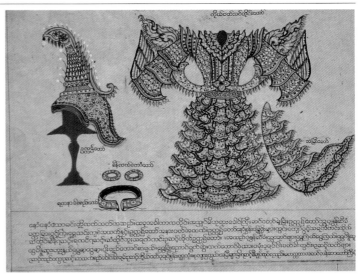

16. A *malika* costume permitted to the king,
from *Designs of things in daily use in the Golden Palace*,
a court *parabaik*, Mandalay ca. 1880.
India Office Library, London, Burmese Ms. 199.

17. A *mahatlata* costume for a chief queen,
from *Designs of things in daily use in the Golden Palace*,
a court *parabaik*, Mandalay ca. 1880.
India Office Library, London, Burmese Ms. 199.

was scarcely discernible...His cap or crown *(thara-poo)* was a round tiara of similar material, in shape like an Indian morion, rising to a peak crowned with a spire-like ornament several inches high, and having flaps or wings rising over each ear. Over the forehead was a gold plate or frontlet."[27]

He was less impressed by the queen's appearance: "The Queen was not seen to such advantage. This was partly owing to the character of her headdress, which would have been a very trying one to any lady. It was a perfectly close cap, covering ears and hair entirely, and rising above into a conical crest strangely resembling in form a rhinoceros horn, or the large nipper of a crab's claw, with the point curved forward into a volute. Close lappets fell along the cheeks. The rest of her Majesty's dress had rather an Elizabethan character. The sleeves and skirt appeared to be formed in successive overlapping scolloped lappets, and the throat was surrounded by a high collar, also scolloped or vandyked, and descending to the waist. At the waist she wore a stomacher or breast-plate of large gems. Both cap and robe (**1, 14**) were covered and stiffened with diamonds, or what appeared to be such".[28]

Provincial ministers and their wives, when attending a court function, wore the ceremonial costumes and paraphernalia of their rank (**10**). The costume of the ministers and courtiers consistently drew comment from Western dignitaries: "It consists of a long robe either of flowered satin or velvet, reaching to the ankles, with an open collar and loose sleeves; over this there is a scarf or flowing mantle, that hangs from the shoulders, and on their heads they wear high caps made of velvet, either plain, or of silk embroidered with flowers of gold, according to the rank of the wearer" (**15, 22**).[29]

Symes's account is confirmed by Yule, who includes a description of the ministers *(woongyis)* sent to escort the English visitors from their residence in Amarapura to the Palace in 1855: "They were all in their court robes, and were so disguised thereby that at first I recognised none of the party. The head-dress is very outré, consisting of a sort of high mitre of crimson velvet, curving back into a volute and encircled at the base with a coronet of tinsel spear-heads. The robe is a heavy, wide-sleeved mantle of crimson velvet, laced with a broad edging of Benares brocade. It seems to be 'ton' to wear the mitre excessively tight on the head, and some of the officials carried a little ivory implement like a paper-knife, which was used (after the fashion of a shoe-horn) for drawing on the cap and for packing away recusant locks of hair. The *tsalwe*,[30] with its cords in number according to the dignity conferred on the wearer, and a trumpet-shaped ear-tube of gold, four or five inches in length, are also essential features in the court costume." (**11, 19**)[31]

King Thibaw (r.1875-85) had manuscripts *(parabaiks)*[32] in his library illustrating and describing in minute detail the costumes and paraphernalia allowed for the members of his court and for those of the provincial governors. From the Victoria & Albert Museum's 'Court Costume' *parabaik* we can see that ministers were awarded one and sometimes two sets of costumes: one to indicate their civil rank and, if applicable, one to indicate their military rank. Ministers wore military or civilian versions according to the occasion while attending the king at court or as his representative abroad (**13**).

Whereas the everyday garments of the court and the people were the same apart from the costliness of the fabric, the Burmese robe of state or insignia was exclusive to the royal

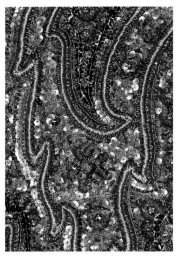

20. Above: Detail of *zardozi* work.

19. Left: The 'military' court dress of an *Atwinwun* (Secretary of State) of the Mindon-Thibaw period (1850-1880) consists of a *watlum* (long robe) of green and plum-coloured velvet lined in pink silk with a deep border of gold brocade and silver gilt spangled embroidery. Under this was worn a long-sleeved front opening shirt of fine white muslin. The minister also wore a diamond-shaped 'cloud collar' and a breastplate, both formed by rows of overlapping pointed scallops thickly embroidered with silver-gilt sequins. Victoria & Albert Museum, London, inv.nos. IM 44 A-1912, IM 44 B-1912.

22. Right: A high hat of crimson velvet decorated with applied gilt-foil ornaments completes the Chief Minister's costume. Victoria & Albert Museum, London, inv.no. IM 43D-1912.

family and to those on whom it was bestowed by the king as a special favour. Not simply highly decorated ordinary dress, the robe of state was a separate form of attire. Besides being sumptuously decorated it was distinctive in that its form was decidedly non-utilitarian and lacked the ease and comfort of everyday dress. Furthermore it was worn over the elements of everyday dress. Whereas the latter closely resembles basic dress forms of the early Indian tradition, robes of state drew on a wider range of sources. Court costumes had to be different to demonstrate superiority to those of the common people, and these differences lay both in the form of the costume and the materials used.

The use of imported textiles, and local textiles imitating foreign imports, to distinguish royal from commoner is well attested throughout Southeast Asia[33] although detailed knowledge of the trade into Burma remains slight and early records are difficult to interpret.[34] Burmese emissaries to foreign countries were expected to observe the customs and practices of the countries they visited. In 1833 a mission from the Court of Bagyidaw to Peking was instructed to "note and bring back with you...what the Emperor of China worships in order to obtain *neibban*...as well as an account of his queens, concubines, kinsmen, children, nobles & officers, and their equipage, dress and ceremonies."[35] It does appear that by the 19th century a number of key influences were at work. Velvet for example was imported from the Middle East by the Toungoo kings of Pegu in the 16th century, and imported velvets continued to be associated with court dress in the 19th.[36] Also introduced from further west were Indian brocades, gold braids and trimmings used for royal robes of state. Yule describes a row of young princes sitting in the audience chamber "in surcoats of silver and gold brocade with gay silk putsos [for court occasions]... the *Ein-she-men* (crown prince)...wore a dress of Benares gold brocade, and a mitre similar in general form to those worn by the courtiers, but of much richer material and set with precious stones."[37]

The source of the elaborate embroidery on the robes of state (**20**) is more difficult to ascribe to a single source. It is clearly related to the embroidery known in India as *zardozi* work, a type of appliqué made from a variety of silver or gilt materials.[38] Embroidery in gold has a long history in the Indian context, but the particular forms that appear in 19th century Burma appear to combine influences from India of the 18th and 19th century with embroidery methods and designs of Chinese inspiration.

It is when we turn to the form of the Konbaung insignia, however, that we face the most complex questions. Nineteenth century Burmese ceremonial dress contains items not seen in depictions of 17th or 18th century rulers of Pegu and Ava, which themselves have been argued to have both Chinese and Central Asian origins. The elaborate, stylised robes of state of the Konbaung dynasty have a parallel in the state robes of the Thai Chakri dynasty of the 18th and 19th centuries. The robes of state of the two courts were similarly fashioned but had different forms of applied decoration. In Thailand, this style can be traced back to the 17th century through literary references, sculpture, painting and old costumes and textiles in the National Museum in Bangkok. Though particular elements such as the scalloped collar seem to be influenced by Imperial Chinese court costume, the search for earlier parallels soon leads from secular to religious imagery. Indications of the origins of these forms of royal costume are to be found in sculptural depictions both of the Hindu deities Shiva or Vishnu and of the Bodhisattvas.

From the 9th century onwards the monarchs of Southeast Asia extended the idea of the righteous ruler (*dhammaraja* and *chakravartin*) first developed under the Mauryan ruler Ashoka, and began to claim both Bodhisattva status and identification with Hindu deities. The Ayutthyan kings of Thailand (15th-18th centuries) claimed the status of Bodhisattva and their culture had a clear impact on that of Burma. At the same time in the 17th century the image of the crowned Buddha, as subduer of Jambhupati, gained popularity (**21**).

The concept of monarch as deity was never explicitly accepted in Burma, but for some sections of the Burmese community it was a popular fact.[39] Certainly the marked similarity in design between royal thrones and shrines for the image of the Buddha, between the costumes of crowned Buddhas and the royal insignia of the Konbaung kings, between the queen and depictions of dancing and flying *apsaras* (courtesans of the gods and seducers of men) and the fact that the *konbaungset* (chronicle of the Konbaung Dynasty) states that the king is dressed as Brahma and the Queen as queen of the *devaloka* (place of the gods) at the coronation ceremony,[40] indicates that in art and in late ideas of kingship the two ideas tended to converge. The elaborate insignia dress, with its wing-like projections suggestive of minor deities (**16**), was not merely intended to distinguish king and queen from their courtiers, but to suggest a positive identification with the gods themselves.

Notes see Appendix

21. Above: The Buddha as King, wearing the ceremonial robes of a king of the Konbaung Dynasty. Carved teak figure, overlaid and decorated with gesso-like ornament in *thissi-***lacquer and composition, gilt and jewelled with artificial gems. Burma, 18th century. Victoria & Albert Museum, London, inv.no. IM 40-1912.**

DYEING UNDER FIRE

The following articles look at two UNESCO-sponsored short-term projects that were organised in the early 1990s in Mazar-i-Sharif, the capital of Balkh Province in northern Afghanistan. Rather like the Turkish DOBAG project in western Anatolia, both involved the setting up of workshops to revive the use of natural dyestuffs and weaving techniques, drawing on rapidly disappearing traditional local knowledge. Unlike DOBAG, however, the Mazar projects were conducted in a war zone.

4. Above: Hajji Abdul Raouf and his wife making heddles by hand, using cotton thread.

3. Left: After the mud wall hardened, the cauldrons were filled with water. Pir Nazar then added dried water-melon seeds *(tokham karbouza)*, wrapped in muslin cloth.

1. Preceding pages, left: Silk yarns, both natural white and coloured with the vegetal dyestuffs madder, wild delphinium *(isparak)*, pomegranate and indigo; with madder husks in the foreground.

I: THE IKAT PROJECT

By Harriet Sandys
The author describes her search for the ikat weavers of Kortchangee, their journey to Mazar-i-Sharif, and the seven weeks of weaving and dyeing that followed.

2. Preceding pages, right: Mohammed Saleh, son of Hajji Abdul Raouf, heating dye in a small pot over an open fire.

In the spring of 1989, while working with Afghan refugees in the Northwest Frontier Province of Pakistan, I discovered several families of silk weavers living in a refugee camp about twenty-five miles south of Peshawar, on an arid tract of land in the shadow of the Kohat mountains. They had fled their homes and villages in Afghanistan during the 1980s to escape the war, and the men, all skilled weavers, had taken jobs as road labourers on the Grand Trunk Road around Lahore, miles away from friends and family.

With funding from the Swedish Government, these silk weavers were supplied with looms, dyes and silk yarn. They gave up their work on the Grand Trunk Road, returned to their homes in the camp and began to weave silk shawls which were sold through Save the Children, USA, in both Peshawar and Islamabad. It was at about this time, during a visit to the weaving project in Pubbi Jalozai refugee camp by a representative of UNESCO (United Nations Educational, Scientific and Cultural Organisation) that I was asked if I would organise and implement a similar project inside Afghanistan.

The project was to be administered by UNESCO and UNOCA (United Nations Office of the Co-ordinator of humanitarian and economic assistance programmes to the people of Afghanistan) as part of the UN's 'Operation Salam', co-ordinated by Prince Sadruddin Aga Khan, to encourage Afghan refugees to return to their homeland after the withdrawal of Soviet troops in January 1989. The aims of the project were two-fold. First to continue a project started by UNESCO the previous year in Mazar-i-Sharif, teaching vegetable dyeing of yarn for carpets (see Part II), and second, to locate the last remaining ikat weavers, so that they could pass on the knowledge of silk weaving, and in particular the resist-dye technique of ikat, to young men and women.

For some time I had known about the existence of ikat weavers living in a small village called Kortchangee, which lies to the north of Aq Chah in Jowzjan Province, northwest

5. When the silkworm makes its cocoon it secretes a thin layer of the natural gum sericin. This binds the fibres together to create the hard shell of the cocoon.

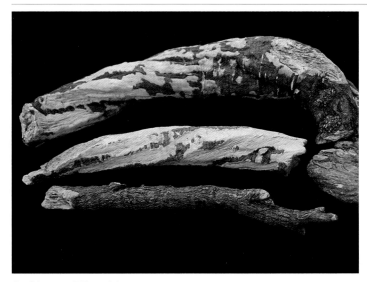

6. Above: The rhizome root of the dicotyledon known as *ashlone* or *chagon*.

7. Far right: The weavers thread each group of 24 warps through the holes in a smooth wooden bar.

8. Right: *Ashlone* or *chagon* is burned, resulting in a clinker-like alkaline product, *ashkar*, used for de-gumming raw silk.

9. Pot (*qum*) used for fermentation of a mixture of water, unripe mulberries, madder root and baker's yeast. After three days, the silk threads are added to the pot and left to steep for four days.

Afghanistan. It was during a visit to Paris some years earlier that I had seen a short documentary made in Kortchangee in 1972 by a French anthropologist, Annie Zorz. She had filmed and recorded the story of a small group of Ulutepe Karaja Turkoman ikat weavers who, during the 1930s, had fled their farms in the rich alluvial plains around Samarkand to escape Stalinist repression and famine brought about by the introduction of collective farming. They sought refuge in Faryab in Afghanistan, and were only able to regroup in villages insufficiently supplied with water. To support themselves and their families they therefore relied on womens' carpet weaving in addition to a little animal husbandry and agriculture.

Gradually these Turkoman moved west to the village of Kortchangee and took up their old tradition of sericulture and silk weaving, specialising in the production of head-shawls for women. During this time an Uzbek craftsman from Bukhara, Said Murat Urgunci, arrived at Kortchangee. There he taught some of his neighbours a technique they didn't know, the decoration of fabric by resist-dyeing the warps before weaving. I began to question the silk weavers in Pubbi Jalozai camp, hoping to learn more of this small group of ikat weavers, who were by now elderly men, living in Kortchangee. I wondered how many were still alive. Had they managed to survive the war? Were they still producing ikats? The Pubbi Jalozai weavers assured me that they personally knew a master or *ustad* with the knowledge of ikat weaving still living inside Afghanistan.

Late in November 1990, I visited Bernard Dupeigne at the Musée de l'Homme in Paris to make further enquiries about the Kortchangee weavers. He had accompanied Annie Zorz in 1972 and had subsequently written an article entitled 'L'Artisan dans l'Afghanistan'. One particular artisan, Hajji Abdul Raouf, had the knowledge of ikat (*abr'*) and another very basic method of tie-dyeing cloth after weaving called *yufak yagliq* in Turci or *sarandoz* in Dari. Makhkamova refers to this simpler plangi technique, which probably existed in Central Asia before the arrival of ikat, as *bandan*. Brightly coloured tie-dyed shawls are presented by a girl to her husband's family on the first occasion that she visits his home after the wedding ceremony. They are also used by nomads to cover their possessions during migration, thereby disguising their poverty.

Dupeigne felt, however, that after twelve years of war in Afghanistan it would be impossible to locate either Hajji Abdul Raouf or the weavers from Kortchangee. Two months later, as war loomed in the Gulf, I arrived in Kabul. The city was experiencing its worst winter for

11. Above: A wooden pole is passed through the centre of the silk skeins and the silk dipped repeatedly into the alkaline solution, which strips the gum from the fibres leaving the silk ready for dyeing.

10. Left: Weavers standing on the mud wall around the edge of the bath *(aujakh)* containing an alkaline solution.

twenty-five years and was buried under a metre of snow. Telephone lines were dead and the inhabitants of the city were busy sawing branches off fallen trees to use in wood-burning stoves to keep themselves warm. Even the dull thud of incoming artillery shells ceased as the heavy snowfall prevented movement by Mujaheddin in the surrounding mountains.

With all offices and shops closed, I was invited by Ewaz Badghissi, a carpet dealer in Kabul, to spend the day with his family. Ewaz and his wife, Hajji Bibi, are Ersari Beshir Turkoman from the village of Murachaq in Soviet Badghis. All the family, including children and grandchildren, and the war orphans given a home by Hajji Bibi, weave carpets using vegetable-dyed wool and silk. It was here, surrounded by all generations of this extended Turkoman family that I met Hajji Abdul Raouf, aged 76 and living as a refugee in Kabul. I gave him a copy of the article 'L'Artisan dans l'Afghanistan', which contained photographs of himself and of the silk weavers of Kortchangee, taken in 1972. He recognised many of the weavers whom he assured me were still living in Kortchangee and agreed to locate them.

Together with the Badghissi family, Abu Ali, Chief Technical Advisor for UNESCO, Ziaudin Zia of the Carpet Export Guild in Kabul and Hajji Abdul Raouf, it was agreed that the UNESCO silk weaving project should start in April at the end of Ramazan, in the north of Afghanistan. The town of Mazar-i-Sharif in Balkh Province, just sixty miles south of the border with Uzbekistan, was chosen as the location for the project. And so in April 1991 I left my house in London, boarded Ariana Afghan Airlines in Prague, and flew via Moscow and Tashkent to Kabul.

No one had thought to warn me that on 27 April the Mujaheddin annually celebrated the Saur Revolution by rocketing the city. More than eighty artillery rockets fell on us that day, so it was with some relief that I boarded the UN aeroplane for Mazar-i-Sharif a few days later. Compared to Kabul, where rockets landed daily, Mazar was peaceful, the roar of MIG fighter jets taking off from the nearby airport and circling the town before flying south to bomb mud villages the only reminder that Afghanistan was still in the grip of civil war.

12. An assistant winds the bundles of silk yarn on to the *qaleb*.

In Mazar, Mujaheddin, militia and Government soldiers lived a wary coexistence, for all Afghans regard the beautiful blue mosque and shrine of Hazrat Ali (fourth Caliph of Islam), which dominates the city centre, as one of the most sacred sites in the whole of Afghanistan. In addition, silk weaving and silk production have been known in this region for more than a thousand years; the ancient ruined city of Balkh, situated just to the north, was once an important trading centre on the Silk Road before its destruction by Genghis Khan in 1218.

On arrival in Mazar, Ewaz Badghissi, Ziauddin Zia and Hajji Abdul Raouf visited more

13. Above: The strong natural yellow of yarn dyed with *isparak* (wild delphinium) will be used for two of the four ikat bands.

14. Right: The two yellow bands are tied in various places and dyed with two chemical colours, purple and red. The two natural white bands are tied and dyed red and green.

15. Once the silk is wound onto the *qaleb*, the frame is laid flat and the master-weaver marks out the areas to be tied on the warp bundles. These areas are bound with long strips of cotton to prevent dye penetrating the yarn.

than fifteen caravanserais in an attempt to find a suitable site. Inside courtyards, secluded behind heavy wooden doors and high mud walls, I had my first glimpse of the familiar old Afghanistan, far removed from the rusting Russian helicopter gunships, lorries, empty petrol drums and paraphernalia of war that litter the outskirts of Mazar.

Young Turkoman girls dressed in pink and green flowered dresses played together in the bright sunshine, their shaven foreheads and long plaits covered by embroidered caps decorated with large triangular amulets. Sitting on wooden balconies above the courtyard, women were busy hand-spinning wool for carpet warps. From beneath tall head-dresses covered with striped red and yellow silk shawls, they watched the men load bales of Afghan carpets and precious firewood onto the backs of Bactrian camels. Beneath the walls, in shadows cast by the turrets of the caravanserai, old men, the cotton wadding falling out of their patched, worn *chapans*, sat cross-legged on raised wooden tables, sipping green tea from Gardiner porcelain cups.

During April and early May, rain and fierce gales swept through Afghanistan, bringing severe flooding and misery to a country already devastated by war. The mountains surrounding Mazar gradually changed to a vivid emerald green and the slopes became carpeted with small red field poppies. The Turkoman shopkeepers in the old bazaar were a valuable source of information as they exchanged news with farmers coming into town from outlying areas. It was through them that we learnt that floods had swept away half the small town of Aqcha in a single night.

At this point the whole UNESCO project hung in the balance. The weavers from Kortchangee would have to negotiate mud roads blocked by landslides, flood water and government checkposts during their journey from their village in Mujaheddin-held territory. After ten anxious days of waiting, Mohammed Saleh (Hajji Abdul Raouf's son), Abdul Subkhan, Abdul Karim, Pir Nazaar, Tulak and Khudai Qul arrived from Kortchangee. Together with other weavers from Balkh, Faryab, Jowzjan, Kabul, Herat, Badghis, Parwan and Samangan, they began to organise the workshop in the assembly hall of the Sultan Razia Girls' Secondary School. The hall was ideal for use as a temporary workshop, being large with a high ceiling, cool and well ventilated. More importantly, the weavers, looms and silk were protected from the elements. The weavers were from many different tribes and consisted of eight Uzbeks, sixteen Tajiks, ten Ersari Beshir Turkoman and one Saryk Turkoman.

Throughout the seven weeks of the project I was assisted by the Badghissi family. Hajji Bibi introduced me to the traditional and ancient Central Asian method of de-gumming silk

17. The dyed warps are threaded through the heddles and reed of the loom, a process that takes six weavers approximately three days to complete.

16. Untying the cotton bands from the freshly dyed warp threads.

using a strong alkaline solution prepared by dissolving *ashkar*, a coke or clinker-like substance, in a bucket of water (**8**). *Ashkar* is produced by burning the dried branches and rhizome root known as *ashlone* (Dari) or *chagon* (Turci). It has a curiously shaped root stock which lies deep below the soil, enabling it to survive extremes of temperature and climate. This plant grows abundantly in sandy loam and salt desert and occurs everywhere in Badghis Province in both northern Afghanistan and Russia.

Wahida, Hajji Bibi's daughter, became my interpreter and close companion, and helped us to set up a small natural dye workshop using madder, pomegranate, walnut, almond bark, straw and a wild delphinium called *isparak* (Dari). Each day schoolchildren, together with Turkoman carpet weavers from Faryab, and women from the Rural Rehabilitation Centre engaged in carpet weaving, and watched and participated in the dyeing of wool and silk.

With the introduction of strong chemical dyes into Afghanistan from Romania, Poland and China, carpet weavers and dyers have largely abandoned the method of scouring wool before dyeing or using mordants. Alum or *zarmch* (Dari) was found in the bazaar in rock crystal form. We brought it back to the workshop, ground it into powder using a pestle and mortar, and demonstrated the mordanting process. When treated with alum before dyeing, both wool and silk emerged from the madder dye vats a soft orange-pink. Hajji Bibi then demonstrated another method. First, she dyed the yarn in madder without using a mordant, removed it from the dye vat and plunged it into an alkaline solution prepared from *ashkar*. The colour changed dramatically in seconds from salmon pink to deep burgundy; a colour typically used in Turkoman carpets.

Ewaz Badghissi demonstrated a fermentation process using a traditional pottery jar, called a *qum*, which was set into the ground in direct sunlight. This was filled with water, unripe mulberries and madder root (**9**). Baker's yeast was added and the pot tightly covered. After three days, fermentation was well under way with a thick froth at the neck of the *qum*. The silk was placed in the *qum*, where it was left to steep for about four days. At the end of this period the silk was removed from the *qum*, having taken the red dye from the madder.

Ziauddin Zia and Ewaz Badghissi were invaluable in helping to organise the workshop, purchasing items and liaising with the weavers. Without their constant assistance it would have been quite impossible to carry out the project. Word soon spread throughout the neighbouring provinces that UNESCO were once more back in Mazar. Turkoman carpet weavers

18. Right: The warps are placed on the loom for weaving. Any broken threads are mended by rubbing the ends between finger and thumb. A pit loom is used, the heddles operated by foot pedals and the shuttles passed from hand to hand. The woven cloth is wound onto the roll bar in front of the weaver.

19. The final result: a completed ikat strip.

began to arrive from far and wide asking for a demonstration from Hajji Bibi on the dyeing of wool and silk using vegetable dyes. They had seen carpets woven by the weavers trained in May 1990 by UNESCO consultants Roland Gilles and Jim Williams, and wanted to learn the recipes so that they too could use vegetable dyed wool when weaving their carpets.

I left Afghanistan in July 1991 to return to the UK, somewhat despondent at the realisation of the enormous forces ranged against the continuation of ikat weaving in Afghanistan. The following year Kabul fell to the Mujaheddin, and United Nations personnel withdrew from Afghanistan. As a consequence of twelve years of war, sericulture and silk weaving has been affected by the destruction of the economy and the devastation of the countryside through prolonged high altitude bombing. The livelihood of the Turkoman, the traditional wearers of silk ikat, has been so badly affected by constant war that they are too poor to purchase such luxury fabrics. The knowledge and skills of ikat dyeing and weaving still survive, but there is no local demand for the product. Even the famous brightly coloured striped chapans worn by the men of Mazar-i-Sharif are now woven from cotton.

Although it has been estimated that there are some eight million mulberry trees in Afghanistan, bombing of the *karez*, the underground canals which channel snow melt from the mountains, has meant that in certain areas mulberry trees have died through lack of irrigation. Fighting between government forces and the Mujaheddin made it difficult for farmers in the rural areas to purchase fresh stocks of silkworm eggs sent out from the sericulture centres in Kabul and Mazar to provincial towns held by government forces. Often children were sent into the bazaars to purchase seed because it necessitated crossing over from Mujaheddin-held territory into government areas.

As a result farmers tried to breed their own silkworms, but this resulted in inbreeding, and the silkworms fell prey to viral infections. They either died before being able to construct a cocoon or produced poor quality silk thread which broke easily when reeled. Although this silk yarn is unsuitable for fine ikats, it is ideal for use in the weaving of traditional head-shawls and for rugs, hence the increase in the number of silk carpets being produced today in Afghanistan.

On a visit to Peshawar in January 1994, I was encouraged to receive news that the silk weavers from Pubbi Jalozai refugee camp had returned to northern Afghanistan with their families, and were continuing to weave silk head-shawls for the local market.

MICHAUD- JOHN HILLELSON AGENCY

II: THE CARPET PROJECT

By Roland Gilles & Jim Williams
*In May 1990, the authors closed the shutters of their oriental carpet gallery on the Left Bank
in Paris, near Notre-Dame, and set off for Mazar-i-Sharif in northern Afghanistan. Their
mission, to set up twin workshops on natural dyes and carpet weaving for UNESCO.*

When we first proposed this project to UNESCO – in the person of Mr Vencatachellum, Head of Culture and Handicrafts – many objections were raised. After all, what could two Paris carpet dealers possibly bring to Afghan weavers? In reply, we explained that the scheme was not about teaching the Afghans how to weave carpets, but about demonstrating simple and inexpensive ways of improving their carpet production.

Afghan crafts, partly ruined by war, had succumbed to the dead hand of commercialisation even before the beginning of the conflict. To breathe life back into this art, our plan was to reintroduce some of the traditional Afghan designs, whose simple borders and well spaced field patterns could then serve as a model for future production. At the same time we planned to bring back the strong colour values of the old tribal rugs by returning to the use of natural dyes made from products available on the local markets in Afghanistan.

This project formed part of a vast programme of aid to Afghanistan called Operation Salam, administered jointly by UNESCO and UNOCA. This enterprise may seem a bit surreal given the circumstances. By May 1990 the Soviets had withdrawn their troops and the country was no longer at war, but it was far from enjoying peace. The victorious Mujaheddin remained entrenched around Kabul, and we expected to see the regime fall at any moment. Our arrival was badly timed. The government was holding its first great assembly (*Loia Jerga*), while the Resistance shelled the city to remind everybody they were there.

Mazar-i-Sharif seemed to us a haven of peace after Kabul, at least during the daytime. On the turquoise domes of Imam Ali's mausoleum, the white doves had completed their pilgrimage (**1**). This city of Afghan Turkestan, dedicated in equal measure to religion and trade, was certainly not the worst place to carry out this project. In the local shops, silk cocoons, handspun wool, and all kinds of natural dyestuffs were available alongside wine-red carpets.

Our workshops were scheduled to last only three weeks, and it would have been impossible to go ahead without the collaboration of a local Afghan organisation. We had chosen to

PHOTOGRAPHS ROLAND GILLES & JIM WILLIAMS

2. Threading the warps on the large double vertical loom. Near the bottom of the loom, two cords divide the warp into front and back threads.

3. Right: The women's workshop; preparing balls of warp threads.

1. Left: The Tomb of Hazrat Ali, the Prophet's son-in-law and the Fourth Caliph of Islam, in Mazar-i-Sharif. This magnificent mausoleum was built in the 15th century by the Timurid Sultan Hussein Baiqara (1462-1506).

4. Mordanting the wool with *zarmch* (alum).

work with the Afghan Carpet Exporters Guild, which had existed prior to the war and had continued to function through successive governments. The guild's board of directors included Ewaz Badghissi, a well known carpet merchant and producer of Kabul, whose Turkoman wife, Hajji Bibi, is an outstanding carpet weaver. They were to come to join us in our workshops with a group of their best apprentices.

Our workshops were set up in the open air, on a property situated on the Reservoir Road just outside Mazar. We arrived to find nothing apart from the materials we had asked the guild to acquire and the 39 participants they had recruited from all over Afghanistan. All the masterweavers were of Turkoman origin, as were the majority of the apprentices. There were however, a certain number of Hazara, Uzbek and Tajik weavers.

The section of the courtyard that the workshops occupied was on two levels. The higher part, shaded by a magnificent mulberry tree, was reserved for the looms of the women. Just below were the boys' looms, and a few steps away was the dye workshop which communicated with a woodshed, firewood being essential for the heating of the dye baths. This made it easy for the weavers to come and watch the dyeing operations and note down the recipes. The only drawback to this site was the lack of running water inside the dye workshop. We were obliged to bring water from a stream just outside the main entrance.

The workshops were built and functioning in three days. In the dye workshop the first task was to dig out and build ovens out of brick and dried earth to house the dye vats. At the same time the weavers were setting up their looms, five in number: three of traditional horizontal type, a small metallic vertical loom, and a large wooden double vertical loom which could carry two carpets, one on each side. The weavers at this curious loom were obliged to raise their seats as the carpet progressed; it thus combined the characteristics of the continuous warp Tabriz loom and the short warp Hamadan type loom.

Without appearing to hurry, the artisans completed the considerable task of stringing the warps in a single day, thus avoiding shrinkage of the warp threads in the humid night air, a problem which leads in its turn to pockets of uneven tension. On the large vertical loom they started by marking five centimetre sections on the upper loom beam with small nails, and between each section they stretched the warp thread forty times (**2**).

Horizontal and vertical looms require different techniques of stretching the warps. On the horizontal loom the warp is wound around the two beams in a figure of eight. This configuration allows the shed stick to be inserted directly. On a vertical loom, the weavers pass the warp thread alternately over and under two cotton cords that are strung across the loom near the bottom, forming the shed stick opening. When the warp is completely stretched, the two cords are brought together, forming the bottom of the carpet.

It was without a doubt the first time that the boys had worked with women weavers, and while the women masterweavers were safeguarded by their venerable age, the same was not true of the apprentices. In the workshop the atmosphere was one of great good humour, but, alas for the boys, they had no chance of access to the women's workshop, which Mr Badghisi had encircled in several bands of cloth.

In fact, it was out of the question to trifle. The young female apprentices worked under the orders of Hajji Bibi and Ogul Jamal (Beautiful Flower), and the young male apprentices

6. Above: Sirajuddin controls the temperature of the madder root bath, which must never be allowed to boil.

5. Left: Fermentation dyeing; after ten days the wool is removed from the jar where the dye is fermenting.

under the direction of Qurban Ali and Najaf Ali, all of whom were skilled and methodical Turkoman weavers. It was the masters themselves who fixed the heddles on the third day.

In the dye workshops we taught two methods of dyeing. One is the rapid, classic procedure involving premordanting the wool, and then steeping it in heated dye baths (**4, 6**). The second method, slower but more economical because it does not require firewood, is that of fermentation vat dyeing (**5**). This last method was taught us by Anne Rieger, a masterdyer from Paris, and we have practised it successfully for ten years.

On the first day of the workshop, before the unbelieving eyes of our participants, we put fruit peel and madder root to steep in one large jar and delphinium in another. It takes at least ten days to obtain a good fermentation, and we counted on the solar heat to carry out the process. But it turned out that the earthen jars, porous on the outside and glazed on the inside, remained as cool as a cellar. Hand-testing the contents, we felt it was probably the coolest place in Mazar-i-Sharif.

As time was short, we concentrated on the first method, which enabled us to dye 150 kilogrammes of wool in fifteen days. Wool put into skeins was mordanted in baths of alum (**4**), which were brought to boil for one hour while we prepared a dye decoction in the neighbouring vats. The cooled, mordanted wool was put to steep in the dye bath, which was brought to the right temperature (**6**).

In accordance with the principles of the mission, we only used dyestuffs available on the local market in Mazar. Dried and ground madder root (*royan*) gave us reds, delphinium flowers (*gul zard*) gave us yellows, walnut husks (*pust charmaz*) the browns. To these basic dyes were added pomegranate husks, mulberry wood and fruit. Only indigo (*nil*) was a problem. We found natural indigo agglomerated to lime and sold as a medicine for its scarring virtues, but this was unsuitable for dyeing purposes. After some experimentation we obtained the best results with Chinese indigo bought in the bazaar, and then treated with sulphuric acid. We very much regretted however not having brought with us sufficient quantities of natural indigo.

There were not really any masterdyers in our workshop, and we had continually to adjust quantities of dye stuffs and mordants to obtain the best colours. As each important dye operation was carried out we asked the weavers to join the dyers to observe. We felt it would be advantageous for the weavers to know how to dye, since this knowledge could give more autonomy to home workshops and encourage artistic creativity. In this respect, fermentation dyeing aroused much interest. After ten days, we withdrew the wool from the fermenting baths (**5**), then alkalinised the baths and dipped the wool again for a short time to develop the colour. We were delighted when we achieved a crimson red from this dye bath which was similar to the red of old Tekke Turkoman carpets. Our best dye apprentice, Khal Mohammed, who was a shopkeeper in the bazaar, immediately started practising this dye method in his private workshop.

In the weaving workshop we had nothing to teach but everything to observe. However, since our plan was to return to some of the antique designs, we wanted a certain number of traditional structures to be observed, such as wide coloured kilim ends and reddish brown

7. Roland Gilles (left) and Jim Williams in the dye workshop in Mazar-i-Sharif.

8. Above: *Pardah* (ensi) made in our workshops arriving at UNESCO in Paris.

9. Right: Khal Mohammed matching the colours to be used in one of the carpets.

10. Ogul Jamal trimming the pile. On the horizontal loom the asymmetric knot is made by hand without the aid of a hook.

weft threads. The Turkoman women entered fully into the project. In accordance with regional carpet tradition they alternated two types of wefts, a thick, taut weft (*arach*) and a thinner, loose weft *(put)*. As the finely spun wool for the *put* was not available, they had wool fleece purchased in the local sheep market, which they washed, carded and spun with surprising rapidity.

The final activity in the workshops, entrusted to Najaf Ali, consisted of transcribing onto graph paper the carpet designs chosen. We had brought with us a series of photos of twenty-five traditional Afghan carpets, and we asked the masterweavers to choose five of these to transfer to the looms. For the large double loom the boys chose an Ersari Beshir carpet with a floral design, and an Ersari with four tangent güls for the horizontal loom. The women chose an Ersari *pardah* (ensi) with two superimposed niches, an Uzbek caisson carpet, and an Ersari *gülli-göl* design.

All these were 19th century designs, part of the tribal tradition of Afghan Turkestan and with the characteristics that we wanted to reintroduce. Their fields were enclosed within a single main border, rather than the five or six disparate borders as is usually the case in modern Afghan carpets. The fields were decorated with vigorous and well-spaced patterns, and not overcrowded with rigid, hybrid designs. All these qualities were perfectly understood by the weavers.

Those working on vertical looms used the Turkish (symmetric) knot, and those on horizontal looms used the Persian (asymmetric) knot, as was traditional (**10**). At the end of sixteen days' work, the weavers had knotted about forty centimetres of carpet, and the border and first field designs could be seen. This was a remarkable feat after only ten days of knotting, three days of kilim weaving and three days preparing the looms.

In spite of heat and fatigue, good humour reigned in the workshop. The young mothers stopped work from time to time to breast-feed their babies, husbands came to check on their wives, who immediately gave them a skein of wool to wind for use on the looms. The children all tried to make themselves useful by untangling skeins of wool. Tea was distributed to all the weavers, and punctuated the rhythm of the work.

Although this was a temporary workshop, created in exceptional conditions, it reflected the evolution of Afghan carpet production. For long carpets had not been made solely by Turkoman women on horizontal looms in the home, but were more and more often produced in urban workshops by young male apprentices using vertical looms and the Turkish knot. Our mission was not to change the methods of production, nor to attempt a return to a purely tribal tradition which was already very weakened when the Turkomans arrived en masse in northern Afghanistan in the 1920s and 1930s. We simply wanted to demonstrate that it is possible to create a small, quality production which could serve as a model for others. We believe that such a production could open new markets and new prospects.

It may be unrealistic to try to restore the now interrupted tradition of the oral transmission of skills, but it is nevertheless possible, with weavers as skilled as the Afghans, to arouse artistic creativity by the use of good wool and good dyes. In carpets, as often in paintings, the beauty of the colours is a fundamental stimulus to creation.

IKAT CHAPANS

Since the collapse of the USSR and the consequent 'free' movement of peoples and goods from and to the independent republics of Central Asia, a new wave of desirable woven artefacts has emerged onto the world textile market, via a 'Turkic pipeline' which has its Western terminus in the Grand Bazaar in Istanbul. Among the materials thus available are expressive resist-dyed silk *ikat* coats, or *chapans*, made in Uzbekistan in the 19th and early 20th centuries. Worn by both men and women, some examples, as in the Turkish private collection featured here, show skill and artistry of the highest order.

The Malay word *ikat* has been generally adopted in international textile terminology to describe the resist-dye technique employed in the production of these luxurious silk robes (known as *chapan, khalat, yaktak or munisak*) and related dresses (*koilak*), wall-hangings (*pardah*) and coverlets, although in Uzbekistan the local term is either *abr* (Persian for 'cloud') or, in Turkic languages, *ipekshahi*. In a complicated and time-consuming dyeing process, once largely the preserve of the Jews in cities such as Bukhara, Tashkent, Kokand and Samarkand, sections of the silk warp threads (which carry the design) are tightly bound with cotton-thread resists in a planned sequence for immersion in successive colour vats. This takes place before the warp threads are placed on the loom for weaving, and requires immense skill and patience. The typical 'blurring' effect occurs where areas of colour meet other colours or undyed sections.

AKBAR'S COURTIER

A Silk from Fatehpur-Sikri

By Catherine C. McLean

Most of us give little thought, as we walk round an exhibition, to the enormous effort of preparation that for months, sometimes years, has been going on in the background. In the case of fragile objects the decision to travel from the home institution is very likely to be a controversial one. Some pieces need costly and elaborate conservation before public display can be contemplated. The following study describes the philosophical and material issues that arose when the Conservation Department of the Los Angeles County Museum of Art decided to stabilise and mount a rare Mughal compound-weave silk hanging in preparation for a travelling exhibition.

1. Left: *Courtier with a Wine Cup*. Mughal India, Fatehpur-Sikri, Akbar period, ca. 1570. Compound-weave silk hanging, 1.24 x 2.16m (4'1" x 7'1"). The final appearance of the textile after conservation. Los Angeles County Museum of Art, inv.no. M.73.5.702.

To set the groundwork for the discussion of an early Mughal textile, it may be useful to begin with a brief historic overview.[1] Jalal ad-Din Akbar, known as Akbar, was the third ruler of the Mughal Dynasty and thus the supreme Muslim power in India. He was only fourteen years old when he inherited the throne, in 1556, upon the death of his father Humayun. By that age he had already seen his family struggle for many years to regain their empire, centred in the north-central part of the subcontinent. In 1555 with support from Shah Tahmasp, the ruler of Safavid Iran, Humayan had gathered an army and returned to India to claim what he believed was rightfully his.

During Akbar's reign, from 1556 until his death in 1605, the empire was expanded to include most of the Indian subcontinent. His marriage in 1562, to the daughter of the leader of one of the most powerful Hindu Rajput clans, formed an important political and religious alliance. After the birth of his son Prince Salim, later to be the Emperor Jahangir, Akbar founded the city of Fatehpur-Sikri, which served as the Mughal capital from 1571 until 1585. This new centre, built between two major cities, Agra, the old political capital, and Ajmer, the spiritual centre of the dynasty, was to emerge as the focus of Mughal India.

Akbar's keen interest in the arts, literature, astrology and metaphysics was a legacy inherited from both his father and his grandfather. His formal education began at the age of four, and, although he never learned to read or write, he surrounded himself with poets, artists and scholars, many of whom were Iranian. A military and administrative genius, Akbar was known for his intellectual curiosity and religious tolerance. His patronage of the arts led to the formation of an imperial library and workshops at Fatehpur-Sikri. The library was the centre of manuscript production and painting, while the imperial workshops produced a variety of items, from perfume and guns to textiles for tents, clothing and palace furnishings. Surviving textiles are rarely inscribed, so attributions are based on comparison to dated manuscripts and contemporaneous architectural details.

Most of the valuable textiles at Fatehpur-Sikri were kept in a private storehouse in the complex that was destroyed by fire in 1579. Records state that approximately ten million textiles were burnt or lost, no doubt an exaggeration on the part of the Mughal chroniclers.

2. Left: The Mughal silk hanging in 1973, at the time of its acquisition by the Los Angeles County Museum. The textile is wrinkled and distorted, showing partly completed restoration work.

Today, few textiles can be securely attributed to the imperial city, and few carpets can be found in museums around the world.

A compound-weave silk hanging of a *Courtier with a Wine Cup* from the Los Angeles County Museum of Art was recently attributed to the imperial workshops at Fatehpur-Sikri and has been dated to the early 1570s (**1**). On 23 October 1924, Sotheby, Wilkinson and Hodge, auctioneers in London, offered the textile for sale. A photograph taken around this time by the auction house appeared in the January 1925 issue of *Rupam, A Quarterly Journal of Oriental Art*. It is the earliest photograph available to us, and shows the textile to be in fairly stable condition (**3**). The cape has scattered losses, primarily in the centre; and the eyes, eyebrows and nose of the figure are clearly visible. By using this photograph and examining the textile today, one can trace a rough outline of the previous restoration that was carried out. In 1924, the textile had two large vertical lines of deterioration, one through the centre of the figure and a second to the viewer's left. Close examination of the line of deterioration to the left indicates that the piece was not cut completely from top to bottom; the horizontal wefts remain continuous in several areas. Due to later restoration, the central deterioration is much more difficult to examine. It is possible that the textile was once divided into two pieces at this point, and the fine vertical warps have begun to break in many areas. Deterioration of this type is particularly visible to the left of the figure, near the waist.

By the time of the Sotheby's sale, steps had been taken to stabilise the textile by sewing it to a red cotton plainweave fabric with cotton floss. The sewing resembles coarse vertical lines of quilting and is clearly visible in the 1924 photograph. Although this stitching is unsightly, it is the main reason why the textile survived in one piece: without the backing, much more serious damage would have occurred. Note that the textile does not display any large areas of reweaving or darning, and that the edges have a light-coloured binding.

In 1973, the Los Angeles County Museum of Art acquired this textile from the collectors Nasli and Alice Heeramaneck in New York City. A photograph taken at the time (**2**) shows that between 1924 and 1973 the textile had been extensively restored. The losses in the vertical cuts are filled with coarse darning. The turban and plume are altered. The shirt and trousers are covered with a surface of darning in a twill weave to simulate the original compound-weave textile; and the cape and face are left partially rewoven. The partially rewoven areas have only the weft yarns in place.

The surface of the textile is worn, revealing elements of the compound weave that were not originally visible. It was intended to have a multicoloured border composed of predominantly white, blue, green and yellow yarns. Many of these weft yarns have worn away, revealing the red satin ground below. The central figure stands in an architectural niche, the background of which was once a solid red satin weave. Much of this surface has been lost, revealing the continuous coloured weft yarns that were not intended to be seen. More of the warps have broken, leaving behind long loose floats of the multicoloured wefts. The warps had held the wefts in a rigid order, the uppermost wefts forming the image. Without the warps, the wefts are free to mix, and this results in a blurred image which is sometimes impossible to read.

When acquired by the museum, the surface of the textile was fragmented and unstable. It was realised that conservation would be time consuming and would require a large work surface, so until such time and space could be found, the textile was rolled face out on a tube and placed in storage. Although not on display, the textile was well known and highly regarded by scholars in the field of Mughal art, and early in 1985, the Asia Society in New York requested that LACMA loan them the piece for their autumn exhibition, 'Akbar's India: Art from the Mughal City of Victory'. Though aware of its condition, the museum agreed to the loan in the belief that there was sufficient time to stabilise the hanging, and because it would allow scholars the opportunity to see it in the context of the varied artefacts of the Mughal period, a rare occurrence in itself. The treatment described below was the outcome of this loan request. It was designed keeping in mind that the textile would travel to three venues: New York, Cambridge, Massachusetts and Houston.

Conservation treatment began in February 1985. The examination and initial discussion of treatment with curators Thomas Lentz and Edward Maeder and conservators Pat Reeves, Ann Svenson, Philip Sykas and William Leisher took nearly a month. During this time, the main questions concerned how much of the original compound weave survived below the restoration, and how much, if any, of the restoration should be removed. These questions sparked lively debate, and several viewpoints were well supported. The broad spectrum of philosophies extended from the idea that all previous restoration should be removed, since it is a visual distortion of the image, to the belief that very little should be done owing to the textile's fragile nature. Foremost in everyone's mind was the question whether textile conservation of the time would be able to devise a suitable treatment for the piece; if not, should a method of easily reversible stabilisation be done in the hope that the future would bring better solutions? Before us lay a textile that had suffered from past restoration, and no one

3. Above: Photograph taken by the auctioneers when the damaged and partly stabilised Mughal textile was offered for sale in London by Sotheby's, Wilkinson and Hodge in October 1924. The image was first published in the January 1925 issue of *Rupam, A Quarterly Journal of Oriental Art.*

wanted this damage and distortion to proceed any further.

At every step in the treatment, a small area was treated first, and then discussions about appearance and long-range effects were held with curators and conservators. Close examination revealed that, for the most part, restoration of the figure had been done in silk floss that matched the colour of the original weft yarns. The turban was blue-green, with yellow-orange through the centre; the shirt, trousers and shoes were various shades of blue-green; the cape was yellow. The restorer had planned to recreate the final colour of the cape by blending warps and wefts of slightly different shades. The wefts were orange-yellow, the warps a cool lemon-yellow; mixed together, they would match the original fragments below. Unfortunately, the restoration was completed only in a small area near the shoulder, leaving most of the cape an inappropriate orange-yellow.

After much discussion, the area of restoration on the cape was removed. Incomplete restoration on the sash, sword, belt, buckle and ankles was also removed. On the hands and face the light-coloured floss was left because the original flesh tones were worn away, leaving a blotchy red-and-blue surface. Without the hands and face clearly defined, the figure would be difficult to identify. Attempts to remove the bluish-red restoration in the borders and background were difficult. It was found that removal of these yarns caused much damage to the original weaving, and consequently the red areas of reweaving and darning were left.

Once the final appearance of the textile was established, stabilisation could begin. Since the textile was wrinkled and distorted, blocking was the first step. The textile was humidified by placing damp linen cloths beneath and creating a Mylar tent above. Due to the double thickness of the textile, a light misting with deionised water facilitated the blocking. Guide lines were established so the main vertical and horizontal elements could be lined up. At the same time the loose wefts were aligned.

After blocking, the job of securing loose wefts began. This was essential, since any vibration would move these wefts and more warps would be strained and broken. A very fine two-ply silk was used to secure the wefts. The span stitch was nearly invisible and the undyed silk thread blended well with the multicolored wefts. The wefts were secured to the red backing fabric, a laborious task that took 85 hours to complete. At this point, nothing further was done to change the appearance of the textile. The compensation for losses and disguising of splits were considered, but it was thought that this would have the unwanted effect of further highlighting the old restoration. The final appearance of the textile is shown in (**1**).

The mounting of the textile for travel and exhibition became the next topic of discussion. Depending upon the specific needs of a textile, modern conservators have many different mounting methods from which to choose. Generally, they look for a method that is independent of the mending, gives adequate support, protects the textile from harmful environmental conditions, is easily reversible, and does not allow the glazing material, such as glass or Plexiglas (Perspex) to touch the surface of the textile.

Several museums, including the Metropolitan Museum of Art in New York and The Textile Museum in Washington, D.C., have used a temporary mounting technique called pressure mounting. This involves placing a very fragile textile onto a specially padded surface and then setting a glazing material directly on top. With the glazing well secured, the textile is held in place by light surface pressure. Although much progress has been made in this technique, it is important to emphasize that pressure mounting is not for the novice. There are many pros and cons, and the decision to use it on the Mughal textile was not an easy one, as its improper use can result in irreversible damage to a work of art. Uneven and/or excessive pressure can cause fibres to break, while insufficient pressure can allow the textile to slip in its frame. Sudden environmental changes can cause a dramatic rise in relative humidity within the mount, which could then cause condensation on the inside of the glazing material, which is an ideal place for mould growth to begin. The technique described below took into consideration each of these concerns.

The padded surface on which the Mughal textile rests is composed of several elements.

4. The padded well of the pressure mount.

First a sealed wooden strainer with cross bars was made. Then ³/₁₆" thick Gatorfoam (sanded to improve adhesion) was attached to one side of the strainer using a PVA emulsion. Weights were left on overnight, and the next day the edges of the Gatorfoam were trimmed with a mat knife and sanded.[2] As a precaution against any potentially harmful components, 5mm thick Mylar *(Melinex)*, a polyester film, was placed on the Gatorfoam.[3] The next layer was designed to counteract changes in humidity. Silica gel in 20" square sheets (Artsorb) was cut to fit and sewn together with edges butted to cover the entire mount. The sheets were preconditioned to fifty per cent relative humidity. This was covered with two ¹/₈" layers of Pellon, a non-woven polyester fabric.[4] The first layer was smaller than the second, creating a slight mound in the middle. This was to offset any possible bowing of the glazing material; by building up the centre, even pressure on the textile could be maintained. To hold these bottom layers in place, washed white cotton batiste fabric was placed on top, stretched around to the sides of the strainer and stapled in place (**5**).

Prevention of excess pressure on the edges of the textile was the next concern. Following the contours of the textile, a pattern ¹/₄" larger than the hanging was traced on to Mylar, then a mat was cut from acid-free single-wall corrugated cardboard. Supported on a sheet of clear Mylar, the textile was easily slid over the mat to check for a proper fit. The mat was covered with a layer of ¹/₈" Pellon the same shape as the mat but cut to extend ¹/₄" over the mat's centre to soften the hard, though bevelled, edge. Then the entire mount was covered with a sheet of ¹/₄" Pellon. These last two layers of Pellon were basted together with white cotton thread. To secure the package, it was covered with another layer of cotton batiste that was stapled to the back of the strainer (**6**). For smaller mounts the batiste layers may be unnecessary, but they lessen the risk of sliding layers.

5. Pressure mount layers (from bottom to top): wooden strainer, Gatorfoam, Mylar, Artsorb, small layer of Pellon, large layer of Pellon. These layers were covered with a layer of cotton batiste.

The final layer was the mounting fabric that would show around the edges of the Mughal textile while on display. A commercially dyed deep red cotton/polyester plainweave fabric was selected. Like the cotton batiste, it was stretched around the strainer and stapled to the back. Care was taken not to stretch the mounting fabric too tightly so that the art object could be pressed down into the padded well (**4**) without too much pressure.

While lying on a sheet of clear Mylar, the Mughal textile was positioned on the padded mount. Then, holding the textile at one end, the Mylar was slid out from the opposite end, leaving the textile in its correct position. Because of the textile's size and weight, there were concerns that light pressure alone would not hold it in place. As a precaution, it was sewn to the mount with five vertical rows of running stitches and one horizontal row across the top, done in cotton thread. Next, ¹/₄" thick Plexiglas was placed on top of the textile and screwed around the edges, through the mounting fabric, into the strainer. A wooden frame, designed to cover the screws holding the pressure mount together, was placed on top. For stability, the frame was screwed to the strainer around all four edges.

The textile successfully travelled by truck to three venues, New York, Cambridge, and Houston, over a period of nine months. Upon its return it was found to have sustained no visible damage.[5] A pressure mount is normally used only for a short display period, the textile then being rolled or placed horizontally in storage, but owing to the large and fragile nature of the Mughal textile, it has been retained in the mount since 1985. Very few textiles at the Los Angeles County Museum of Art have been pressure mounted. In several instances the mounts have been opened to permit the replacement of layers with more inert materials, and at such moments the decision to continue pressure mounting the tex-

6. Next layers of the pressure mount: cardboard mat, Pellon mat, full layer of Pellon, cotton batiste.

tile is always carefully weighed. More recently, conservators have turned their attention to the use of passive mounts for textiles, including horizontal and slant board display, and the development of other temporary mounting techniques.
Notes see Appendix.

Superb magical bronze armlet to clear the path for the Oba during the celebration, Benin.
Remarkable combination of brass and copper, the overlapping finals cast as crocodile heads, 12cm diameter.

Such mastery of mixed casting techniques would have been available to the casters in Benin City
during the 'revival' period of Akenzua I and Eresonyen (end of the 17th/ beginning of the 18th century).
There is also a pair of bracelets cast in copper and bronze in the Ife Museum
(see Werner and Willet, 1975, Pl. 5) and a bracelet in 'The Perls Collection - Royal Art of Benin',
The Metropolitan Museum of Art, New York, 1992, by Kate Ezra (p. 186, no. 78).

The crocodile is regarded as the messenger of Olokun, god of great waters.
Chambers (Ben-Amos and Rubin, 1983, p. 94) gives a resumé of the prominent role of crocodiles
in the corpus of Benin bronzes, and suggests that the heads are used as a metaphor for power.

Slit-tapestry kilim, eastern Anatolia, 155 x 202cm
Published in: *Yayla, Form und Farbe in türkischer Textilkunst,* 1993, Werner Brüggemann, pl. 55

Holger Ungerer • Taubendorf 3, 84140 Gangkofen, Germany • Tel/Fax 49-8735-606 • By Appointment Only

Small Medallion Double Niche Ushak Rug with Palmette Border
16th Century, 1.16 x 1.62m (3'10" x 5'4")

Provenance: Consul Otto Bernheimer Collection, Munich
Published: *Alte Teppiche des 16.-18. Jhdts. der Firma L. Bernheimer*, Otto Bernheimer, Munich 1959, plate 34
HALI, Issue 58, volume 13, number 4, page 58
Comparative examples: The Metropolitan Museum, New York (Ballard Collection, inv. no. 22.100.111, Dimand & Mailey figure 169)
The Philadelphia Museum of Art (McIlhenny Collection, inv. no. 43-40-59, Ellis no. 27)

UMBERTO SORGATO

20122 MILANO – VIA CERVA, 18 – TEL. 02 - 784323

Teresa Coleman Fine Arts Ltd

Embroidered silk panel with gold couched dragons
Chinese, mid 17th century, size: 79 x 78 inches

37 Wyndham St.
Hong Kong
tel: (852) 526 2450   fax: (852) 525 7159

Cakrasamvara Mandala
embroidery on silk
Sino-Tibetan
14th century
233 x 178 cms

Anna Maria Rossi & Fabio Rossi

91c Jermyn Street
London SW1Y 6JB
phone 071 321 0208
fax 071 321 0546

exhibition 15th-30th June 1994
catalogue available

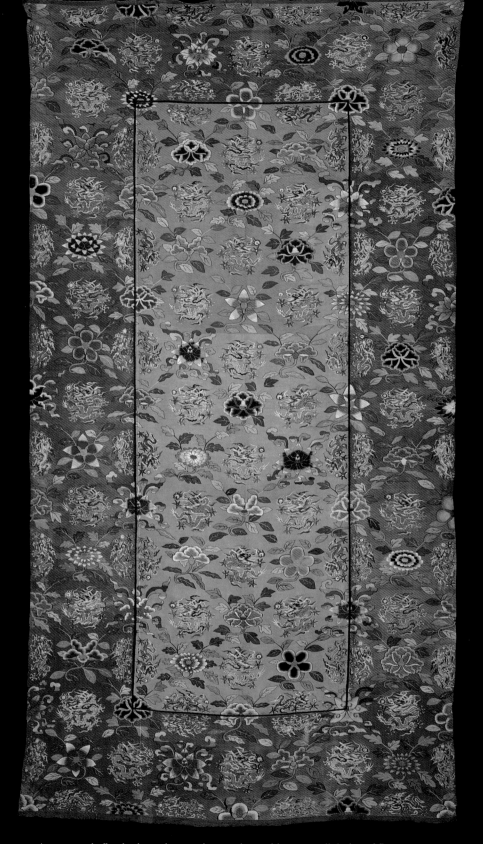

An extremely fine kesi panel woven in one piece, with an overall design of flower sprays
and five-clawed dragons on a red and biscuit-coloured ground.
Chinese, 16th/17th century. Height: 246cms. Width: 125cms.

EXHIBITION OF CHINESE TEXTILES
5th-16th December 1994

BY APPOINTMENT TO
HER MAJESTY THE QUEEN
MEDALLISTS
SPINK & SON LTD. LONDON

BY APPOINTMENT TO
H.R.H. THE DUKE OF EDINBURGH
MEDALLISTS
SPINK & SON LTD. LONDON

BY APPOINTMENT TO
H.R.H. THE PRINCE OF WALES
MEDALLISTS
SPINK & SON LTD. LONDON

SPINK

SPINK & SON LTD, 5, 6 & 7 KING STREET, ST JAMES'S, LONDON SW1Y 6QS. TEL: 071-930 7888. FAX: 071-839 4853. TELEX: 916711.
English Paintings and Watercolours · Oriental, Asian and Islamic Art · Textiles · Medals · Coins · Bullion · Banknotes

MICHAIL

di SORGATO DAVID e C. snc.

ISLAMIC ART AND FINE RUGS

White ground Agra, India, early 20th century, 4.24 x 5.75m (13" x 18'10")

ISLAMIC ART
Via Santo Spirito 19
20121 Milano, Italia
Tel e Fax (02) 7600 1064

FINE RUGS
Via Caminadella 18
20121 Milano, Italia
Tel e Fax (02) 8645 3592

OTTOMAN ART
ANTIQUE CARPETS AND KILIMS

Karakeçili rug, Balıkesir area, west Anatolia, 19th century
1.16 x 1.37m

GALLERY: VIA DELLA SPOSA, 15/A - 15/B, 06123 PERUGIA, ITALY   TEL/FAX: (39 75) 573 6842
RESTORATION WORKSHOP: VIA DELLA SPOSA, 16, 06123 PERUGIA, ITALY

Bilverdi village carpet (Heriz district), 266 x 346cm, 1880-1900

Bukhara silk chapan
Uzbekistan
second half 19th century

Ottoman embroidery, silk on cotton
Turkey
18th century
180 x 115cm

BIDJAR "TRICLINIUM", Persia Nord Occidentale, XIX Secolo, cm. 600 X 340

Il Mercante d'Oriente®
Tappeti • Tessili • Arazzi

Tiziano Meglioranzi
Il Mercante d'Oriente • C.so S.Anastasia, 34 • 37121 Verona (Italy) • Tel. 045/594152 • Fax 045/8011085

Samarkand
Galleries

Afshar Rug, Niriz, South Persia, Circa 1900, 2.03m x 1.60m (6'8" x 5'3")

Exemplary Antique and Contemporary Oriental Rugs & Carpets
Specialising in Tribal Weavings

Brian W. MacDonald, 2 Brewery Yard, Sheep Street, Stow-on-the Wold, Gloucestershire GL54 1AA
Tel/Fax: (0451) 832322

Linda Wrigglesworth
Chinese Costume and Textiles

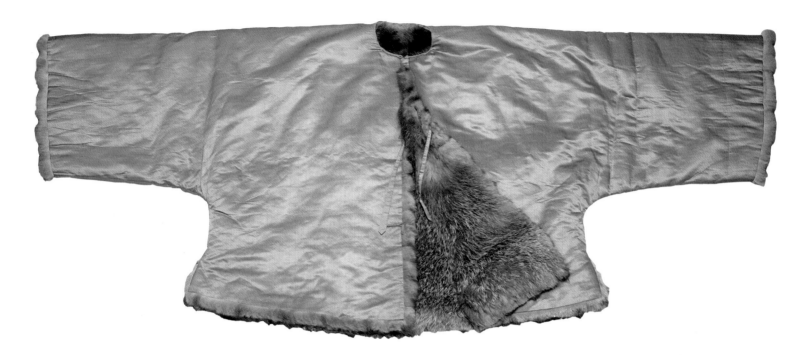

Li Hung Chang, 1896

A most handsome jacket worn by Li Hung Chang, the Senior Manchu Official, Viceroy of Two Provinces. Li Hung Chang was resident in Canton in 1900, a most powerful man and one of the plenipotentiaries in negotiations with the western world following the Boxer Rebellion. He was instrumental in forming a western modern Chinese army by employing foreigners such as General Gordon and Robert Hart. He was a senior advisor to the Empress Dowager Tzuxi. The photograph of him, was published in a book by Morse titled 'The International Relations of the Chinese Empire', published by Longmans, Green and Co., 39 Paternoster Row, London, New York, Bombay and Calcutta, 1918.

The rich blue satin silk has a lustre and richness of the best quality silk available at that time. Lined with wolf, to which the Chinese gave a special name, and edged with ermine. China, Late 19th century.
Size: this robe has a grandeur – 77cms collar to hem, 177cms cuff to cuff.
Provenance: Purchased from Mr & Mrs Drake whose father (Mr Drake) was a missionary in China and was given the jacket from Li Hung Chang's grand-daughter between 1930 and 1950 in Beijing.

Exhibitions 1994

Olympia, London, 2nd – 12th June

Linda Wrigglesworth, London, 9th – 24th June

Susan Scollay, Melbourne, 24th July – 3rd August

Great Sydney Showground, Sydney, 11th – 14th August

★Sherman Galleries, Sydney, 24th August – 10th September

Cintra Galleries, Brisbane, 15th – 24th September

★Linda Wrigglesworth, London, 17th October - 4th November

★*Textiles, Costume and Carpets from Japan*

Appointments to see the collection can be made weekdays 10.30am - 6.00pm. Weekends by arrangement.
Restoration, mounting and appraisal services also available.

'The Ground Floor Suite', 34 Brook Street, London, W1Y 1YA, England.
Tel: 071-408 0177 Fax: 071-491 9812

MEYER MÜLLER

since 1870

Gaschgai old
circa 1920
2.20 x 1.91 m, 7.3 x 6.3 ft.

Khamse antik
circa 1850
1.90 x 1.30 m, 6.3 x 4.3 ft.

Melas antik
circa 1850
1.63 x 1.13 m, 5.4 x 3.7 ft.

Gaschgai old
circa 1900
2.30 x 1.47 m, 7.6 x 4.9 ft.

Teppichhaus Meyer-Müller AG, Uraniastrasse 40, CH-8001 Zurich, Switzerland
Tel: 0041 (1) 221 05 21, Fax: 0041 (1) 221 09 40

EDITOR'S CHOICE

The following pages illustrate just a few of the most important and intriguing oriental rugs and textiles that have been offered on the international market during recent years through the pages of HALI. They have been chosen to convey something of the depth and richness of Eastern woven art.

Azerbaijan medallion and cartouche carpet, Tabriz, northwest Persia, early Safavid period, ca. 1500. Wool pile on a cotton foundation, 3.02 x 7.42m (9'11" x 24'6"). The Michaelian/Beghian carpet, which during the Ottoman period made its way to the Ghazi Husain Pasha Mosque at Tashlija in Herzegovina, is one of the grandest and most important Persian 'classical' weavings to come onto the market in recent years.

The endless repeat field design, which underlies the elegant sixteen-pointed central medallion and disappears beneath the imposing 'strapwork' border, can be seen as a floral variant of a geometric pattern derived from architectural tilework, specifically the Seljuk star-and-cross design. A radical alternative theory is put forward by the present owner, who interprets the design as an abstract avian representation with symbolic relevance to pre-Islamic Iranian religion. He has also speculatively back-dated the weaving to around 1465, associating it with the suite of carpets reputedly commissioned for the Blue Mosque in Tabriz by Saliha Khanum, daughter of the Kara Koyonlu ('Black Sheep') Turkoman Shah Jihan, and the subsequent destruction and looting of the city by the Ottomans under Sultan Selim in 1514 (see E. Herrmann, *Asiatische Teppich-und Textilkunst 4*, Munich 1993, pp.14-17).

The pair to the carpet is in the Museum für angewandte Kunst, Vienna. Fragments of a third are divided between the Kunstmuseum, Dusseldorf and the Wher Collection, Switzerland. The present whereabouts of three other closely similar carpets are unknown, and at least three small fragments are thought to be in the Türk ve Islam Eserleri Museum, Istanbul. Eberhart Herrmann Teppichantiquitäten, Munich.

Left: Medallion and animal carpet, Esfahan, central Persia, Safavid period, ca. 1600. Wool pile on a wool, cotton and silk foundation, 2.34 x 4.80m (7'8" x 15'9"). Shah Abbas the Great (r.1588-1629) established his court in Esfahan in 1598, bringing together the finest crafts-men in workshops within the palace to produce car-pets for the court, for pre-sentation to foreign visi-tors and as diplomatic gifts for Persian ambas-sadors to carry abroad. The earliest Esfahan designs were based on carpets made in Tabriz in the first half of the 16th century and in Kashan in the second. Examples such as the Rothschild carpet shown here have a characteristic palette, a brilliance of drawing and design remi-niscent of the famous Kashan silk rugs and a close stylistic affinity to much of what is assumed to be 16th century Kashan production, suggesting that they may be among the earliest products of the Esfahan looms. The Textile Gallery, London, in association with Dani Ghigo, Turin.

Right: 'Lotto' arabesque rug, Anatolia, 16th cen-tury. Wool pile on a wool foundation, 1.24 x 2.26m (4'1" x 7'5"). Named for the Italian Renaissance artist who depicted this and other carpet types usually, but not definitiv-ely, associated with the west Anatolian weaving workshops at Ushak, 'Lotto' arabesque rugs are ubiquitous among the ranks of Turkish 'classical' weavings. This excellent example stands out for its exceptionally rich colour, superb lustrous wool and outstanding condition. Galerie Sailer, Salzburg.

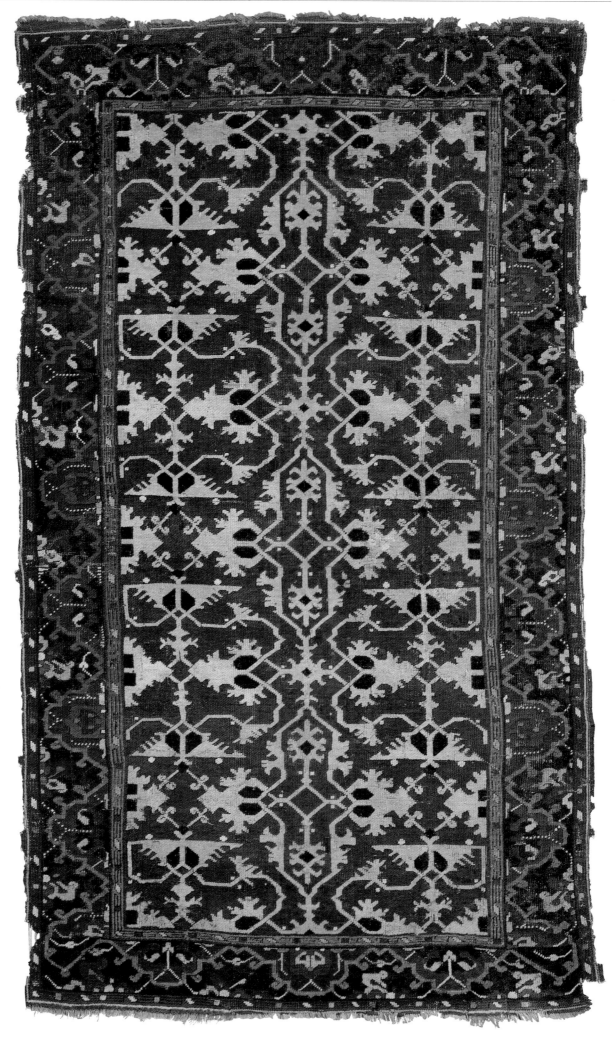

Left: Northwest Persian (?) long rug with 'Zoroastrian' flame-palmette design, early 19th century. Wool pile on wool foundation, 1.43 x 2.70m (4'8" x 8'10"). This rare, enigmatic and beautiful village carpet is only tentatively attributed to northwest Persia and does not fit readily into any of the conventional categories. However, much of our knowledge is discovered in the exceptions, the mysterious unknown types that inspire avid speculation. Formerly in the Meyer-Müller Collection, Zurich, its very unusual field and border designs, coupled with outstanding aesthetic and material qualities, make it the sort of carpet that attracts the attention of dealers and collectors who are drawn to rare weavings at the outer limits of the subject. Ronnie Newman, Ridgewood, New Jersey.

Right: Bakhtiari *khersak* (bedding rug), Zagros region, west-central Persia, 19th century or earlier. Wool pile on a wool foundation, 1.50 x 2.53m (4'11" x 8'4"). *Gabbeh*, called *khersak* by the Farsi speaking Luri and Bakhtiari nomads, are coarsely woven, shaggy piled weavings, produced by tribal weavers for their own use. Examples as old and dramatic as this are very rare. However, more recent material, ranging in date from the latter part of the 19th century to the present, has emerged as an extraordinary commercial phenomenon on the oriental carpet market, rising from complete obscurity to seemingly insatiable demand in less than a decade. Galerie Neiriz, Berlin.

Left: Avar *davaghin* (slit-tapestry kilim), Daghestan, northeast Transcaucasus, second half 19th century. Wool warp and weft, 1.40 x 2.85m (4'7" x 9'4"). This dramatically graphic flatweave, and the Azerbaijan kilim illustrated opposite, are top quality representatives of the significant numbers of such weavings to emerge during the 1990s from the Caucasian regions of the former Soviet Union. Of previously unknown or very unfamiliar types, these desirable domestic heirloom pieces have been forced onto the Western market, via east Anatolia and the Istanbul bazaar, by their owners' economic circumstances. Clive Loveless, London.

Right: Azerbaijan kilim, south Transcaucasus (?), 19th century. Wool warp and weft, 1.65 x 2.30m (5'5" x 7'6"). The technical and stylistic distinctions between antique Caucasian and northwest Persian tribal and village weavings are far from clear-cut. Many writers, dealers and collectors adhere to 20th century lines of geopolitical demarcation in their attributions, despite the existence of a cultural and historical continuum in what may be called 'Greater Azerbaijan'. This splendid and very unusual kilim, despite the suggestion that it may be a Shahsavan tribal weaving, is closer in its fairly coarse structure and colours to so-called Kazak village weaves of the southern Caucasus than to the rather finer flatweaves associated with the northwest Persian nomads. Richard Purdon, Burford, Oxfordshire.

Above: Shakhrisyabz suzani, Uzbekistan, first half
19th century. Silk embroidery on a plainwoven cotton
ground, 1.83 x 2.16m (6'0" x 7'1"). Suzani (the word
means 'needle' in Farsi) are the dowry covers and hangings worked by the townspeople of Uzbekistan and
Tajikistan. They combine a variety of influences, indigenous and cosmopolitan, in their predominantly floral
designs. Some of the most beautiful examples are
attributed to the town of Shakhrisyabz, south of
Samarkand. Paul Jarl Rognlie, Petaluma, California.

Right: Bukhara suzani, Uzbekistan, mid 19th century.
Silk embroidery on a plainwoven cotton ground, 1.80 x
2.71m (5'11" x 8'11"). A fine example of an extremely
rare design type of embroidered dowry cloth. It has
been suggested that the unusual 'leaf' forms surrounding the loosely drawn eight-pointed 'star' medallions in
the field may be a rare, symbolically significant, representation of 'fish and ponds', used in combination with
the more typical floral repertoire. Esther Fitzgerald in
association with Shirley Day, London.

Serapi Carpet
Azerbaijan
19th century
400 x 303cms

BATTILOSSI
TAPPETI D'ANTIQUARIATO

Gallery: Torino, Via Giolitti 45/F, Tel. 011 817 0722 Telefax. 011 812 3890   Restoration Studio: Torino, C.so Cairoli 4, Tel. 011 882576

Three Medallion Carpet

Khotan, Eastern Turkestan

early 19th century

183 x 407cm

John Eskenazi Ltd.

New addresses

15 Old Bond Street

London W1X 4JL

Telephone 44 71.4093001

Fax 44 71.6292146

Via Borgonuovo 5

20121 Milano

Telephone 39 2.86464883

Fax 39 2.86465018

John Eskenazi

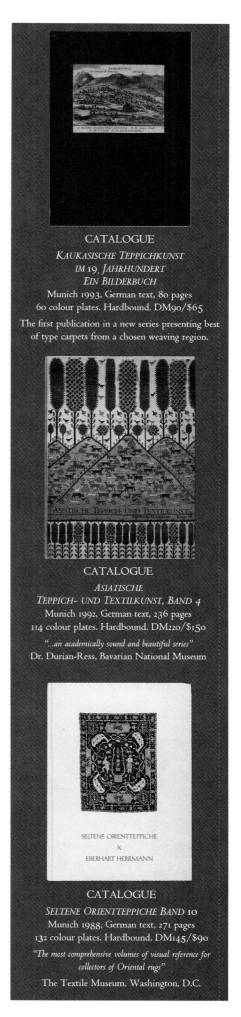

Penny Oakley
LONDON

Panel of stencilled, resist painted and dyed cotton (detail). India, Golconda, 1650-60, 85 x 31cm; 33 x 12in.
other examples:-
Spink & Son, cf: *The Art of Textiles*, London, 1989, no. 95
The Textile Museum, Washington D.C., cf: *Master Dyers to the World*, Mattiebelle Gittinger, Washington D.C., 1982,
figs. 61 and 65.

BY APPOINTMENT ONLY

27A COLLINGHAM PLACE, LONDON SW5 0QF TEL: 071-370 7160 FAX: 071-373 5654

Yves Mikaeloff

Old Master paintings and drawings carpets, tapestries furniture & porcelain

will be exhibiting at

The Grosvenor House Art & Antiques Fair
9th - 18th June 1994
Grosvenor House, Park Lane, London W1A 3AA
and
XVIIe Biennale Internationale des Antiquaires
Carrousel du Louvre, Paris
10th - 24th November 1994

---

10 et 14 rue Royale, 75008 Paris France Tel: 33 (1) 42 61 64 42 Fax: 33 (1) 49 27 07 32

RONNIE NEWMAN

An Extremely Rare Ming Dynasty Throne-back, circa 1600
3'2" x 2'9$\frac{1}{2}$" (0.95 x 0.85m)

P.O. Box 14 • Ridgewood, New Jersey 07451 • USA • Tel: (201) 825-8775 • Fax: (201) 825-8719 • By Appointment

MOSHE TABIBNIA
ARTE TESSILE ANTICA
TAPPETI ARAZZI - TESSUTI

INTERNO DEL NEGOZIO - ARAZZO BRUXELLES XVI SEC. CM. 267x252
AUBUSSON FRANCIA XIX SEC. CM. 380x300 - HERIZ PERSIA XIX SEC. CM. 395x300

VIA BRERA, 3 - 20121 MILANO
TEL. 02/8051545 - FAX 02/8051549

EUROPE

BRUSSELS

The first quarter of the 16th century saw one of the richest and most exuberant periods in the history of northern European tapestry weaving. As Gothic decorative ideas began to be infused with the new values and ideas of the dawning Renaissance, designers and weavers in the work-shops of Brussels achieved a supremely confident synthesis of composition, colour and technical skill.

Pre-Renaissance Tapestries

by An Volckaert

STYLE

The transition from the Middle Ages to the Renaissance represents, from a cultural-historical point of view, a steady shift towards new values, standards and conventions. In the art of tapestry, too, a new graphic language appeared on the scene and the iconographic repertory shifted. In tapestry jargon this phase has come to be referred to as the 'pre-Renaissance', an expression taken from Ghislaine de Boom's *Marguerite d'Autriche-Savoie et la pré-Renaissance* (1935). She characterises the period as a time when "...se prolongent les dernières lueurs du Moyen Age, où s'annonce l'aube victorieuse de la Renaissance" [...the final glow of the Middle Ages still lingered, as signs of the triumphant dawn of the Renaissance appeared].

This transitional period, roughly corresponding to the first quarter of the 16th century, and thus to the regency of Margaret of Austria at Malines (1507-1530), is chiefly associated with Brussels tapestries. Unfortunately few written records are preserved from this time and, in addition, prior to 1528 the weavings carried no identifying marks. Ornamental inscriptions occasionally provide a possible clue to identity, as for instance on the tapestry *The Bearing of the Cross* (**7**). It is, therefore, on the basis of a general consensus that a number of stylistically related tapestries are attributed to the Brussels workshops. Indeed, it was there that several cartoonists worked in a common style.

Fortunately, a few works are identified quite explicitly and thus act as key pieces – for example *The Legend of Notre-Dame-du-Sablon* (**4**). This set of four tapestries was commissioned by François de Taxis, the founding father of the postal system, who was resident for a while at the court of Maximilian of Austria in Innsbruck and of Margaret of Austria at Malines between November 1516 and November 1517. The set was completed sometime in 1518. Destined for the burial chapel of the de Taxis family in the church of *Notre-Dame-du-Sablon* in Brussels, the tapestries include several allusions to de Taxis – in a portrait, a coat of arms and a motto – as well as to other key figures from the House of Habsburg. There is much evidence to indicate that Bernard van Orley might be responsible for the designs: he had already painted an altar-piece for the same church, and had been since 1518 court painter to Margaret of Austria. It is not often that a pre-Renaissance piece is documented in such detail, and partly for this reason it was one of the most significant hangings to be included in the 1976 Brussels exhibition 'Tapisseries bruxelloises de la pré-Renaissance', which offered a striking overview of the period.

A PRE-RENAISSANCE STYLE

While any generalisation risks being reductive, it is nevertheless reasonable to say that the pre-Renaissance style has a number of clear general characteristics. One example which corresponds stylistically to the pieces that occasionally appear on the art market and which does, indisputably, have many pre-Renaissance features, is *The Story of Esther* (**2**). This demonstrates the general tendency for the main emphasis in a composition to fall on the central figures – in this case Queen Esther and below her, in the foreground, a man at a writing table. These in their turn are surrounded by figures who have a more minor, not to say ornamental role, certainly functioning within the context of a prevailing *horror vacui*, yet without creating any sense of over-elaboration.

The void around the figures is filled with tufts of grass and, in the top left- and righthand corners, a limited vista over the landscape. The line of the figures and the décor has a pronounced verticality which is somewhat modified by the prominence and serene gestures of

1. Preceding pages: ***Bathsheba Invited to the Palace of David*. From the series of ten tapestries *The History of David and Bathsheba*. Brussels, 1515-1525, after cartoons by Jan van Roome, possibly woven in the workshop of Pieter van Aelst, in collaboration with Pieter de Pannemaker. Gold, silver, silk and wool, 4.60 x 7.20m (15'1" x 23'7"). The weavers' masterly interpretation of the damasks, brocades, silk, ermine and jewels is characteristic of the treatment of costume in pre-Renaissance times. The heavily wadded, sculptured fall of the drapery emphasises the dignity of these courtiers. Seen together, the set of ten pieces is overpowering, not just in the minutiae, but as a whole, being in its entirety 75 metres long, 4.5 metres high, and containing over 600 figures, with lavish use of gold and silver thread. The unknown patron was clearly a man of great consequence. Castle of Ecouen, France.**

2. Left: ***The Story of Esther*. Brussels, 1510-1525. Silk and wool, 2.52 x 2.84m (8'3" x 9'4"). In a scene that provides a monumental witness to life at the time of Margaret of Austria, the stately pose of the courtiers is fixed by virtue of their sumptuous costumes. The decorative elaboration of the figures that fill the composition responds to the pre-Renaissance *horror vacui*. Formerly Oxburg Hall, Norfolk, and Seligmann Collection, Paris. Photo courtesy Blondeel – De Wit, Belgium.**

3. *The Triumph of Fame*. Brussels, 1500-1504. Silk and wool, 3.57 x 3.37m (11'8" x 11'1"). The cartoon, in the style of Perugino, shows the personification of Fame surrounded by literary figures of the ancient world – Ovid, Virgil, Dares, Josephus and Justinus. The combination of an antique theme with pre-Renaissance forms results in anachronisms which will later disappear when form and content are united in the full realisation of the Renaissance style. Formerly: probably collection of Isabella the Catholic of Spain and collection of the Marquis de Castro Serna Spain. Photo courtesy Blondeel – De Wit, Belgium.

4. *The Statue of our Lady arriving in Brussels.* **From the series of four tapestries** *The Legend of Notre-Dame-du-Sablon.* **Brussels, 1516-1518, after cartoons attributed to Bernard van Orley. Silk and wool, 3.45 x 5.00m (11'4" x 16'5"). Like the three others in the set, this tapestry is conceived as a triptych and exudes an atmosphere of the late Middle Ages. Just as in painted and carved retables, this layout dictates a hierarchy as regards content: the arrival of the statue of the Virgin Mary is the central focus, both in the literal and figurative sense, while the side panels depict scenes of secondary importance. One particularly striking feature is the portrayal of François de Taxis, as the patron, no less than three times, with only slight variations in his conventional pose. Surrounded by a language of forms characteristic of the late Gothic era, the colonnade shows the first signs of a Renaissance style. Musées Royaux d'Art et d'Histoire, Brussels, inv.no. 3153.**

the central figures. The facial expressions of the women are fairly wooden, the only expressive elements being a few head or hand movements. It is in the decorative interpretation of the costumes, the skilful transformation of one fabric into another that the richness of effect of such tapestries lies.

A sense of perspective is suggested by ranging the figures above each other and by positioning the horizon quite high on the panel. The use of colour is confined to contrasting tones of red, blue, yellow and a touch of green, while a very fine brown line is used to outline the figures. All these compositional elements are still strongly linked to the graphic language of late Gothic realism. At the same time the first signs of a Renaissance style are beginning to appear in this series with the use of small pillars, often hybrid in character, to enclose or divide up the composition. The designs of these are often based on the art of the gold- and silversmith, which introduced the *antijckse* style in the Netherlands and flourished in Brussels. It was not however until 1525-1530, when the Renaissance in Flanders was approaching its height, that compositions of panoramic landscapes with anatomically detailed figures and a very evident mathematical perspective came into use.

One of the most influential factors in the assimilation of a Renaissance style in tapestry design was the impact of Raphael's cartoons for *The Acts of the Apostles.* Commissioned by Pope Leo X, this series of tapestries brought a new vision to the Brussels workshop of Pieter van Aelst, the best known of the Flemish masterweavers, who realised the series between 1516 and 1521. The commission acted as a direct and challenging encounter with Italian Renaissance values.

CLASSICAL & BIBLICAL THEMES

As well as beginning to adapt stylistically to classical Renaissance ideas, Brussels tapestries begin to show a distinct preference for classical themes. This is very evident in, for instance, *The Triumph of Fame* (**3**), possibly the same piece that is described in the statement of assets and liabilities drawn up on the death of Isabella the Catholic, queen of Castille from 1474-1504. The iconography of this tapestry is linked to the work of the poet Petrarch (1304-1374) and of the artist Giulio Romano (1499-1546). Arising from a renewed interest in antiquity and its triumphal, imperial processions, the theme of the Triumphs was very popular in the 15th century in Italy and, indeed, played an important part in Florentine social life. It even found its way into the theatrical performances of royal households.

The personification of Fame is shown here with an entourage of ancient poets, including Ovid and Virgil. The banderole "Thus are the deeds of the ancients immortalised by fame" speaks of the ephemeral nature of life on earth, and the consequent need for a higher set of values. Fame effortlessly triumphs over the Three Fates of Greek and Roman mythology, spinners of the destiny of mankind. They can be seen again in a tapestry at the Victoria & Albert Museum (**8**), in which, set against a millefleurs background, Cloto, Lachesis and Atropos trample the figure of Chastity.

The Bible remained a perpetual source of inspiration in the pre-Renaissance period. Certain themes such as *David and Bathsheba* (**1, 6**) were interpreted time and again in masterly weaving, often for royal collections. The Old Testament theme of David's sinful love for Bathsheba was popular as early as the late 15th century, offering a moral allegory of kingly infidelity and instability.

It is noticeable that in these tapestries biblical and classical themes are expressed in a contemporary style; figures are interpreted as refined princes and courtly ladies, their acts and attire adapted to the conventions of late medieval society. The palace in the *David* tapestry of Ecouen (**1**) reminds us, for example, of the old palace of the Dukes of Burgundy, "*la cour des bailles*", on the Coudenberg in Brussels. It was not until the Renaissance that, in tapestry design at least, this disjunction was abandoned.

THE BEARING OF THE CROSS

Sumptuously woven with gold thread, the magnificent tapestry *The Bearing of the Cross* (**5**), constitutes a supreme moment in the art of tapestry of the pre-Renaissance, indeed, of Flemish tapestry as a whole. The technical virtuosity of the weaving is borne out by the inscriptions 'AELST' and '1507'. The cartoons for the first edition were woven in the workshop of Pieter van Aelst, the foremost supplier of tapestries to the Emperor and the Pope. As well as the Raphael series mentioned earlier, *The Acts of the Apostles*, he produced the series of *Panos de Oro* (Golden Weavings) for the wife of Philip the Fair, and *Los Honores*, an allegory of the power of worldy sovereigns, for the then ruler, Emperor Charles V (Charles I of Spain).

The Bearing of the Cross is again one of a series, probably of four tapestries. Together with *The Descent from the Cross*, it is now in the collection of the Spanish Patrimonio Nacional, one of the most impressive collections of tapestries anywhere in the world. These scenes from the Passion of Christ, first mentioned in the statement of assets and liabilities drawn up on the death of Margaret of Austria in 1530, entered the Spanish Collection after Charles V made a present of the complete set to his wife Isabella of Portugal. In the 19th century Isabella II gave two pieces from the set to an Italian diplomat, and they subsequently found their way into national collections, one in the Rijksmuseum in Amsterdam, and one in the Musées Royaux d'Art et d'Histoire in Brussels.

The exquisite details, the vitality of the dazzling and colourful procession and the serene expression of the suffering Christ and the women who surround him are remarkable. At the centre is Veronica, who hands Christ her kerchief to mop his brow. In sharp contrast the executioner, seen kicking Christ in the loins, is an aggressive burlesque figure which evokes imagery of the suffering Christ in northern European art. The story continues in the top panel, which records events at Calvary, with Christ on the cross along with the two thieves. The soul of the repentant thief, flanked by the sun, is carried to heaven; that of the unrepentant thief, flanked by the moon, to hell. The horseman carrying a lance is the centurion

5. Left, and detail title page: *The Bearing of the Cross*. From the series of four tapestries, *The Passion of Christ*. Brussels, workshop of Pieter van Aelst, 1511-1518, after a cartoon from 1507. Gold, silk and wool, 3.01 x 3.09m (9'10" x 10'2"). Pieter van Aelst, the weaver par excellence to emperors and popes in the first quarter of the 16th century, created fabrics of exceptional quality. Striking in *The Bearing of the Cross* is the subtlety with which composition and expression are used to structure the journey of Christ to Cavalry. Shown in the 1993 exhibition 'Golden Weavings' in Munich, Mechelen and Amsterdam. Royal Collection, Palacio Real, Madrid, inv.no. 216.5915.

6. *The History of David and Bathsheba.* **Brussels, 1500-1525. Silk and wool, 3.20 x 3.40m (10'6" x 11'2"). The History of David and Bathsheba can be counted among the most popular themes used in pre-Renaissance times, reflecting the moral and political aspirations of the court at the end of the 15th and the start of the 16th century. Other examples of the theme can be seen in the National Museum, Stockholm; the National Museum, Warsaw; Brussels City Hall; the Palacio Real in Madrid and the collection of the princes of Hohenzollern in the castle of Sigmaringen. Henry VIII of England had no fewer than seven sets of David tapestries. Photo courtesy Blondeel – De Wit, Belgium.**

7. Opposite: *Judith and Holofernes.* **Tournai, probably workshop of Arnould Poissonnier, 1510-1522. Silk and wool, 3.57 x 2.32m (11'8" x 7'7"). The scene is explained by the banderole: "Her beauty and her timidity pleased Holofernes." Judith and Holofernes themselves have their names on their costumes, as does the eunuch who stands between them. While the pre-Renaissance period is mainly associated with Brussels weavings, other centres such as Doornik were also actively producing extremely decorative tapestries. Photo courtesy Blondeel – De Wit, Belgium.**

8. *The Three Fates*. Flanders, beginning 16th century. Silk and wool, 3.07 x 2.64m
(10'1" x 8'8"). In ancient times the Fates held the key to the destiny of man. They
are Cloto, who spins the thread of human fate, Lachesis, who dispenses and maintains
it, and Atropos, who cuts it, thus determining an individual's moment of death. Here
they trample the prostrate figure of Chastity. This theme from antiquity is seen ana-
chronistically against a millefleurs background. Victoria & Albert Museum, London,
inv.no. 65.1866.

9. *The Allegory of Time*. Tournai or northern France, 1525-1550. Silk and wool, 1.94 x 2.78m (6'4" x 9'2"). Tapestries with a moralising theme, acting as a mirror for their viewers, were much appreciated in the 16th century. On this tapestry, with its still obvious splendour of colours and its flamboyant drawing, the allegory of Wisdom points to the words on the banderole "Si tu pretens a honneur parvenir es deux recorde et prevoi ladvenir" (If you aspire to honour, look to both sides and foresee the future). Both iconography and design are unique. Photo courtesy Blondeel – De Wit, Belgium.

Longinus, whose blindness, according to a story that originates in Jacobus de Voragine's 13th century *Golden Legend,* was healed by Christ's blood. In the top lefthand corner the scene of Abraham preparing to sacrifice Isaac foreshadows the sacrifice of Christ. Italianised pilasters with genii and baluster pillars give a graceful outline to the composition.

OTHER CENTRES
Brussels is unanimously identified with the pre-Renaissance style. During the first quarter of the 16th century other centres tended to be rather provincial and noticeably less influenced by the political, economic and artistic climate. Some extremely decorative designs were nevertheless produced in other workshops. Tournai, past its heyday by the end of the 15th century following the death of one of its great weavers, Pasquier Grenier, maintained a reputation in the early 16th century thanks to the workshop of Arnould Poissonnier, to which we can attribute *Judith and Holofernes* (**7**), woven to the same cartoon as the piece in the Musées Royaux d'Art et d'Histoire in Brussels. The flat composition, the narrow perspective and the highly stylised shapes are still very medieval, while the Renaissance-influenced realism in the fall of the pleated costumes and in the reproduction of the furniture is striking.

From an artistic standpoint, the pre-Renaissance was a brief but influential period in Flemish tapestry weaving, which was to assure Brussels' position of eminence for the coming decades. During the ascendancy of the Tournai workshops, the Brussels weaving guild slowly developed to become the undisputed centre of production in the Low Countries. Further advances beginning in the 1530s were fuelled by the economic prosperity that marked the reign of Charles V, as well as by the city's new status as capital of the Netherlands. The religious upheavals of the 1560s halted this period of growth, but Brussels nevertheless held its position in the market until tapestry weaving finally began to decline in the 18th century.

EMBROIDERY IN BRITAIN
1200-1750

The work of British embroiderers survives from as far back as the 9th century. By the late 13th century the sophisticated and immensely costly products of the English embroidery workshops were highly sought after by leaders of Church and State. London's Victoria & Albert Museum, which houses the national collections of British art and design, have an unparalleled collection of embroidered textiles, evoking the changing designs and techniques of over a thousand years of craftsmanship.

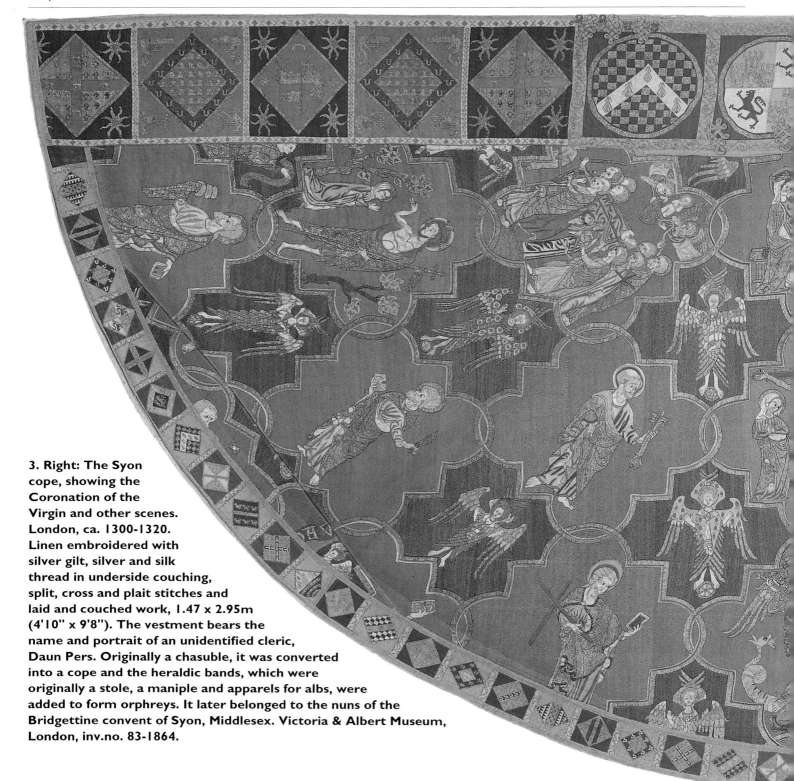

3. Right: The Syon
cope, showing the
Coronation of the
Virgin and other scenes.
London, ca. 1300-1320.
Linen embroidered with
silver gilt, silver and silk
thread in underside couching,
split, cross and plait stitches and
laid and couched work, 1.47 x 2.95m
(4'10" x 9'8"). The vestment bears the
name and portrait of an unidentified cleric,
Daun Pers. Originally a chasuble, it was converted
into a cope and the heraldic bands, which were
originally a stole, a maniple and apparels for albs, were
added to form orphreys. It later belonged to the nuns of the
Bridgettine convent of Syon, Middlesex. Victoria & Albert Museum,
London, inv.no. 83-1864.

1. Preceding pages, left: The Clare chasuble, showing the Crucifixion, the Virgin and
Child, St Peter and St Paul, and the Stoning of St Stephen. London, ca. 1272-1279.
Satin embroidered with silver-gilt, silver and silk thread in underside couching, split
stitch and laid and couched work, 1.20 x 0.81m (1'5" x 2'8"). The chasuble formerly
bore heraldic shields indicating that it was commissioned by Margaret de Clare, wife
of Edmund Plantagenet, nephew of King Henry III. The couple were married in 1272.
Victoria & Albert Museum, London, inv.no. 673-1864. All photographs courtesy the
Board of Trustees of the Victoria & Albert Museum.

2. Preceding pages, right: The John of Thanet panel (detail), showing Christ enthroned.
Probably London, ca. 1300-1320. Silk twill embroidered with silver-gilt, silver and silk
thread and pearls in underside couching and split stitch, 1.00 x 0.42m (3'3" x 1'4").
Probably part of a cope, it bears the name of John of Thanet, a monk of Canterbury
Cathedral, who died in 1330. Victoria & Albert Museum, London, inv.no. T.337-1921.

I: THE MIDDLE AGES

By Donald King

As well as reflecting late classical themes, medieval embroidery in Britain was much influenced by the ornament and illustrative style of manuscript painting, becoming ever more elaborate and lavish in the golden period of the early 14th century.

Weaving and needlework have been practised in Britain since remote antiquity. As a province of the Roman Empire, England is known to have possessed a state textile factory and there is documentary evidence for the export of British woollen textiles in that period. During the Middle Ages, immense quantities of high quality wool were exported from Britain to various weaving centres in Europe, where it was used for the production of the finest grades of cloth. Unpatterned woollen and linen cloth in many

different types and colours were also woven in Britain, while many patterned textiles were imported. These included silk textiles with repeating patterns, woven on the drawloom in Italy, Spain, Byzantium, or the Islamic world, and pictorial wall-hangings, woven by the tapestry technique, and imported in the later Middle Ages from France and Flanders.

Only two classes of patterned textiles are certainly known, from surviving examples, to have been produced in England during the Middle Ages. The first were narrow tablet-woven bands or ribbons, from a few millimetres to about three inches wide, patterned with geometric labyrinths or interlace, and occasionally small plants and animals.

The second, far more important both artistically and economically, were embroideries. The oldest significant embroideries which can be attributed to English workers are some pieces preserved at Maeseyck in Belgium, dating from about 850 AD.[1] Their designs of arches and circles containing animals and interlace, very closely related to the ornament of contemporary Anglo-Saxon manuscripts and sculpture, are the earliest examples of the animal patterns of which many are to be found in later English embroideries.

In an entirely different style are the figures of prophets and saints to be seen on an early 10th century stole and maniple at Durham Cathedral.[2] The ornamentation of vertical bands by means of standing figures one above another was derived from late classical textiles and was to remain an important feature of English embroidery until the end of the Middle Ages.

4. Altar frontal or dossal fragment, showing two kneeling couples who are identified by inscriptions as Henry and Joan Smyth and Thomas and Joan Smyth. Possibly Worcestershire, ca. 1470-1500. Velvet, with applied motifs of linen embroidered with silver-gilt and silk thread and sequins in couched work and split stitch, 70 x 68.5cm (28" x 27"). Victoria & Albert Museum, London, inv.no. T.194.1911.

Considerably later in date, and very different in scale, technique and style is the great embroidered frieze at Bayeux depicting the Norman invasion of Britain in 1066,[3] in which the designer excels in organising the complex story into lively pictorial episodes, foreshadowing the narrative skill which appears in many later English embroideries.

In contrast, embroideries of the Romanesque and early Gothic periods aim at effects of sober magnificence and are apt to seem severe, even a trifle monotonous.[4] The figures and ornaments, rather stiffly drawn in styles related to those of contemporary manuscript painting, are executed almost entirely with gold thread, in the technique known as underside couching, on backgrounds of silk cloth in deep tones of red, blue or purple (2).

During the 13th century English gold embroidery, most of which was produced in workshops in the City of London, acquired an international reputation. In 1263, a certain Gregory of London was working in Rome as gold-embroiderer to the household of Pope Alexander IV. The great Vatican inventory of 1295 recorded well over a hundred examples of English embroidery, far more than of any other type. In the late 13th and early 14th century the London embroidery workshops reached the zenith of their achievement, and their products were sought after by great potentates throughout Europe. This was a period of luxurious taste in England, corresponding to the Decorated style in English Gothic architecture and the rich illuminations of the so-called East Anglian manuscripts. The elegantly posed embroidered figures, with their ample garments with convoluted folds and serpentine hems, are identical to those depicted by the painters and miniaturists who worked for the English court and the nobility. No doubt the embroidery designs were supplied by the same artists (1, 5).

As in the preceding period, the figure subjects in the embroideries were enclosed within coiling vine stems, within geometrical frames, or within Gothic arches. These three types of composition are exemplified by the three great copes in the collection of the Victoria & Albert Museum, the Jesse Cope, the Syon Cope (3) and the Butler-Bowdon Cope, as well as by many smaller embroideries.

From the middle of the 14th century onwards, although the English workshops continued to be extremely active, making large quantities of excellent embroidery, they were no longer called upon to produce work of such luxurious quality as in the preceding period. Economic resources were now diverted from luxury goods into military expenditure; the wages of skilled workers rose; and at the same time the embroidery workshops had to meet increasing competition from imports of Italian patterned silks. The English workshops responded by simplifying their techniques; underside couching, for example, was replaced by surface couching. Designs were also simplified and repeated. Large pieces, such as copes and altar frontals, were no longer embroidered throughout to specially commissioned designs but decorated by embroidering standardised motifs on linen, which might be large and elaborate, or small conventional motifs such as flowers. These were then cut out around their outlines, and applied to a silk or velvet background (4).

The long tradition of religious embroidery in England was brought to an abrupt halt by the Reformation. The Reformed Church had no use for embroideries with sacred subjects, which ceased to be made. Of the vast stocks of medieval examples then existing, many were destroyed to recover the pearls and the gold thread while others were exported to Catholic countries overseas. A few were preserved by English Catholic families for occasional clandestine use by visiting priests. It is from these sources that the V&A have assembled their unique collection.

Some of the richest of medieval embroideries were produced for court costumes or for furnishing items, but almost none of this work now survives. A hint of the nature of secular embroidery can be gleaned from the scrolls and animal patterns of the Clare chasuble (2) and the John of Thanet panel (1), or the heraldic work of the Syon cope (3).[5] The professional workshops certainly found little difficulty in making the transition to the new secular styles of ornament, but their monopoly was to be increasingly challenged by the work of skilled amateur embroiderers.

5. Chasuble orphrey (detail) showing Christ carrying the cross. London, ca. 1315-1335. Linen embroidered with silver-gilt, silver and silk thread in underside couching, split stitch and laid and couched work, 33 x 19cm (13" x 7"). The arms are those of the Wokyndon family, benefactors of St Paul's Cathedral. Victoria & Albert Museum, London, inv.no. T.31-1936.

II: POST-REFORMATION

By Santina Levey

The Reformation marked a change in the production and use of embroidery in Britain. Open to influence both from Europe and the East, embroiderers produced work mainly for domestic use in an unbroken tradition that still flourishes today.

TUDOR & JACOBEAN WORK (1550 TO 1660)

The embroidery which survives from the reigns of Elizabeth I (1558-1603) and James I (1603-1625) is almost entirely secular. While on the one hand the Reformation had ended the demand for ecclesiastical embroidery, on the other, the growth of a stable society meant that prosperity was expressed by the building and furnishing of new houses.

Textiles in domestic use included tapestries from Flanders, silks, velvets and other woven

1. Applied and embroidered cushion cover (detail). Probably London, second half 16th century. Velvet, cloth of silver and silk on satin with embroidered details. 53.5cm (21") square. Victoria & Albert Museum, London, inv.no. T.22-1947.

2. Embroidered woman's informal jacket (detail of back). England, first quarter 17th century. Linen with silk and metal thread in chain and detached buttonhole stitches, 38 x 28cm (15" x 11"). Victoria & Albert Museum, London, inv.no. 919-1873.

fabrics and trimmings from Italy and rarer items, mainly carpets, from the Near and Far East. Some embroidery was also imported – silkwork from Italy, whitework from Flanders and canvas work from France, including the pictorial valances frequently found in English and Scottish houses and once thought to be British – but most of the embroidery was produced in Britain. The inventories of the period describe embroidered furnishings made with a wide variety of materials and techniques. Rich woven fabrics were applied one to another and minor details were added in silk or metal thread (**1**). Woven grounds were also decorated with applied embroidery worked on linen canvas and innumerable small flowers (called slips) were embroidered on linen canvas for use in this way. Inventories are full of entries such as "An other long quition [cushion] of crimson velvet set with slips of needlework".[6]

Woven silks and velvets were used for one other group in which the ground and the embroidered decoration were of equal importance. The patterns, which were usually small and linear, were worked mainly with silver-gilt and silver thread and were embellished with spangles, seed pearls and other ornaments. This technique was used both for furnishings and for dress, although the tendency to salvage the valuable materials means little has survived.

Embroideries made of less valuable materials survive in greater numbers, particularly those worked on linen canvas, with the ground entirely covered by embroidery in wool or silk, normally in tent, cross or gobelin stitches. This was popular for small items such as pincushions and purses. Also long-lasting are the embroideries worked on an exposed linen ground. Surviving pieces include examples of the large number of decorated towels, table and cupboard cloths, coverlets and pillows which are listed in the inventories and the many shifts, shirts, caps, coifs, jackets and other linen accessories worn during this period (**2**).

Linen was worked with coloured silks and gold thread, and also in monochrome, notably with black silk. White-on-white embroidery differed from the other monochrome embroideries by its frequent combination with drawn-thread work and cutwork, techniques which, in the most elaborate examples, overlapped with needle lace.

While some Elizabethan and Jacobean designs reflected the international repertoire, others were peculiarly English, or combined the two. Although grotesques (**1**), arabesques,

strapwork and other elements of Renaissance ornament were known to English designers, they were seldom used in their pure form. More typically English are the embroideries at Hardwick Hall which combine grotesques and lattice patterns with naturalistic flowers.

The arabesque underlies many English embroidery designs. The influence of the simplified forms of flower-decorated arabesques, often combined with strapwork, that were published in Continental pattern books from the late 1520s onwards, can be seen in many English embroideries. Another popular design both in Continental and in English embroidery was the zig-zag or curvilinear flowering stem. The English preferred the more coiling and flowery version which, when adapted to form an all-over pattern, became the most characteristic of all English embroidery designs of the period (**2**).

Diapers and lattices adapted from late medieval geometric patterns and Renaissance strapwork were frequently combined with small floral motifs and in some English examples the floral ornament almost obliterated the underlying design. More exclusively English were

3. Embroidered long pillow cover showing scenes from the Book of Genesis. England, late 16th or 17th century. Linen worked with silk and metal thread in stem, chain, back, cross and speckling stitches. 52 x 90cm (20" x 35"). Victoria & Albert Museum, London, inv.no. T.116-1928.

the patterns composed of isolated motifs. Most popular were the little floral slips.

There is also evidence that canvas work embroidery was used extensively for bolder pictorial subjects, as on the border of the Bradford table carpet which depicts mankind's progression from the wild state to civilisation, set within a pastoral landscape. Many canvas work pieces are decorated with coats of arms, reflecting a strong interest in genealogy.

By the early 17th century embroidery patterns were being provided by the print sellers, who offered not only books of designs, but patterns printed directly on cloth. Other printed sources were the illustrations of emblem books, of certain classical works and of the Bible. Any craftsman who was a competent draughtsman – writing master, master plasterer, wood-worker – was likely to be pressed into service for the embroiderer from time to time.

Little detailed information is available concerning the relative roles of professional and amateur embroiderers and the relatively large quantity of domestic (and probably amateur) embroidery which has survived tends to overshadow the rarer professional work. Members

of the Broderers' Company, which was incorporated in October 1561, were responsible for all ceremonial embroidery, including work for the London Livery Companies and for the royal household, but virtually nothing is left of this work. Professional embroiderers were employed in the large country houses, but their work is hard to distinguish from that of skilled amateurs. Documents of the period record the important part which embroidery played in the lives of most well-to-do women; standards were high and a thorough grounding in embroidery techniques was part of the basic training of girls from an early age.

LATER STUART & HANOVERIAN WORK (1660 TO 1750)

Embroidery continued to make a major contribution to furnishings and dress throughout the 17th century and during the first sixty years of the 18th century. Canvas remained the basic material for furnishings, from large items such as floor carpets and wall hangings to cushions and sets of seat furniture down to smaller pieces such as hand screens. However, silk and velvet grounds became less common and, during the second half of the 17th century, fine silk-on-linen embroidery was then replaced by crewel wool embroidery on a heavy linen-cotton twill. Fine linen returned to favour in the early 18th century when it was embroidered with both fine wool and silk. During the 18th century, silk thread was used either alone or in combination with metal threads for many professional embroideries, including bed sets composed of coverlet, valances, bolster and pillows and costume items, notably dresses.

Embroiderers of the later 17th century drew upon a slightly different repertoire of stitches. Tent and cross stitch remained the basic stitches for canvas work but rococo stitch was popular for details and for smaller items. The jagged arrangement of upright stitches, now called Hungarian, Florentine or Flame stitch, was used extensively in the late 17th and early 18th century, when it was known as Irish stitch. This period also saw the introduction from the

4. The Abigail Pett hangings (detail). England, late 17th century. Linen and cotton twill embroidered with crewel wool in long and short, stem, satin, feather and herringbone stitches, laid and couched work. 51 cm (20") high. From a complete set of bed curtains and valances inscribed on one valance with the embroiderer's name. Victoria & Albert Museum, London, inv.nos. T.13 to I-1929.

East of chain stitch and the extensive use of quilting, which was normally worked in white on white. A technique which was particularly popular around 1700 was knotting: with the aid of a shuttle, a series of knots was tied in lengths of plain or coloured thread and the knotted lengths were then used for fringes or couched work.

Some designs of the Jacobean period were carried over into the second half of the 17th century, mainly in the samplers and small embroideries worked by young girls. Slips, bird and animal motifs continued to be used, as did pictorial subjects illustrating Biblical stories or personifications of the Senses, the Virtues or the Seasons, all based on printed sources.

The designs of the painted cotton palampores of India, themselves a mixture of oriental and Western elements, were very influential at this time. The Baroque leaves of crewel work hangings are sometimes filled with tiny plant forms which are derived from the leaves of palampores and are quite unlike the geometric patterns of earlier English fillings.

English embroiderers particularly liked exotic chinoiserie birds and these appear in a number of late 17th and 18th century pieces (5) as do – although more rarely – representations of imported Chinese objects. Woven silks also influenced design in the 17th century, and increasingly in the 18th century. This was particularly true of professional embroidery which was used as an alternative to patterned woven fabrics, notably for elaborate bed sets and court dress of both men and women.

The difference between professional and amateur embroidery became more marked during the 18th century. Although standards remained high, the amateurs gradually restricted themselves to a narrower range of techniques and a smaller group of objects – pictures, chair seats and dress accessories. This trend was accentuated towards the end of the century as the Neo-Classical style gained ground and surface decoration dwindled in importance.
Notes see Appendix

5. Embroidered curtain (detail). England, early 18th century. Linen and cotton twill worked with crewel wool in brick and stem stitches with French and bullion knots. 241 x 211cm (95" x 83"). Victoria & Albert Museum, London, inv.nos. T.172-1923.

Crewelwork Curtain (detail) finely embroidered in silk and wool on linen dimity ground, English or Scottish, c. 1730.
A set consisting of 2 Curtains and a Pelmet: Curtains 94" x 99" each, Pelmet 10½" x 216"

Cora Ginsburg, Inc.

Fine Textiles, Needlework and Costume

19 EAST 74TH STREET, NEW YORK, NY 10021 TEL 212-744-1352 FAX 212-879-1601
By Appointment

GALERIE CHEVALIER

ANTIQUE TAPESTRIES, RUGS
17, Quai Voltaire - 75007 PARIS - Tel. (1) 42 60 72 68 - Fax (1) 42 86 99 06
11 East 57th Street - New York, NY 10022 - Tel. (212) 750-5505 - Fax (212) 750-6234

A rare Peruvian tapestry
Colonial Peru, 17th or 18th century, llama wool weft on cotton warp
H. 226cm x W. 216cm / H. 7ft 5in x W. 7ft 1in

CHEVALIER
CONSERVATION

CLEANING, RESTORATION, CONSERVATION
OF ANTIQUE AND CONTEMPORARY TAPESTRIES, ORIENTAL RUGS, SILK RUGS, KILIMS,
AUBUSSON, SAVONNERIE AND NEEDLEPOINT RUGS, ANTIQUE TEXTILES

FRANCE: 64, bd de la Mission-Marchand - 92400 COURBEVOIE - Tel. (1) 47 88 41 41 - Fax (1) 43 34 08 99
USA: 500, West Avenue - STAMFORD, CT 06902 - Tel. (203) 969 1980 - Fax (203) 969 1988

GALERIE RUF

13TH – 20TH CENTURY EUROPEAN TEXTILES
18TH – 20TH CENTURY EUROPEAN COSTUMES

Lady's costume,
comprising caraco
jacket and petticoat
printed cotton
France, ca. 1785

Red silk velvet on yellow silk
ground, gold brocaded
Italy, first half 16th century
80 x 280cm

D-76437 RASTATT, BRAHMSWEG 3, GERMANY
TELEPHONE: +49-7222-28353 FAX: +49-7222-29034

By appointment only

HADJER et FILS

ANTIQUE CARPETS - ANTIQUE TAPESTRIES

Member of the
French Antique Dealers Association

102, Rue du Faubourg St. Honoré, 75008 Paris, France
Tel: (1) 42 66 61 13   Fax: (1) 42 66 66 03

Joseph Lavian

member of
THE ORIENTAL CARPET CENTRE

An early Louis XV Aubusson 'Teniers' tapestry, circa 1730
2.64 x 2.20m (8'8" x 7'3")

A large selection of very fine tapestries depicting pastoral and
mythological scenes are available now, including Aubussons, Brussels
and Flemish tapestries ranging from the 16th to the 18th century

Antique and Modern Oriental Carpets, Rugs and Kilims,
Aubusson Tapestries and Textiles,
A Comprehensive Range, Always in Stock

WESTERN
HEMISPHERE

THE MOMENT OF GREATEST SANCTITY

A Pacatnamu Ritual Textile

By Christopher B. Donnan

Pacatnamu is a spectacular archaeological site of pyramids and courtyards, located at the mouth of the Jequetepeque River on the North Coast of Peru. During excavation of a walled enclosure within one of the open courts, archaeologists found a large number of textile fragments and miniature garments. One of these has a complex iconography showing ceremonial activities that may once have been part of the social and religious life of the inhabitants of Pacatnamu.

1. Left: Aerial view of Pacatnamu.

2. Above: Slit tapestry fragment with cotton warps and wool wefts. Peru, North Coast, 1000-1300 AD. 23cm (9") square, excluding tassels.

Dominated by precipitous cliffs on two sides and guarded by high city walls on the third, the sprawling architectural complex of Pacatnamu (**1, 9**) has a core area of approximately one square kilometre. The site is dominated by more than fifty truncated pyramids that support elaborate summit structures and sanctuaries. Flanking the mud brick pyramids are attendant complexes of spacious courts, corridors, and elite quarters, and cemeteries are scattered inside and outside the city's perimeter walls.

Because of the arid climate and Pacatnamu's location high above the valley floor, archaeological preservation is extraordinary. Walls often stand to nearly their original height, painted façades survive, and elaborate tombs preserve their full contents — coffins of cane, gourd and ceramic vessels, jewellery, and exquisitely woven garments, which comprise the largest collection of ornate textiles ever discovered in northern Peru.

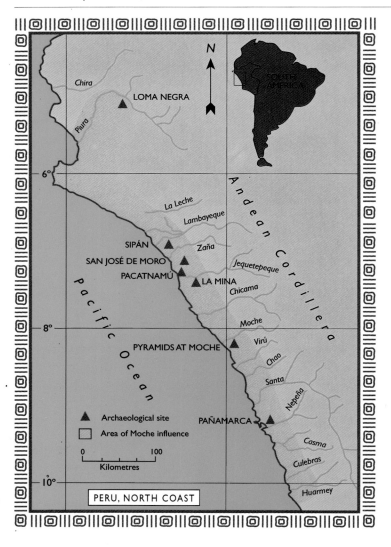

Huaca I is the largest and most impressive pyramid at Pacatnamu and is the centre of an architectural complex that dominates the central portion of the site (**9**). On the south side of this pyramid is a quadrangular walled enclosure, each side measuring approximately 170 metres. Its huge perimeter walls and single narrow doorway assured restricted access to its interior, which was divided into numerous rooms and open courtyards (**9, 10**).

AN ELABORATE TEXTILE

The obvious importance of this quadrangle and its relatively good state of preservation encouraged the team to undertake a major excavation of the area. In the process, a remarkable textile fragment with complex iconography was uncovered (**2, 4**). The textile depicts several individuals who appear to be engaged in ceremonial activities. Since other archaeological material excavated inside the quadrangle indicates that these kinds of activities actually took place there, this textile provides a fascinating glimpse of how the quadrangle may have functioned, as seen through the eyes of the ancient inhabitants of Pacatnamu.[1]

The textile was found near the southwest corner of the quadrangle, in an open courtyard where a U-shaped structure is located (**10**). It was associated with many other textile fragments and miniature garments (**3, 5, 6, 7, 11**), which appear to have been looted from their original context and left scattered on the floor of the courtyard. These textiles were remarkably well preserved because they lay adjacent to a wall and had been covered with windblown sand and melted adobe as the wall subsequently eroded.[2]

The original location of the textiles is not known, but it is likely they came either from the circular pits in the floor of the courtyard in front of the U-shaped structure, or from beneath the structure itself. The fill in these areas contained numerous fragments of textiles, shells, gourds, and ceramic vessels. Of the more than one hundred textile fragments found in these areas and on the patio floor, the elaborate textile discussed here is unique in having complex iconography illustrating numerous figures involved in a variety of activities.

The textile is a slit-tapestry with cotton warps and wool camelid wefts. The long slits are sewn closed with an overcast stitch. The garments worn by some of the individuals depicted have a three-dimensional quality created by weft-looped pile, and a similar effect is achieved for the thatch on the roofs of the two structures, where bands of wool fringe have been sewn onto the textile after it was woven. The original selvedges are preserved along the bottom and left side, but the top and right side are torn. An elaborate border is sewn along the bottom of the piece, and several multistrand tassels extend below it. This border continues beyond the left selvedge, suggesting that there was originally another panel of cloth. Some loose threads and sewing holes along the left selvedge provide further evidence of this.

The border with fringe along the bottom, and the evidence for at least one additional vertical panel, suggest that the textile may originally have been part of an elaborate shirt. Sleeved shirts with elaborate tapestry weave central panels are known to come from the lower Jequetepeque Valley, and some are so similar in colour, construction and iconography, that they are thought to have been looted from Pacatnamu.

DATING

It is difficult to assign a precise date to the textile, but it clearly belongs to the Lambayeque occupation of Pacatnamu that occurred after 1000 AD. Fragments of ceramics found in the looted pits and presumed to be associated with the textile include double spout and bridge bottles of reduction-fired blackware, a form generally associated with the Late Intermediate Period occupation of the North Coast

Also, the manner in which figures are depicted on this textile is similar to that found on other textiles from the Jequetepeque Valley thought to have been woven during the early part of the Late Intermediate Period. Thus, it is reasonable to suggest a date of between 1000 and 1300 AD for this textile.

The predominant figures on the textile are the two, shown frontally, seated under

3. Below: Slit tapestry miniature tunic with vertical neck and arm openings.

4. Right: Drawing of the design on the elaborate textile fragment (2).

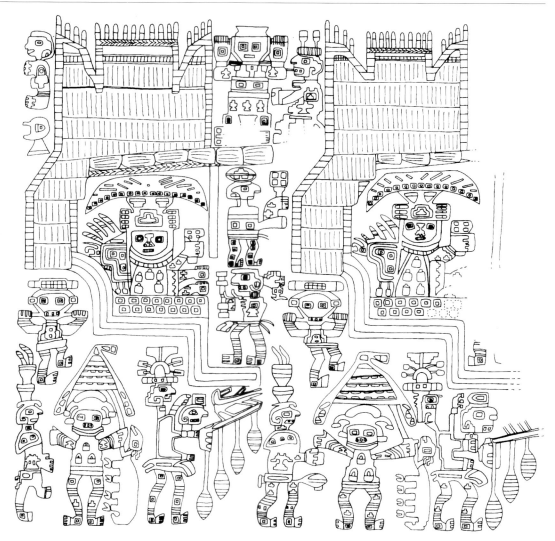

5. Below: Miniature sleeveless tunic at the moment of discovery. It consists of a plain-weave cotton panel with a wool tapestry band sewn along the centre line.
10.5 x 8cm (4" x 3").

6. Below: Elaborate plain-weave panel with cotton warps, striped woollen wefts and wool tassels.
9.8 x 9.1cm (9¹/₂" x 9³/₄").

tall thatched roofs. They wear large crescent headdresses and elaborate clothing, including a birdlike element that projects from their backs. Each holds a decorated goblet, raised as though a toast is being proposed. The stepped line patterns beneath the figures suggest raised platforms or elevated architecture on which the thatched roof structures were built. Symmetrical notches on top of the thatched roofs are identical to those on some architecture depicted on Lambayeque ceramics (**8**).

Below and to the left of each of the seated major figures is an individual whose face, arms, hands and torso are presented frontally, and whose legs and feet are shown in profile. The hands are raised; one leg is extended with the foot on the ground, the second is elevated with the knee bent. The intent of the weaver may have been to imply movement, possibly dancing, and these figures will henceforth be referred to here as 'dancers.'

Beneath and to the right of each dancer is an individual in frontal view, holding a white llama with his left hand.[3] The llama almost certainly has been or is soon to be sacrificed. It is suspended from a rope tied around its neck which extends upward to a large triangular element. To the left of each llama holder is what may be an attendant figure, shown in profile, who is helping with the llama sacrifice. To the right of the llamas are weavers, shown standing and in profile. In front of each is a loom, indicated by a diagonal line extending upward from their hands, with a series of bobbins hanging from it.[4] The multiple bobbins suggest the weaving of tapestry. Each of the weavers has a human head projecting from the wrist nearest the loom.

The activities of the other figures depicted on this textile are more difficult to interpret. Those seen in profile, standing one above the other between the major figures, may be attendants. The one at the top appears to be holding a goblet similar to those held by the major figures. At the top of the textile, between he thatched roofs, are two figures, one of which is shown in frontal view with hands raised alongside his head. To the right, and facing him, an individual is shown standing in profile with his arm extending forward. A similar figure is shown in the upper left corner of the textile, with an enigmatic object beneath him.

7. Right: Small rectangle with slit-tapestry chequer-board pattern in alpaca and cotton, found along the perimeter walls of the courtyard. 35.5cm (14") wide.

ARCHAEOLOGICAL CORRELATIONS

Excavation inside the large quadrangle provided striking correlations to the activities and objects depicted on the textile. The elevated architecture where the two principal figures are seated is analogous to the elevated architecture located near the entrance to the quadrangle (**10**), the summit of which is approximately three metres above the floor of the quadrangle, and can be reached only by two narrow ramps. It had at least eight rooms, including one with a series of niches along one side.

The smaller rooms and portions of the large patio area were probably roofed, and some of the roofs may have been gabled and covered with thatch, although no good evidence of roofing was uncovered. This elevated architecture clearly had limited access and probably served either as a residence for individuals of high status, or as an area for performance of ceremonies. In either case, it would have been an appropriate location for ceremonial drinking by high-status individuals, and as such, provides an interesting parallel to the analogous structure depicted on the textile.

8. Below: Lambayeque ceramic bottle depicting a structure with a gabled roof. The two notches at the top of the roof are similar to those shown on the textile.

Assuming our identification of two of the individuals as dancers is correct, it is clear that their activity could well have taken place inside the large quadrangle, where there are numerous large rectangular plazas of varying sizes and forms (**10**). These plazas are flat, with clean clay floors that would have been ideally suited for the performance of dance.

The depiction of two individuals sacrificing llamas is of particular interest because sacrificed llamas, carefully wrapped in textiles, were found ritually buried beneath the floors of two of the rooms inside the quadrangle. In each instance a single llama was found; its chest had been cut open but there was no other evidence of trauma. The llamas were less than one year of age; one had white fur, and the fur of the other was a light tan colour.[5] It is possible that the ritual sacrifice of llamas within the quadrangle took place in ceremonies similar to the one shown on the textile.

The two weavers depicted on this textile have particular significance because abundant weaving materials were found inside the quadrangle. Many balls of yarn, bobbins, and spindles were uncovered, and the yarns they contained were identical in fibre, spin, thickness, and colour to those used in the textiles excavated inside the quadrangle. This suggests that at least some of the textiles found in the quadrangle were actually woven there. As noted above, the multiple bobbins hanging from the looms depicted on the textile suggest the weaving of tapestry. Most of the textiles found inside the quadrangle are tapestries. The activities of the other figures depicted on the textile cannot be identified, but there is nothing to suggest that what they are doing could not have taken place inside the quadrangle.

WRITTEN EVIDENCE

Historic documents from the Early Colonial Period confirm that some of the activities depicted on this textile were staged in monumental architecture at important sites on the North Coast of Peru. One of the most interesting of these documents was written by Pedro Cieza de Leon, who travelled in Peru in the late 1540s, visiting

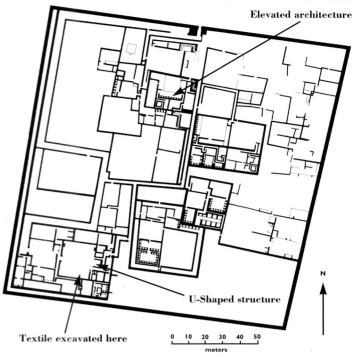

Elevated architecture

N

U-Shaped structure

Textile excavated here

0 10 20 30 40 50
meters

9. Above: Aerial view of Huaca I, with the quadrangle on the south side in the foreground.

10. Above right: Plan of the quadrangle on the south side of Huaca I.

11. Below: Human figure of slit tapestry with cotton warps and both cotton and wool wefts, probably made to be sewn on the front of an elaborate shirt. Herght 11.9cm (5").

the Jequetepeque Valley in September 1547.

In reference to the local rulers, he states they were well served by women and men, were carried on litters, and had guards for their custody and the custody of their houses.[6] They had dancers, musicians, singers, the most beautiful women of the valley, big 'houses' or palaces with matted roofing and adobe columns, big courtyards, and in the interior of the houses they had courtyards where they held their dances and festivities.

At meal time, great numbers of people congregated with the lord, and they drank *chica* (corn beer) and had their meals together. The entrances were always protected by guards who controlled the people entering and leaving the lord's house.[7] Many other early documents allude to these and similar activities and imply the importance of elaborate palace and ceremonial complexes.[8]

In essence, everything depicted on this textile appears to be taking place in an urban setting, adjacent to elevated, high-status architecture. Individuals appear to be engaged in ceremonial activities, using various types of appropriate paraphernalia. It is not clear whether the distinct activities are meant to be occurring simultaneously, sequentially, or in various combinations, but their juxtaposition suggests that all were enacted in relatively close proximity.

CEREMONIAL ICONOGRAPHY

When one considers how the ceremonial activities are depicted on this textile, it is clear that we are witnessing each at their 'moment of greatest sanctity'. Thus with the depiction of drinking, we are not shown the preparation of the beverage, nor the filling of the goblets, but rather the toast, presumably either immediately before or after the beverage is consumed – clearly the 'moment of greatest sanctity' for ritual drinking. With dance, we are not shown the preparation for the dance, nor activities that occurred after the dance was performed, but the dance itself. Clearly, this was conceptualised as the 'moment of greatest sanctity' for this activity.

Similarly, with llama sacrifice we are not seeing the selection of the animal, nor its ritual burial, but instead the moment immediately preceding or following the sacrifice – again, its 'moment of greatest sanctity'. This being the case, it is particularly interesting to consider the two individuals who are weaving. Presumably, we are also witnessing them at their 'moment of greatest sanctity'. They are not shown spinning yarn, nor are they holding completed textiles. They are weaving, and this strongly implies that individuals entered the quadrangle in order to engage in weaving as religious rite.

The correlation between what is shown on the textile, the objects that were excavated, and the information contained in historical documents, suggests that the staging of these ceremonial activities was a primary function of the quadrangle. Thus we are able to postulate that various individuals entered the quadrangle to perform ritual activities, and that these activities included drinking, dancing, sacrifice, and weaving. This remarkable textile allows us to view these activities through the eyes of the people who practised them centuries before the arrival of Europeans.

Notes see Appendix.

FROM THE INFINITE BLUE

Mapuche Textiles from Southern Chile

By Vanessa & Andrés Moraga

When seen at a distance, from across the horizon of the Pampas or the undulating heights and valleys of the lower Sierra, the monumental blue and white geometric forms of Mapuche chief's ponchos must have had a striking visual impact. Radiating power, they proclaimed at a glance the identity and status of their owner. But these dynamic textiles were more than visual insignia or badges of prestige. As the most highly developed and pre-eminent Mapuche art form, they were invested with the deepest spiritual and cultural ideas of the people. Like all Andean textiles, they eloquently and elegantly transcended their utilitarian role, mediating between the living and the dead, and encoding a vision of the sacred and the mythic. In so doing, Mapuche textile artists created a singular abstract language that explored the essential nature of colour, shape and the geometry of space.

3. Above: *Cacique Araucano.* **From Robert Gerstmann,** *Chile,* **Paris 1932, pl.164.**

1. Preceding pages, left: Mapuche chief's ikat poncho (*trarikanmakuñ*), late 19th century. 1.57 x 1.65m (5'2" x 5'5"). The vivid stripes, similar to those in ceremonial belts (16), derive from natural dyes which were rapidly replaced by anilines after 1860. By experimenting with spatial relationships and positive/negative inter-play, Mapuche textile artists found an inherent rhythm and dynamic potential in the repetitive, angular designs.

2. Preceding pages, right: *Cacique Currilan,* **ca. 1870-1880. Archive photo by B. Herrmann.**

4. Below: *Ruca Araucana.* **From Gerstmann,** *Chile,* **pl.163.**

"The first Mapuche spirit came to earth from the infinite blue. Upon death, after crossing a river, one arrives in a blue land where all the ancestors reside. This colour does not exist in our world, only in the sky and in the souls of the Mapuche."
Elicura Chihuailaf, contemporary Mapuche poet.

The history of the Mapuche people of southern Chile is among the most unusual in the annals of the conquest of the Americas. Renowned for fiercely resisting the expansion of the Incas' southern empire into the heartland of present day Chile, the Mapuche subsequently waged a bitter defensive war against the Spanish for more than three centuries, and were only decisively defeated at the end of the 19th century. Their indomitable spirit and military tenacity was commemorated in the earliest work of Latin American literature inspired by the conquest of the New World – the poem *La Araucana* (1569-1589) by Alonso de Ercilla, a Spanish soldier-poet who participated in the campaign to conquer Chile. Ercilla apparently coined the name 'Araucanian' from the Mapuche words *rau* and *co*, a place of muddy water, but its true etymology, rooted in the Quechua name for the unyielding peoples of central Chile, *auka* – enemy or rebel – is more evocative of the Mapuche's singular and bellicose history.[1] Although widely adopted after the 16th century, the colonial appellation was never used by this Andean people, who call themselves *Mapuche* or 'people of the land'.[2]

Not nearly as well known is their textile tradition, one of the most cohesive and distinctive in South America. The dazzling brilliance of the weaving arts of the central Andes and the Peruvian coast has tended to focus interest and research on those areas. However, an investigation of the textiles made by the Mapuche, primarily their chiefs' ponchos, deepens our understanding of the links and aesthetic influences between all Andean cultures, from those based in major centres such as Chan Chan, Pachacamac, Cuzco and Tiahuanaco, to the most remote nomadic tribes such as the Tehuelche of Patagonia.

Throughout the pre-Columbian and post-conquest eras, the history and development of Mapuche society was shaped by the eccentric features of Chile's geography. The modern nation of Chile occupies a narrow strip of land, about a hundred miles wide, squeezed between the Pacific Ocean and the Andean Cordillera. Some three thousand miles long, it is bounded by the uninhabitable Atacama Desert in the north, and the vast cool rainforests and windswept plains of Patagonia in the south. For at least a thousand years, the Mapuche inhabited a fertile temperate zone, which extended in pre-colonial times from the Valley of Quillota, just north of Santiago, to the southern Chilean archipelago and the island of Chiloe. Sixteenth century chronicles describe this as a beautiful region, set at the foot of the Andes amid lakes and volcanoes, and covered in a forest so dense that it was almost impenetrable. However, by the end of the War of Pacification in 1882, Mapuche territories had been reduced to a system of reservations in the area between the Bio-Bio and Calle-Calle Rivers. As with nearly all native American peoples, the loss of their lands led inexorably to the depletion of their tradition, wealth and power and to their present day impoverishment.

The origins of the Mapuche are subject to debate. It is believed that they were originally nomads who migrated from east of the Andes between 700 and 1,000 years ago, mixing with settled indigenous populations. These local groups were culturally more advanced and are known to have produced painted ceramics with anthropomorphic and zoomorphic forms which were used in ceremonial and funerary practices. However, Mapuche culture has been moulded by a number of diverse influences. Their aesthetic tradition and mastery of complex weaving techniques in particular reflects their extensive contact with the pre-Columbian cultures to the north. But it was the period of Spanish colonisation which had the most profound impact on their society and their art. The confluence of these distinct historic forces, which merged with an autochthonous tradition, is critical to a proper understanding of their place in the Andean world.

PRE-COLUMBIAN ANTECEDENTS

The Incas initiated the expansion of their empire beyond the recently conquered *Colla* kingdom near Lake Titicaca during the reign of Tupac Yupanqui, circa 1460. They occupied the vast desert areas which stretched towards the 'Valley of Chile', as well as the few coastal settlements near Arica which could support life in one of the most arid terrains on earth. Making use of ancient trade routes which hugged the mountains in northern Chile and linked these distant villages, the Incas constructed roads, rest stops (*tambos*) and military outposts to consolidate their political control of the region. Throughout their empire they created systems that would greatly facilitate the Spanish conquest less than a

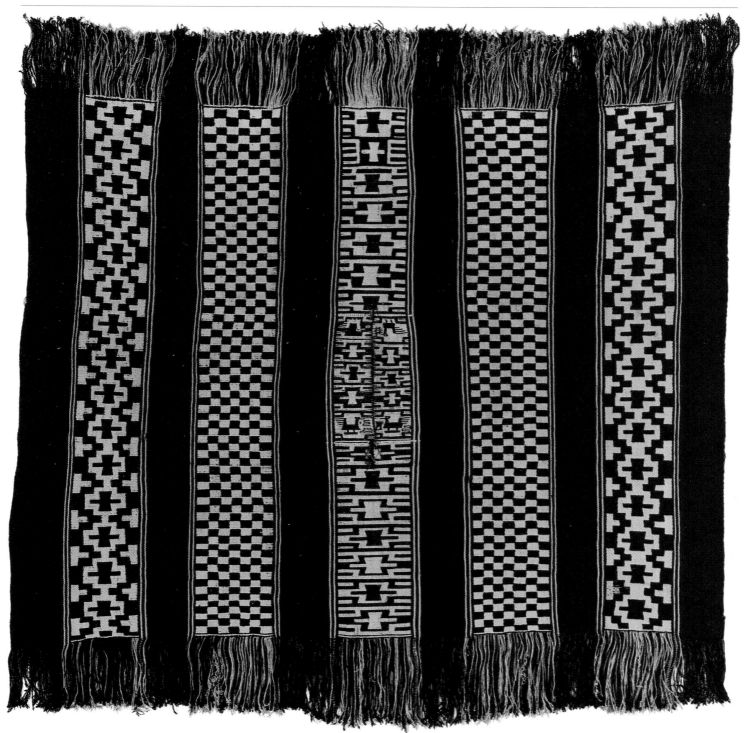

century later. Indeed, it was only at the periphery of Incan influence that the Spanish were forced to conquer local peoples for themselves. In 1540, the conquistador Pedro de Valdivia retraced the Incas' route, stopping at the *pukara* of San Pedro de Atacama, located in an area where a rich tradition of textile art had flowered under Tiahuanaco influence, and finally reaching the frontier zealously defended by the Mapuche.

The rain-drenched climate of the south has destroyed potential archaeological evidence of early Mapuche textiles, so it is almost impossible to ascertain what the Mapuche were wearing prior to the arrival of the Spanish and the first written records. Fray Diego de Rosales, a Jesuit missionary who arrived in Chile around 1629, provided a comprehensive view of the varied styles of indigenous dress at the time: "The clothing of the Chilean Indians is diverse, depending upon region, because some are dressed in wool, others in skins or feathers or bark-cloth, while some are painted with mud and are naked save for a loincloth to cover their decency. This was the manner of dress until the Spanish arrived in their lands bringing sheep whose wool they now use. Before they had used a fibre called Ñocha…This is the clothing of those Indians who inhabit the two extremes of Chile, one very warm, the other very cold. But those in the center…go dressed in wool dyed in brilliant colours."[3]

It is generally assumed that the Mapuche acquired much of their weaving skill and iconography from contact with the Incas; the persistence of Quechua-derived words for garments

5. Mapuche chief's double-cloth poncho (*niminma-kuñ*), ca. 1850-1880. 1.42 x 1.40m (4'8" x 4'7"). This masterpiece of Mapuche weaving reportedly belonged to a chief who signed the 1882 Peace Treaty with the Chilean government: 19th century ponchos in good condition are rare, due to the practice of burying chiefs with their most important textiles. The unique bird and figural motifs around the neck may be talismanic or power symbols.

167

6. Mapuche chief's ikat poncho (trarikanmakuñ), ca. 1850-1880. 1.42 x 1.32m (4'8" x 4'4"). Judging by its technical virtuosity and the quality of the wool, this may be one of the oldest surviving Mapuche textiles. The ikat pattern re-invigorates an archetypal Andean design that was interpreted over the millennia. Studies of Andean textiles suggest that the very weaving techniques imposed their conceptual patterns onto the cloth. The design is also evocative of the ancient agricultural terraces built on the steep Andean mountainsides.

and adornment such as *ikulla* for mantle and *tupu* for mantle-pin suggests this is plausible. Mapuche weavings were probably originally based on plant fibres, as an offshoot from basketry; and they may have used the wool and skins of wild southern camelids like the guanaco. The greater availability of wool from domesticated llamas and alpacas brought by the Incas doubtless stimulated the development of new types of weaving. Mapuche design concepts, however, have a more ancient source, rooted, as with all Andean cultures, in the Early Horizon developments along the coast and mountains of Peru.

The primary motif in Mapuche textiles – the stepped-cross or pyramid and its many variations – is found throughout the Andes in all chronological horizons. It appears in innumerable sites and contexts, ranging from petroglyphs and earthworks to stone reliefs and textile art. One of the earliest uses of this symbol, circa 1000 BC, is seen at Chavin de Huantar, the most important religious site in the northern Peruvian highlands. A stone slab in the Chamber of Ornamental Beams depicts a fanged fish surrounded by stepped-crosses and circle-cross motifs. A ceremonial mortar found at the same complex, sculpted in the form of a jaguar, is embellished with similar crosses. Mortars of this type were used to grind psychotropic snuff – apparently an important aspect of the Chavin cult. It is believed that the tradition of inhaling hallucinogenic powders, and its associated iconography, was a cultural trait originating in the tropical lowlands east of the Andes, the source for such substances.

Since it is possible to trace the continuous use of this archetypal element on both sides of the Andes, this archaic Amazonian connection becomes important when establishing another possible path for the transmission of this motif to the Mapuche – via their contact with nomadic tribes who had migrated to Patagonia along the eastern side of the continent. We will examine this influence below in terms of the visual and thematic parallels between the ikat designs in Mapuche chiefs' ponchos and the schematic paintings on Tehuelche hides.

The stepped-cross assumed an architectonic dimension during the next major pan-Andean cultural phase, which emerged at Tiahuanaco in the southern highlands, where it was carved into temple walls, and also rendered as a three-tiered platform supporting the image of the paramount staff-bearing deity on the Gateway of the Sun. The concept of designating sacred space in terms of a stepped shape, and the shift from the linear plane to a monumental expression, culminated in the Incan *usnu*, a ceremonial throne cut into the living rock.

The Chavin period established the interchangeability of textile and lithic designs in ancient Andean art. This process reached its apogee in the spread of Huari and Tiahuanaco religious iconography through the textile medium. Textiles with interpretations of the quintessential stepped motif are myriad.[4] Scaffold-woven tunics with their individually shaped segments are one example of the use of stepped patterning not only as a surface design element but as the fundamental building block of the textile structure itself. The basic organisation of these Nazca-Huari 'patchwork' tunics, which may also be embellished with large-scale tie-dye patterns in different colours, is similar to certain ikat-dyed Mapuche ponchos. Although this pan-Andean context for their textile designs is clearly important, it is difficult to establish whether the Mapuche had assimilated these influences before the arrival of the Incas. It is likely they were linked to these earlier artistic traditions through their closest neighbours to the north, the Diaguita, who were renowned for high quality pottery painted with complex interlocking designs in red, black and white. Few textiles have survived, but Diaguita ceramics, dating to between 1200 and 1470 AD, are rich in the exploration of geometric themes and are a direct precursor to the patterns on Mapuche textiles (**8, 9, 10, 11**).

As the stepped-cross and other geometric patterns were diffused over time and place, their primordial symbolic content was either concealed or re-imagined within a local vernacular. The language of seemingly enigmatic abstract symbols and signs that later Andean cultures such as the Mapuche inherited was nevertheless imbued with spiritual and aesthetic resonance. As the post-conquest artistic tradition shows, these fundamental Andean conceptual and visual systems not only endured, but continued to absorb new cultural references and ideas arising out of their cataclysmic encounter with the European order.

SPANISH INFLUENCE AND THE INTRODUCTION OF THE HORSE

The Mapuche were the first South American people to adapt to the horse. Of all the changes wrought by Spanish contact, none had greater impact on their society than this event. Like the Plains Indians of North America, they soon became accomplished horsemen, and within twenty years were mounting cavalry raids against Pedro de Valdivia's forces. Both the horse and the textiles associated with it became an integral part of Mapuche ceremonial practice and religious belief, and the development of the poncho itself can be traced to this equestrian introduction.

The state of perpetual conflict that ensued between the two forces was marked by intermittent periods of peace, broken treaties, and recurring encroachments into Mapuche territory. But access to horses, and tactical knowledge and weapons gained from deserters, captives and escaped slaves, enhanced Mapuche mobility and strength against the Spanish. They burned Santiago no less than six times, and repeatedly forced the abandonment of Spanish towns and forts in the region of 'Arauco'. In 1724, their status as a *de facto* sovereign nation with established boundaries was acknowledged by the Papal Audience in Lima. War resumed during the period of Chilean Independence, ceasing finally with the Peace Treaty of 1881, marking the Mapuche's final defeat.[5]

These military successes, however, displayed a sense of cohesion unique to times of war. Traditional political and social institutions were loosely structured, reflecting individual independence and the importance of kinship and lineage bonds. The ongoing threat and need for sustained martial organisation had the effect of unifying Mapuche society. It led too to the permanent establishment of the *toquis* – military leaders who were only appointed during times of war, and whose authority was limited to strategic matters. The introduction of concepts of rank and hierarchy into the Mapuche ethos, and the resulting social stratification, was further exploited in the mid 19th century when the Chilean government instituted the hereditary *cacique* (chief) system as part of their strategy of 'pacification'. Mapuche chiefs became numerous, consolidating their authority and wealth through trade, the control of large herds and the accumulation of silver jewellery. The chief's poncho and ceremonial horse-blanket (*chañantuco*) became icons of political power and cultural status. It was at this time that the textiles shown here were produced.

7. *Cacique Lloncon*. From J. Diaz Lira (ed.), *Tipos Araucanos*, Santiago n.d.

8. Diaguita ceramics. From F.L. Cornely, *El Arte Decorativo Preincaico de los Indios de Coquimbo y Atacama (Diaguitas Chilenos)* La Serena 1962, pl.X. The patterns painted on Diaguita ceramics are the closest prototypes for Mapuche textile designs.

9. Above: Diaguita ceramic. From Aureliano Oyarzun and Ricardo Latcham, *Album de Tejidos y Alfareria Araucano*. Santiago 1929, pl.VII, part II. The mythological figure with elaborate eye motifs is depicted wearing a striped shirt with a checkerboard band that closely resembles the design, layout and proportions of Mapuche chiefs' ponchos.

10. Above: Diaguita ceramic. From Oyarzun and Latcham, *Album*, pl.VI, part II.

11. Below: Diaguita Ceramic. From Oyarzun and Latcham, *Album*, pl.VI, part II.

Constant Spanish pressure induced some Mapuche groups to migrate back over the Andes to the Argentinian Pampas at the end of the 17th century. The seemingly endless flat grazing lands had proved an ideal habitat for the horse, which multiplied so rapidly that by 1599 it was estimated that there were over one and a half million wild horses in the territory.[6] The *Indios Pampas*, as the Argentinean Mapuche were called, began capturing these wild horses and trading the mares to their Chilean kinsmen for textiles. Documents show a lucrative trade in ponchos, mantles, saddle-blankets, woven headbands and belts, which were exchanged for commodities, tools and alcohol. The Mapuche on both sides gradually enriched themselves from this commerce. The mid 19th century saw the rise of the greatest Mapuche chief, Cafulcura, who united all the tribes in the southern Pampas and exerted control to the outskirts of Buenos Aires. It took a massive Argentinean army years to defeat this confederation. Some of the most important Argentinean chief's ponchos date to this period.

THE DEVELOPMENT OF THE PONCHO

Of all types of textiles, the poncho is the garment most readily associated with South America in the popular imagination. This impression stems as much from accounts of the picturesque *gauchos* and *huasos* (horsemen and cattle-herders) of Argentina, Uruguay and Chile, as from descriptions of the ceremonial and daily dress of the Aymara and Quechua of Bolivia and Peru. During the wars of independence against Spain in the early 19th century, the poncho became the symbolic garb of the great liberators such as San Martin, O'Higgins and Bolívar, further underlining its cultural and emblematic importance.

Prior to the 17th century, however, there is no mention of this type of large, rectangular, open, sleeveless garment in histories such as those of Guamán Poma de Ayala (1613), with its drawings of Inca customs and styles of dress. Nor is there much archaeological evidence of its existence in the pre-Columbian epoch. Although the poncho may have some isolated antecedents, coastal textile finds consist primarily of small tunics with sleeves, or the Andean *unku*, a sleeveless tunic of various proportions which is sewn up at the sides. The widespread use of the poncho in daily wear thus appears to be a post-contact development.

In *Dress and Ornaments in Ancient Peru* (1929), Gosta Montell proposes that the poncho first evolved in Chile as a result of the Mapuche's rapid adaptation to the horse and the new style of mounted warfare.[7] His theory is corroborated by numerous linguistic references and depictions of the poncho in a Chilean context several decades after the conquest. The earliest colonial records, such as Pedro de Valdivia's letters to King Charles V, noted only that both men and women wore woollen sleeveless garments. Góngora Marmolego (1549-1575) reported that "they go dressed in shirts without sleeves and some wear *zaragueles* (*chiripas* or *mantas*)."[8] These accounts are consistent with the traditional Inca attire which the central Mapuche groups probably emulated.

Although the etymology of the word *poncho* is unclear, its first unmistakable use is found in *My Happy Captivity*, Bascuñan's 1629 narrative of his experiences as a Mapuche prisoner of war. In 1648, another traveller, Marcgrav, published a clear description and drawing of this new type of textile: "The men take a square piece of cloth...In the middle they make an incision, through which they put the head...This piece of cloth is mostly of different colours, white, yellow, blue, and red, and fringed at the corners like a Spanish shawl." Later texts refer interchangeably to this garment and other weavings such as mantles, shirts and vests, as *ciogni*, *chony*, *poncho* or *macuñ*. This lexical confusion, suggests Montell, reflected the transition in the clothing styles at the time, and the emergence of the poncho as the principal item of male apparel. *Poncho* and *chony* are probably collocations; and we know *macuñ* today as the Mapuche word for poncho.

An interesting but more speculative aspect of Montell's thesis is his belief that the poncho arose from a modification of the large trapezoidal-shaped tunic which was unique to the Arica culture of northern Chile during the Gentilar period (1100-1470 AD). He contends that by opening a tunic of this kind along the side seams and altering its shape to a rectangle, the Mapuche would have produced a textile closely resembling the poncho in size and appearance. Of course, a similar result could be had by opening any pre-Columbian tunic – a Nazca *cushma* for example. But Montell's premise seems viable in the light of several visual and technical correlations between Arica tunics and Mapuche ponchos. Both, for example, make use of vertical stripes and warp-patterned bands of varying proportions as their principle decorative device, as well as employing an embroidered reinforcement at the neck opening to resist tearing. Whatever the actual source or process, this innovation on the narrower and restricted proportions of the Andean *unku* was a tactical and technological advance for the Mapuche, ensuring greater mobility in the saddle, while its ample size, tight weave and heavy wool provided protection against the climate.

By the early 18th century, ponchos were being produced for export by the tens of thous-ands in Jesuit workshops or *obrajes* in Chile, becoming a key stimulus for the growing trade circuit between Lima, Potosi, Tucuman and Santiago. It was probably around this time that the style reached Peru and Bolivia, where it had a tangible impact on Aymara and Quechua dress. The fusion of colonial and pre-Columbian ideas represented by the poncho found a ready market in the new *mestizo* and *criollo* class, itself a hybrid of both cultures. The Inca nobility or *curacas*, on other hand, who had been retained by the Spanish to help administer the new colony, still adhered to the pre-Columbian *unku* or tunic, which was worn over their lavish European clothing as a symbol of their indigenous identity.

In the 1780s, after the failure of a series of uprisings in the southern Andes culminating in the rebellion of Tupac Amaru, the wearing of the *unku* and the mantle was outlawed by the colonial authorities. Although this impetus to suppress Andean textiles was a tacit acknowledgement that the magico-religious and political role of cloth had survived the conquest, the promulgation of edicts prohibiting traditional apparel and the ceremonial role of textiles contributed to the widespread adoption of the poncho in the Highlands. However, as Tracht and Adelson point out in *Aymara Weavings*, the earliest Aymara examples were often "little more than disguised tunics", closely imitating the poncho layout and design composition.[9] Here, as among other ethnic groups, the idea of the poncho was grafted onto a living and vigorous weaving tradition, where it took forms that were richly varied and distinct from the original models.

In surveying the evolution of the poncho, therefore, it is important to distinguish between several features: the spread of this garment type throughout Latin America and its many

12. Mapuche chief's ikat poncho *(trarikanmakuñ)* with braided fringe, late 19th century. 1.40 x 1.47m (4'7" x 4'10"). This complex compos-ition, built from nine bands of interlocking ikat patterns, shows a strong conceptual relationship to the schematic painted designs of Tehuelche hides, which the compar-ative ethnologist Carl Schuster has identified as "genealogical patterns" depicting rows of stylised ancestor figures.

regional reinterpretations; those weavings of Chilean provenance that were produced specifically for trade; and lastly, the ponchos the Mapuche made for themselves which reified their most important spiritual and cultural ideas.

CHIEF'S PONCHOS

The best source for the study of 19th century Mapuche textiles is the work of Father Claude Joseph, a Belgian ethnographer who conducted extensive research into Mapuche culture and art during the 1920s. His *Los Tejidos Araucanos* (1928), provides the first systematic approach to textile categories and weaving techniques.[10] Later studies, which focus primarily on 20th century weavings and weavers, tend to have a semiotic or ethno-historical bias, though valuable iconographic information is emerging about Mapuche textile symbolism. Notably lacking, however, is a survey of the earliest Mapuche textiles in museum collections, and a perspective informed as much by aesthetics as by a knowledge of the Mapuche cosmological framework. Joseph had access to a generation of weavers who were still directly linked to the last era of Mapuche autonomy and cultural integrity. After 1882, the loss of their lands and the capacity to raise quality sheep affected wool production and contributed to a rapid decline in the textile arts. As the tradition became increasingly commercialised, the more technically complex and lustrous ponchos were supplanted by coarser weavings with simplified and static aniline-dyed patterns. Nevertheless, Joseph was able to collect older examples of both men's and women's textiles. From this material and information acquired in the reservations, he catalogued the range of natural dye sources, basketry, weaving, spinning, dyeing techniques and implements, and recorded an indigenous weaving vocabulary.

The most esteemed ponchos among the Mapuche were those that demonstrated the greatest mastery of weaving and dyeing. Exceptional skill in these time-consuming arts was one of the few ways a Mapuche woman could achieve renown. Similarly, a man's status was implicit in the ownership of ponchos with a wealth of complicated designs or techniques. Above all, textiles were prized for their sheen and luminosity, an ineffable quality deriving as much from the elasticity and fineness of the wool as from their saturated colour, achieved from repeated immersions in an indigo infusion. Early 19th century accounts indicate that Mapuche textiles were originally ranked by colour, and that in addition to the requisite dark blue, white and red, a turquoise dye was also common. Despite their knowledge of a wide spectrum of natural dyes, Mapuche prestige textiles display an emphatic preference for a reduced palette. This chromatic restraint, combined with a bold geometry, is the keynote of their aesthetic sensibility. The austerity of woman's attire epitomises this sober elegance: two rectangular cloths used as mantle and dress, dyed the deepest indigo *after* being woven, their unalloyed blueness alleviated only by a narrow swath of colour and pattern at the waist, and the contrast provided by large pieces of silver jewellery.

There are three distinct types of Mapuche chief's ponchos: *wirikanmakuñ* or warp-striped (**24**); the *ñiminmakuñ* (**5, 19, 20**), embellished with elaborate complementary warp-patterned or double-cloth bands; and ikat-dyed, or *trarikanmakuñ* (**1, 6, 12, 13**). Certain ponchos (**18**) may combine one or more of these techniques.[11] The use of multicoloured warp stripes or warp-patterned bands on a field of dyed or undyed alpaca or wool is an ancient Andean design concept, particularly identified with Highland (especially Aymara) textiles. The Mapuche interpretation of this layout generally relies upon the sparing use of narrow stripes in vivid colours such as red, pink and orange to offset and enliven zones of solid indigo or ikat designs (**5**).

It seems likely that the Mapuche had a system of colour meaning which, like the imagery seen in belts and men's *ñiminmakuñ*, encoded a subtle and hermetic language expressing both male and female cosmological principles. These warp-patterned designs, reminiscent of Inca, Atacameño and Diaguita prototypes, are the most complicated in the weavers'

14. Mapuche loom with woman's belt. From Oyarzun and Latcham Album, pl.I, part I.

15. Poncho with ikat bands and stripes and a man's belt. From Oyarzun and Latcham, Album, pl.IX, part I.

13. Left: Mapuche chief's ikat poncho (trarikanmakuñ), late 19th century. 2.11 x 1.50m (6'11" x 4'11"). Chief's ponchos with all-over ikat patterning are the rarest Mapuche textiles. The bevelled planes of endless interlocking geometric motifs give palpable form to the concept of the infinite. For the resist-dye process, the loom was warped prior to weaving, and the pattern tied with a coarse yarn (palao) or bark fibre (maki). A white clay resist paste (molle-molle) was applied, and the warps were repeatedly saturated in an indigo dye infusion to achieve the characteristic deep blue colour. Small eccentricities define the weaver's individual style and mastery of this prestige technique.

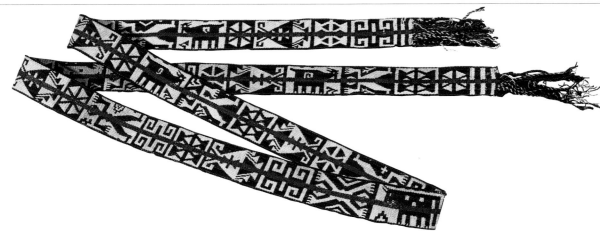

18. Far right: Mapuche chief's ikat poncho (*makuñ*) with patterned bands (*kulatrarin, ñimin* and *wirikan*), late 19th century. 1.85 x 1.55m (6'1" x 5'1"). The combination of three weaving techniques seen in this poncho is extremely rare, and may represent an earlier style which had disappeared by the late 19th century. A similar textile appears in an engraving from Claudio Gay's *Historia Fisica y Politica de Chile* (Paris 1854).

16. Man's ceremonial belt (*traruchiripa*), late 19th century. 2.36 x 0.05m (7'9" x 0'2"). Such belts were used with the *chiripa* or loincloth. The combination of motifs – male, female, animal – evokes the Mapuche cosmological and material order. The geometric motifs may be powerful protective talismans. These diverse elements are connected by a wide, central band which conceptually and structurally unites them. The centre of the belt is marked by a bisected human figure with upraised arms; in pre-Columbian art this pose conveys a state of shamanistic exaltation. There is a technical and design correlation between this belt and the warp-patterned bands on textiles from the Gentilar period (1100-1470 AD), suggesting links between the Mapuche and Arica weaving traditions that are separated by nearly a millennium.

vocabulary. Men's belts are virtually unknown outside of early field photographs and a few Argentinean museum collections formed in the late 19th century (**16**). A piece published in Alfred Taullard's *Tejidos y Ponchos Indigenas de Sud America* (1949) is a rare example of an ikat poncho decorated with two narrow double-cloth bands that are virtually identical to men's belts in technique, proportions, colour and symbolic repertoire. Once owned by the Cacique Namuncurá, it was collected in the 1870s. The designs – checkerboards, labyrinthine key and spiral forms, chevrons, rhomboids, swastikas, animal and human figures – are angular in character, an apparent trait of masculine symbolism. More enigmatic, however, is the inclusion in some warp-patterned ponchos of ornate figural motifs specifically associated with women. Women's belts (*trariwes*), comprise an abundant body of material, reflecting the innate conservatism of Mapuche woman's clothing and the conservation of their traditional forms well into this century. Pedro Mege Rosso's research among contemporary weavers has unravelled the gender differences in Mapuche iconography, and identified the principal 'female' motif as the *temu* or sacred tree. When woven into men's ponchos, however, this motif undergoes a symbolic inversion that is achieved by visually altering it to connote qualities associated with Mapuche maleness. The transformation reflects an intrinsic dualism in Mapuche thought. Whereas in the feminine context the symbol is associated with such qualities as water, fecundity, softness, and continuity, in the man's poncho, it is disassembled and reconstructed in a rectilinear style to generate new 'masculine' meanings such as vitality, potency and strength.[12]

Since this particular motif can also be recognised as a version of the 'squatting ancestor' or splayed-limbed figure prevalent in Arica coca-bags and ritual cloths, its specific Mapuche content appears to be overlaid on an ancient generative and totemic image. Over the millennia this element assumed a more floral form – perhaps a result of colonial influence – but its endurance attests to the survival and regeneration of archetypal pre-Hispanic themes in Mapuche iconography. Moreover, the Mapuche process of truncating or bisecting this anthropomorphic motif along its axis, and doubling or unfolding it to arrive at the rectilinear notches of the stepped cross, replicates the ingenious manipulation of space, volume and symmetry so brilliantly explored in Huari four-cornered hats.

17. Rock engraving, Lake Nahuel Huapi, Argentina. From M.A. Vignati, *Antigüidades en la Region de los Lagos Nahuel Huapi y Traful I-VII*, La Plata 1944, pl.II, fig.1.

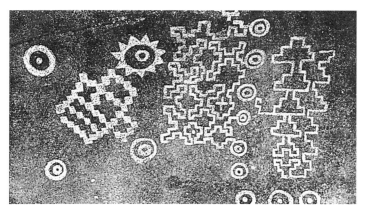

The third type of chief's poncho, the ikat-dyed or *trarikanmakuñ*, was the most prestigious. These pieces are the rarest of Mapuche textiles; in 1930 Samuel Lothrop calculated that they comprised only two per cent of all Mapuche weavings.[13] Woven in one piece on the pre-conquest upright loom, each *trarikanmakuñ* took a specialist weaver up to a year to make. Although the designs are large, as Ann Rowe notes, "most Araucanian ikats are tied so precisely that they look almost as if tapestry woven."[14]

19. Mapuche chief's poncho (niminmakuñ), late 19th-early 20th century. 1.68 x 1.5m (5'6" x 4'11"). Manipulation of squares and rectangles and the varying proportions of the patterned bands create a dramatic optical effect. The rigid geometry and symmetry of the checkerboard columns is modified when worn.

Ikat textiles are extremely rare from the pre-Columbian period; Rowe reports a total of fifteen pieces, mostly Chimu or Inca. Resist-dyed ethnographic textiles are found in two distinct areas: Central America (Mexico and Guatemala) and in the Andes (Ecuador, Chile, Peru and in rare instances, Bolivia).[15] The distribution of ikat thus follows the Pacific coast, forming part of an arc that incorporates Indonesia, Southeast Asia and Japan, where the resist-dyeing technique is also prominent. The origin of these ethnographic traditions in the Americas is unclear. In some areas it may have been a result of European influence, though there is no evidence to suggest this is true for the Mapuche.

The earliest extant Mapuche ikat ponchos probably do not predate the 1850s, but we are not aware of any examples with verifiable accession dates from this period. At this time, ponchos were still buried with their owners in wooden canoes, together with their horse and other paraphernalia. After the 1880s, 'prestige' textiles such as those published here were acquired by European immigrants in the region. Based on its very fine weave and technical

20. Mapuche chief's poncho *(niminmakuñ)*, 19th century. 1.57 x 1.57m (5'2" x 5'2"). The checkerboard pattern, executed in double-cloth, was probably borrowed from Inca textile art. The volumetric quality of Mapuche interlocking compositions, with their strong vertical planes and shifting surfaces, is reminiscent of Inca stone walls which have been described as being "woven together". Collection of The Art Institute of Chicago, Restricted Gift of Mr and Mrs Richard Senior, Mr and Mrs Arthur Kelly and The Textile Society of the Art Institute of Chicago Textile Acquisition Fund, inv.no. 1993.133.

execution, the ikat-dyed poncho shown in (**6**) may well be the earliest in this technique to have survived. Its three broad ikat columns contain an unusual, perhaps arcane, variant of the classic step pattern. This three-band layout, known as *kulatrarin*, is one of two preferred by the Mapuche for their ikat ponchos; the other, much rarer because of its intensive labour requirements, is an all-over stepped-cross pattern known as *sanitran* (**12**, **13**).

LEVELS OF MEANING IN MAPUCHE IKAT PATTERNS

Ikat ponchos of the type depicted in (**12**) and (**13**) are conceived as an infinite field of interlocking repeat linear designs where light and dark, figure and ground, positive and negative, oscillate rhythmically. While for us the powerful geometric configurations have a quality of pure 'abstractness', the comparative ethnographer Carl Schuster understands schematic repeat patterns like these to be "concatenations of human figures" that communicate genealogical themes and ancestral lineages. Schuster has written of the occurrence of such key 'genealogical patterns' in ikat textiles from various cultures. In particular, his essay on painted Patagonian robes (**23**), which identifies the hidden anthropomorphic character of their polychrome designs, supplies an interesting context for the consideration of the basic Mapuche ikat motif. Samuel Lothrop was the first to remark on the affinity between the textile designs of these two southern Andean cultures, as well as with the motifs seen on petroglyphs near Lago Nahuel Huapi in Argentina and engraved talismanic Patagonian stone plaques (**17**).[16]

Schuster believes the blue vertical contoured bands, red and green opposed frets, and yellow zig-zags and ligatures of the Tehuelche horsehide robe are interpretations of a single ancient design that arose in the Palaeolithic era, and was composed originally of tiers of linked human figures, arranged in reciprocal pairs and connected by outstretched limbs (**21**). He finds conceptual equivalents for these endlessly generated stepped motifs in painted otter-skins from the Argentinean Chaco, opossum-skin robes and ritual earthworks of the aborigines, and the tattoos and body

21. Section of the painted decoration on a horsehide robe. Tehuelche Indians of Patagonia. From Carl Schuster, 'Observations on the Painted Designs of Patagonia Skin Robes', in Samuel K. Lothrop (ed.) et al, *Essays in Pre-Columbian Art and Archaeology*, Cambridge 1964, fig.1.

22. Ceremonial pile technique horse-blanket (*chañuntuco*), late 19th century. 0.91 x 0.69m (3'0" x 2'3"). *Chañuntucos* were made for chiefs and wealthy men to display on ceremonial occasions, and during ritual riding displays associated with the agricultural festival *ñillatun*. Their name derives from *chachanun*, meaning 'to throw on the floor'. Traditionally dyed white or deep blue with no design, their only embellishment is the texture of the pile and the long strands of twisted fibres worked into the edges. According to ethnographer Father Claude Joseph, the Mapuche called these fringes *mahull* or *mawell* meaning 'rain'. After its introduction by the Spanish, the horse became an integral part of Mapuche ceremonial and religious life. Archaeological excavations in Neuquén, Argentina have shown that the Mapuche were buried with horses in addition to ceramics, jewellery, pipes and textiles. By the 19th century, the horse had assumed such importance that when a Chief was buried, the skin of his favourite horse was placed on a spear over the grave and left to fly as a banner.

23. *Habits of The Patagonians in 1764,* (showing painted robe). From Pernety, *Histoire d'un voyage aux Isles Malouines*, Paris 1770, pl.xiii.

painting of the Caduveo tribe in the Mato Grosso, Brazil. The complex 'skin-mosaic' is a diagram of 'the social fabric' where "The continuum of human figures finds its most plausible explanation as a symbol of the endless continuity of the genetic process...the component figures of the patterns [representing] members of a social group...visualized both vertically in terms of ancestors and descendants, and horizontally in terms of living relatives."[17]

Stylistic affiliations can be found over a wide area, extending into the Peruvian Amazon, the possible source of Chavin iconography in the Early Formative Period, and of the cult of psychotropic substances in many Andean societies. The Shipibo-Conibo people ascribe the origin of their design tradition to visions experienced under the influence of the hallucinogenic *ayahuasca*, which is said "to produce luminous geometric patterns against the nightly darkness". In their richly inventive pattern language, human figures and cross motifs are often fused. Moreover, as Angelika Bebhart-Sayer notes, the vocabulary of these Amazonian artists is believed to derive almost entirely from "the *joni quene* (human being design): having been abbreviated, varied, ornamented and combined to form new, purely geometric patterns in the course of time."[18] The metaphysical significance of such universal genealogical patterns may lie in the belief that the headless bodies of the design are animated by the head of the wearer, who then appears as the 'tribal ancestor'.[19] If, as Schuster asserts, these designs were first applied to the body, as among the Caduveo tribe of Brazil, they would have been softened by the roundness of the human form. This fluid three-dimensional or volumetric effect is regained in the Mapuche ikat poncho, where the angularity of the technique is transformed through the nature of the cloth itself as it drapes the body. When worn, therefore, the wearer's head would emerge above the stylised ancestor figures of the ikat design.

Since Mapuche ponchos are worn by chiefs, elders and other men of rank (*lonko, ülmen*)[20] on specific ceremonial occasions involving the placation and propitiation of ancestral spirits, this idea seems especially pertinent. As Louis Faron states in *The Mapuche Indians of Chile*, the concept of ancestral spirits is central to Mapuche religious belief; the most important being their former chiefs – elders, lineage founders and military leaders – who assume their place with other deities in the polytheistic pantheon.[21] During funerary rites and the great agricultural/fertility festival known as the *ñillatun*, lineage elders engage in formal orations *(weupin)* recounting their genealogies and linking their family groups to mythical and historical lineage founders. The wearing of ponchos with designs that are visual metaphors for human interconnection reinforces their kinship to these ancestral forebears and alludes to their own place in the social and spiritual hierarchy.

Textiles are also prominent during the *awn* – the ritual purification of the ceremonial meeting or burial ground, characterised by feats of horsemanship and riding displays.[22] Wearing their finest ponchos and mounted on fleecy ceremonial horse-blankets known as *chañantucos*, mounted men – their identities symbolically disguised by masks or facial paintings – perform the *awn* by encircling the field. "So tight is the riding circle of the horse-

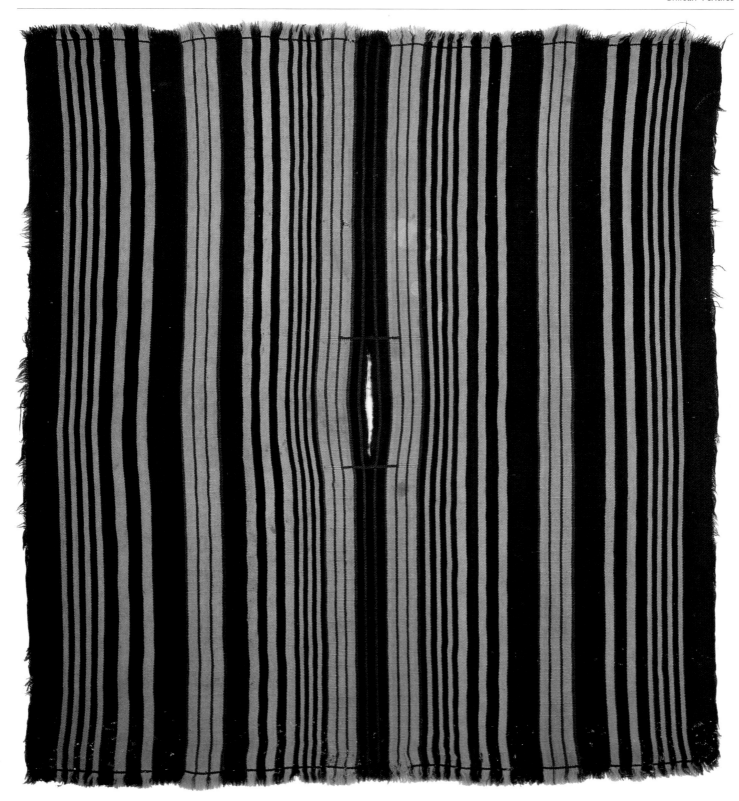

men" remarks Louis Faron, "and so great their speed, the horses are actually leaning inward as they gallop counter clockwise around the sacred ground. The riding is done to clear the field of evil spirits."[23] The sacred space in which the *ñillatun* takes place is demarcated by the carved effigy posts traditionally used by Mapuche shamans or *machis* in trance, divination and curing rites. The notched shaped of these ritual ladders or *rewes* recalls the stepped contours of the classic Mapuche poncho motif. Thus the alignment of textile symbology with the quintessential platform of Mapuche shamanistic practice underlines the cohesiveness of the Mapuche cultural universe and the indivisibility of their spiritual and aesthetic concepts.

Just as lineage orations establish a dialogue between the living and the dead, in the ceremonial context Mapuche textiles mediate between two culturally defined orders: the symbolic realm of the ancestral deities, and the social and natural world. For the Mapuche, as for other Andean cultures, textiles are not only the pre-eminent art form, they chart the topography of cosmological and territorial space along an axis of warp and weft.

Notes see Appendix

24. Mapuche chief's poncho (*wirikanmakuñ*), mid 19th century or earlier. 1.55 x 1.37m (5'1" x 4'6"). The Mapuche conceive of the striped textile ground (*tue*) as a symbolic reference to the Mapu or 'ethnic space' of the wearer. The design may also allude to the furrows of their agricultural fields. British Museum (Museum of Mankind), London.

SEEING AND

BELIEVING

Navajo Blankets

By Joshua Baer

Between 1820 and 1880, a group of weavers living in what is now the Four Corners region of the American Southwest produced a body of artwork that is thought by connoisseurs to rank among the finest aesthetic accomplishments of the 19th century. The author looks briefly at the history of Navajo weaving before turning his attention to the more elusive question of what it means to 'see' a Navajo blanket.

2. Above: Classic serape with a large central diamond. Navajo, circa 1850. 1.35 x 1.73m (4'5" x 5'8"). The reds are ravelled bayeta dyed with cochineal; the blues are handspun wool dyed with indigo; the whites are undyed handspun wool. White-ground serapes are considerably rarer than those with red grounds. Private collection, New York.

3. Right: Classic poncho serape. Navajo, circa 1840. 1.14 x 1.80m (3'9" x 5'11"). The reds are ravelled bayeta dyed with lac; the blues are handspun wool dyed with indigo; the whites are undyed handspun wool. There are less than twenty-five poncho serapes in museum and private collections. The developed quality of the design work in almost all poncho serapes suggests that only the most accomplished weavers produced these impressive garments. Private collection, Santa Fe.

Nineteenth century Navajo blankets were garments designed to be worn around the shoulders, like shawls. Almost all Navajo blankets were woven for trade; that is, the weaver wove the blanket with the intention of trading it for money, livestock, weapons or medicine as soon as it was completed. The widespread assumption that Navajo blankets woven prior to 1850 were worn by Navajos is incorrect; most of this production was, however, traded to other Native American tribes.

All Navajo blankets were woven by women belonging to various clans of the Navajo tribe, an Athapaskan-speaking native American culture which refers to itself as *Dineh*, or 'the People'. American anthropologists believe that the Athapaskans migrated from Eastern Siberia across the Bering Straits and into western Canada sometime between the birth of Christ and 1000 AD. Some Athapaskans remained in Canada, others continued south. In the American Southwest, the Navajo and the Apache are two Athapaskan splinter groups who probably arrived in the Four Corners region between 1000 and 1300 AD. The earliest fragments of Navajo weavings date from the mid 1700s, but it was not until the early 1800s that the Navajo blanket gained its status as a prestige garment.

The two most popular styles of 19th century Navajo blankets were the serape, and the chief's blanket. The word serape comes from the Spanish *zarape*, 'a man's blanket', which

5. Above: Classic Second Phase chief's blanket. Navajo, circa 1855. 1.73 x 1.45m (5'8" x 4'9"). Both the reds are ravelled bayeta dyed with cochineal; the blues are handspun wool dyed with indigo; the browns and whites are undyed handspun wool. Second Phase chief's blankets are a synthesis of classic Navajo design and the vast, spacious environment of the American Great Plains. Private collection, Dallas.

4. Left: Classic serape with a blue field and a large central diamond. Navajo, circa 1860. 1.32 x 1.80m (4'4" x 5'11"). The reds and the pinks are ravelled bayeta dyed with cochineal; the greens and yellows are ravelled bayeta dyed with vegetal dyes; the blues are handspun wool dyed with indigo; the browns are undyed handspun wool. The diagonal steps running through this serape create an optical effect, shifting between foreground and background. Private collection, Aspen.

in turn comes from the Nahuatl (Aztec) *tzalanpepechtli*, 'a woven shawl' (the word serape has no direct connection to the Persian *Serapi*, used by the oriental carpet trade in North America to define a particular quality of northwest Persian decorative carpets).

Navajo serapes were produced during the late 1700s and throughout the 1800s, almost always in combinations of imported and domestic woollen yarns. Trade records indicate that Spanish landowners and merchants living in what is now New Mexico were the Navajo's primary clients for serapes, though the blankets were also popular among non-Navajo native American tribes. Records dating from the 1840s state that Navajo serapes "sell for as much as $100 each among the Mexicans" (Josiah Gregg, 1844).

Serapes were woven vertically, that is, on upright looms that were taller than they were wide. Design elements included diamonds, zig-zags and steps set against horizontally striped fields. Most Navajo serapes were worn around the shoulders, with the central diamonds covering the middle of the wearer's back. An exception was the poncho serape (**3**), which contained an opening at the centre of the serape for the neck and head of the wearer. Most of the twenty-five or so poncho serapes in existence date from the 1820-1840 period and are the rarest major type of Navajo blanket. Child's serapes (**6, 8, 9** and **11**) appeared during the mid 1850s, the 1860s and the 1870s, and generally contained smaller, more delicate versions of the diamonds, steps and zig-zags at work in man's serapes. These smaller blankets were worn so that the central panel of the blanket fell along the child's spine.

Navajo chief's blankets (**1, 5, 10** and **12**) were woven horizontally, that is, on upright looms that were wider than they were tall. The broad, horizontal, blue, brown and white striped pattern which characterises the Navajo chief's blanket was appealing to Plains Indians (Cheyenne, Arapaho, Kiowa and Sioux tribes, among others), who bought, sold and traded thousands of chief's blankets between 1800 and 1860. By the 1840s, the Navajo chief's blanket was such a popular trade item among Plains Indians that it had become a form of currency. The going rate for a Second Phase chief's blanket in the mid 1840s was fifty horses, $50 in gold, or a hundred buffalo hides. After purchasing a chief's blanket for

7. Right: Late Classic serape with a red field, a white terraced grid and 15 small crosses. Navajo, circa 1865. 1.32 x 1.83m (4'4" x 6'0"). The reds are machine-spun knitting yarns dyed with cochineal; the pale greens are machine-spun knitting yarns dyed with vegetal dyes; the blues are ravelled bayeta dyed with indigo; the whites are undyed handspun wool. During the late 1860s and the 1870s, Navajo serapes exhibit design elements which appear more enlarged and expanded than the design elements at work in serapes woven prior to 1860. Private collection, Santa Fe.

6. Above: Classic child's serape with small central diamonds. Navajo, circa 1860. 0.91 x 1.65m (3'0" x 4'5"). The reds are ravelled bayeta dyed with cochineal; the yellow is ravelled bayeta dyed with vegetal dyes; the blues are handspun wool dyed with indigo, the whites are undyed handspun wool. Many collectors regard this child's serape as the finest example of its type. Private collection, Los Angeles.

fifty horses, a Plains Indian could wear the blanket for a year, then exchange it with a third party for another fifty horses, or for $50 in gold. By the 1860s, the demand for chief's blankets had started to come more from Anglo-Americans than from other Indians. To satisfy this Anglo-American appetite for more design and less space, the simple, horizontally striped patterns of the First and Second Phase chief's blankets gave way to the diamonds, half-diamonds and quarter-diamonds of the Third Phase.

   Academics, collectors and dealers of Navajo blankets separate chief's blankets into four specific categories: First Phase, Second Phase, Third Phase and Variants. First Phase chief's blankets contain horizontal stripes, but no vertical or diagonal designs. The Second Phase

9. Right: Classic child's serape with a striped field. Navajo, circa 1860. 0.74 x 1.27m (2'5" x 4'2"). The reds are ravelled bayeta dyed with cochineal; the greens are ravelled bayeta dyed with vegetal dyes; the blues are handspun wool dyed with indigo; the whites are undyed handspun wool. The simplicity and balance at work in this child's serape make it a hypnotic object. Private collection, Santa Fe.

8. Left: Classic child's serape with a white field and small central diamonds. Navajo, circa 1860. 0.79 x 1.27m (2'7" x 4'2"). The reds are ravelled bayeta dyed with cochineal; the greens are ravelled bayeta dyed with vegetal dyes; the yellow is handspun wool dyed with vegetal dyes, probably rabbit brush, the blues are handspun wool dyed with indigo; one of the whites is machine-spun yarns dyed with synthetic dyes that have faded to white; the rest of the whites are undyed handspun wool. When worn around the shoulders, the central panel of this serape would have fallen along the line of the child's spine. Private collection, New York.

has horizontal stripes punctuated by vertical designs, usually in the form of square or rectangular blocks, but no diagonal designs. The Third Phase has diagonal designs against horizontal backgrounds, and these diagonal designs almost always take the form of full, half- or quarter-diamonds. Variant chief's blankets contain elements of the other three phases, but do not conform to First, Second or Third Phase styles. The Variant shown in (**10**), for instance, exhibits a Third Phase top and bottom, above and below a Second Phase centre.

Many people assume that Navajo chief's blankets were either woven by Navajo chiefs or for Navajo chiefs. Neither assumption is correct. Due to the high price of a Navajo chief's blanket, the only Plains Indians who could afford them tended to be the chiefs of their respective clans or tribes. In many cases, Plains Indian chiefs bought the blankets as gifts for their wives and daughters. In 19th century photographs, there are as many Plains women depicted in chief's blankets as there are Plains men. The fact that all the Navajo weavers were women, and that they were all members of the Navajo tribe, is an important historic and

10. Above: Variant chief's blanket with Second and Third Phase design elements. Navajo, circa 1845. 1.68 x 1.42m (5'6" x 4'8"). The red is ravelled bayeta dyed with lac; the blues are handspun wool dyed with indigo; the browns and whites are undyed handspun wool. While almost all chief's blanket variants were woven after 1860, this example was collected in 1849, suggesting that Third Phase design elements are older than is commonly believed. This blanket skilfully combines elements of the Second Phase style (centre) with the Third Phase style (top and bottom).

11. Right: Late Classic child's serape with a red field and green stripes. Navajo, circa 1865–1870. 0.74 x 1.24m (2'5" x 4'1"). Ninety per cent of the reds are ravelled bayeta dyed with cochineal; the remaining ten per cent are machine-spun knitting yarns dyed with cochineal; the greens are handspun wool dyed with combinations of indigo and vegetal dyes; the blues are handspun wool dyed with indigo; the greys are undyed brown fleece and undyed white fleece carded together to create grey. Child's serapes woven after 1865 tend to be more decorative than those from the 1850s and early 1860s. Private collection, Washington, DC.

ethnographic consideration. However, neither the gender nor the race of these weavers is as important as the fact that they were all artists – dedicated, inspired artists who supported their families and enhanced the material wealth of their tribe by weaving blankets.

THE FOUR STAGES OF SEEING

Much has been written about the historical and ethnographic aspects of 19th century Navajo blankets. Virtually all of the two dozen or so books in print on the subject discuss yarn types, dye analyses, design styles, regional idiosyncrasies and cross-cultural influences. However, none of these books contain any discussion of how to look at a Navajo blanket. Evidently, the practice of hanging a Navajo blanket on the wall, lighting it evenly and then standing back to consider its relative merits as a work of art is still too recent to warrant such a discussion.

There is an old Talmudic saying: "We do not see things as they are. We see things as we are." The wisdom of that saying can be helpful in learning to appreciate Navajo blankets. What you and your eyes bring to a Navajo blanket is just as important as any historical or material facts at work in the blanket. Sometimes I think people feel lost when they look at a Navajo weaving because they do not – and cannot – know the name of the weaver, the village she came from or the year in which she wove the blanket. However, it is my belief that the absence of such information makes possible a much deeper relationship between eye and object than can ever occur between the eye and an object that is signed, dated or attributed. The key to that relationship, naturally, is a willingness on the part of the eye to bring a developed appreciation to whatever it sees.

There are four stages involved in developing an appreciation for a Navajo blanket. These stages are not necessarily sequential. Sometimes they overlap, sometimes they parallel each other. But recognition of their identities as stages leads to the discovery of how much depth, and what sort of depth, a Navajo blanket has.

The first stage is *noticing* the blanket. This is a kind of early infatuation between eye and object. Noticing a blanket can happen at auctions, at art shows, in galleries, in private homes, in vaults, in museums, even in magazines or books. A blanket catches your eye, stands out from the rest of your field of vision, and serves notice on you that your attention has been held, even if only for a moment.

Occasionally the blanket you notice will be one you have seen before, but reacted to with indifference. The best Navajo blankets change people's eyes. Once the eye changes, everything the eye sees changes, too. A Navajo blanket that compels attention the second time you encounter it is a blanket worth noticing. By the same token, a blanket that looks the same each time you see it is probably not worth your attention.

The second stage is *seeing* the blanket. Old fans of Carlos Castaneda's books will remember the distinction Don Juan made between looking and seeing. In current American, the art of seeing is revealed by the expression lovers use 'seeing each other'. The less oblique, more urgent, 'When will I see you again?', means that romance has progressed to a more emphatic level. The old cliché 'Seeing is believing' further reveals the art involved in the act of seeing. Belief, per se, is an irrational process. Nobody 'believes' in rational facts because they can be proven and therefore require no leaps of faith. True belief requires confusion, doubt, mystery and paradox. When you see a Navajo blanket, you embrace its unexplained aspects and stop worrying about a factual basis for what you are seeing. You see, you believe, and you appreciate.

Central to the act of seeing a Navajo blanket is the abandonment of the widespread assumption that the blanket 'means' something' Navajo blankets are neither coded messages nor sacred symbols. They do not 'mean' anything. They invite people to see, and then supply their own meanings. Once a degree of personal meaning has been supplied, people often say

There is an old Talmudic saying:
"We do not see things as they are.
We see things as we are."

'That blanket means a lot to me'. Interestingly, they never say exactly what it means.

The third and fourth stages are extensions of the act of seeing, but still deserve individual recognition because of the ways they refine and extend one's ability to assess a Navajo blanket's depth. The third stage is *seeing into* the blanket. Americans often use the expression, 'look into' with the implication that further research is required before a decision can be reached. The difference between looking into and seeing into a Navajo blanket is like the difference between research and experience. When you research a subject, you raise questions and receive answers. When you experience something, you make it a part of your life and accept that, like life itself, it will inevitably raise more questions than it answers.

People who have looked at only a few Navajo blankets often want to know if the lazy lines and the variegated yarns at work in the blankets were put there intentionally, or happened through some kind of 19th century Navajo accident. The question ignores and overlooks the possibility that Navajo weavers wove their blankets in such a way that the very issue of accidental-versus-intentional would not only be raised, but would be impossible to resolve. Why? Because ambiguity makes art more fascinating, and attracts a better quality of attention than art which answers all of our questions.

The fourth stage is *seeing through* the blanket. Seeing through objects often happens in dreams, and certain seers can see through time. Chess masters speak of 'seeing through your opponent's pieces'; poker players say that when you're hot 'You can see through the other guy's hand'. Seeing through a Navajo blanket is like that: a kind of X-ray vision that reveals, among other things, yarns, dyes, spinning techniques, tension problems and on-loom repairs.

Seeing through a blanket can show you where the weaver started weaving, in which direction she wove, and where she finished the blanket. It can also show you what kind of landscape the weaver lived in, how old she was when she wove the blanket, what kinds of prices she got for her blankets, and how many sheep she owned. Old-time American Indian traders will hold a Navajo blanket up to a window, or to a bright light, to see if it contains restoration. That's not the whole process of seeing through a blanket, but it is a good beginning.
Notes see Appendix

12. **Classic Third Phase chief's blanket with three central diamonds. Navajo, circa 1855-1860. 1.80 x 1.42m (5'11" x 4'8"). The reds are ravelled bayeta dyed with cochineal; the greens are ravelled bayeta dyed with combinations of indigo and vegetal dyes; the blues are handspun wool dyed with indigo; the browns and the whites are undyed handspun wool. The concentric, stepped diamonds which characterise Classic Navajo serapes start appearing in chief's blankets during the mid 1850s, creating the Third Phase style. Private collection, Chicago.**

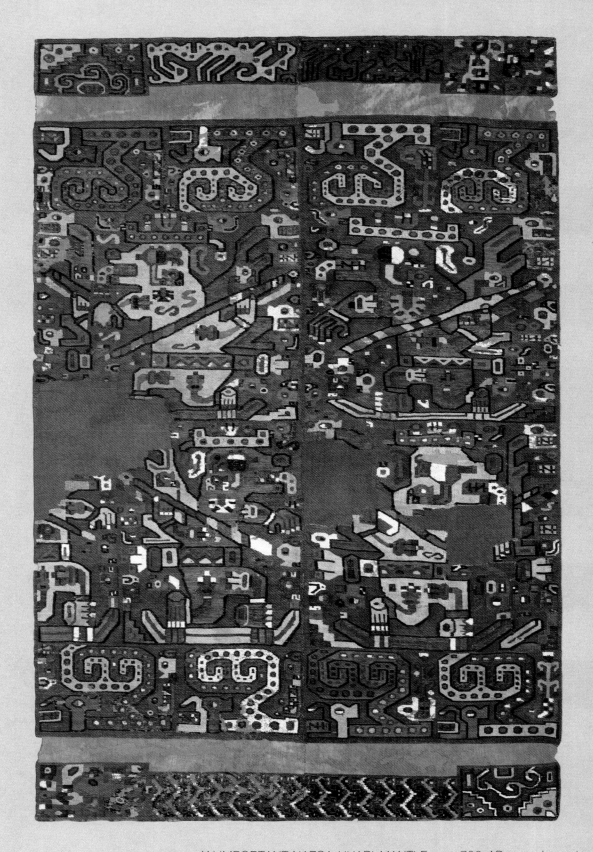

AN IMPORTANT NAZCA-HUARI MANTLE, ca. 700 AD, supplementary decorative weft, Camelid wool on a cotton foundation, South coast, Peru, 109 x 168 cm

This highly important early Huari mantle is the only known example portraying the puma deity in the pose of a spear thrower. The iconography combines aspects of the zoomorphic and the anthropomorphic. The scale of the figures and the complex iconography, together with the richness of symbolic detail, would strongly indicate that this piece was intended for the use of an important warrior-priest serving the Huari theocracy in the south coast colonies. For further analysis of the iconography please see *Tresors du Nouveau Monde* and *Hali's* "Connoisseurs Choice" below.

PROVENANCE: Private European Collection

BIBLIOGRAPHY:
Illustrated: *Hali* 53, vol. 12 no. 5, Connoisseurs Choice, pp. 124-125
José Antonio de Lavalle, *Culturas Precolombinas: Huari*, Banco de Credito del Peru, Lima, Peru, 1986, p. 80
Pre-Columbian Andean Textile Art, Romeo Gigli Gallery, Milan, 1991, Editions Carla Sozzani, pl. 22
Tresors du Nouveau Monde, Musees Royaux d'Art et d'Histoire, Brussels, 1992, p. 419, fig. 451

EXHIBITED:
Milan, Romeo Gigli Gallery, "Pre-Columbian Andean Textile Art", March 1991
London, Rotunda Gallery, Canary Wharf, "Ancient Peruvian Art", May 1992
Brussels, Musees Royaux d'Art et d'Histoire, "Tresors du Nouveau Monde", September 1992

PAUL HUGHES
FINE TEXTILE ART
3A PEMBRIDGE SQ.
LONDON W2 4EW
TEL: 071 243 8598
FAX: 071 221 8785
(By Appointment Only)

MARTIN AND ULLMAN
ARTWEAVE TEXTILE GALLERY

ONE HALF OF A TUNIC, NAZCA, (400 - 600 AD), feathers applied to cotton balanced plain weave ground, 58" x 58" (147 x 147cm)

Outstanding Examples of Antique, Ancient and Ethnographic Textiles.

Conservation and Mounting Services

310 Riverside Drive • New York, NY 10025, USA • Tel: (1 212) 864 3550 • Fax: (1 212) 663 0940
By Appointment Only

A Twilled Double Saddle Blanket with Four Central Diamonds,
Navajo, circa 1890. 34 by 51 inches.
All reproduction rights reserved by Joshua Baer & Company

Joshua Baer & Company maintains the largest inventory of
19th Century Navajo blankets for sale anywhere in the world.
We specialise in building collections of Navajo blankets for
individuals and corporate accounts. We also appraise
Navajo blankets, Navajo rugs and all other types of
antique American Indian art.

JOSHUA BAER & COMPANY
Classic American Indian Art

116½ EAST PALACE AVENUE   SANTA FE   NEW MEXICO 87501   USA

505 988 – 8944

Nazca Tunic with Killer Whale/Profile Head Motif (detail)

ANDRES MORAGA GALLERY

TEXTILE ART

Nazca culture, Peru
Early Intermediate Period, 200-600 AD
Mantle
134 x 190cm (52³/₄ x 74³/₄in)
Balanced plain weave, with warp and weft of camelid wool,
made in sections and sewn together
Published: 'Textile Art/Textielkunst', Kailash Gallery, 1994,
plate 51

Kailash Gallery

a TEXTVRA member

Patrick *and* Rie Ampe

Komedieplaats 7-9-11, B-2000 Antwerpen, Belgium

Tel.:32.3.231.92.46   Fax.:32.3.226.25.05

William Siegal
Fine Tribal Textiles

Specialising in Aymara, pre-Columbian and selected
textiles from Indonesia and Africa

44 Alteza, Santa Fe, New Mexico 87505, USA
Tel: (1 505) 466 4411   Fax: (1 505) 466 3374
By Appointment Only

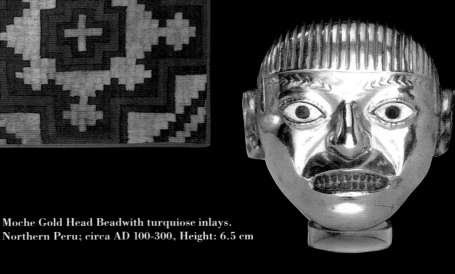

AUCTION
REVIEW

CARPETS

This market report offers readers a very brief, carefully selected overview of oriental carpets sold at major international auctions during the past two years. Our choice is governed by a combination of subjective and objective considerations, with perceived aesthetic quality at least as important a determinant as either market value or art historical significance. Not all areas or types are included, but the selection may nevertheless be seen as representative. There are, of course, many other rugs that have appeared at auction that could undoubtedly be considered the equal of most of those that we have chosen. And it must always be remembered that prices at auction do not necessarily give a true picture of the market or of real values. This is due to the anomalies that the system inevitably produces, because sales tend to be dominated by the carpet trade, and because some rug types are seldom, if ever, consigned for public sale. All prices quoted are US dollar equivalents at the time of the sale, and include the buyer's premiums charged by the auction houses.

1.

2.

AT AUCTION

1. Kuba rug, east Cauc-
asus, early 19th century.
1.00 x 1.18m (3'3" x
3'10"). Rippon Boswell,
Wiesbaden, 15 May
1993, lot 61. Estimate
DM24,500, sold for
DM37,120 ($23,095).

2. Feraghan horse-cover,
west Persia, second
half 19th century.
1.65 x 1.58m (5'5" x 5'2").
Christie's, New York,
6 February 1993, lot 11.
Estimate $5,000-$7,000,
sold for $6,050.

3. Yomut Turkoman
torba, mid 19th century.
1.07 x 0.48m (3'6" x 1'7").
Sotheby's, New York,
16 December 1993, lot 48.
Estimate $2,500-$3,500,
sold for $10,925.

4. Anatolian carpet frag-
ment, 16th/17th century.
1.07 x 2.77m (3'6" x 9'1").
Sotheby's, New York,
16 December 1993, lot 81.
Estimate $20,000-$25,000,
sold for $54,625.

4.

3.

EAST MEDITERRANEAN & TURKEY

East Mediterranean (mainly Cairene) and Turkish rugs are often considered together, despite differences in technique and design, because the weaving traditions converge in the court sponsored workshops of Egypt and Anatolia after the fall of Cairo to the Ottomans in 1513. Unlike their Persian counterparts, however, the majority of carpets from the region that appear at auction reflect the breadth of Turkish production of both pile rugs and flatweaves from commercial workshops and by village and nomad weavers prior to the 19th century.

The distinctive sheen, velvety texture and restricted palette of Mamluk rugs, woven in Cairo between about 1450 and 1550, sets them apart as a group, albeit one which rarely appears on the auction market. Examples differ in format, design and colour range. A marvellous little rug sold in New York in December 1992 for $275,000 (Sotheby's, lot 67) is among the smallest, with a red field dominated by a central star-octagon, symmetrical decorative panels at each end, and the whole framed by a blue major and green minor borders (5).

Almost contemporaneous with the Mamluk carpets are the large format workshop carpets

6.

5. Mamluk rug, Egypt, ca. 1500. 1.45 x 1.88m (4'9" x 6'2"). Sotheby's, New York, 10 December 1992, lot 67. Estimate $100,000-$150,000, sold for $275,000.

6. Kum Kapı prayer rug, Istanbul, ca. 1900. 1.02 x 1.42m (3'4" x 4'8"), Christie's, London, 21 October 1993, lot 428. Estimate £25,000-£30,000, sold for £49,900 ($76,845).

7. Star Ushak rug, west Anatolia, 16th century. 1.19 x 1.83m (3'11" x 6'0"). Nagel, Stuttgart, 23 June 1993, lot 3069. Estimate on request, sold for DM161,000 ($94,275).

8. 'Lotto' arabesque rug, Ushak (?), west Anatolia, early 16th century. 1.22 x 2.09m (4'0" x 6'10"). Phillips, London, 24 November 1992, lot 6. Estimate £20,000-£25,000, sold for £19,800 ($29,955).

9. Bergama rug, west Anatolia,19th century. 1.47 x 2.11m (4'10" x 6'11"). Rippon Boswell, Wiesbaden, 15 May 1993, lot 13. Estimate DM6,000, sold for DM38,000 ($23,650).

5.

7.

8.

9.

woven in Ushak in Western Anatolia. Most of those that appear on the Western market were originally made for export. However, relatively few of these 'classical' carpets are sold at auction and prices are greatly affected by age, condition and quality. Thus while a 'Star' Ushak carpet sold at Phillips, London, in November 1992 for $39,945, six months later a second, smaller, example (bought privately in 1974 for less than $6,000), was sold by Nagel in Stuttgart for $94,275 (**7**). However, $30,000 more ($124,285) was paid at Rippon Boswell, Wiesbaden in November 1993 for lot 132, a 16th century double-niche Ushak (see p.225).

This was one of a number of examples of a fairly rare type, but of variable quality, to appear on both sides of the Atlantic in the past few years, the most recent being lot 70 at Sotheby's, London, in April 1994, which made $48,300.

The 'Lotto' arabesque design was used in different parts of Turkey over two centuries. Despite being severely worn, a small rug (**8**) with a rarely-found 'Kufic' border of the type most common on 'small-pattern Holbein' rugs of the 15th century was sold for $29,955 at Phillips, London in November 1992 (lot 6) while a larger, later, less interesting and extensively restored carpet, was sold by Picard at Drouot, Paris, in September 1993 for $34,780 (lot 298).

Fragments of early Turkish village rugs are a 1990s phenomenon at auction. Part of a rare and remarkable lattice design carpet (**4**) with an outstanding palette and a border reminiscent of a Cairene Ottoman border design, was bid to $54,625 in December 1993 at Sotheby's, New York (lot 81).

Among the most attractive of the 19th century Turkish rugs during this period was a Bergama (**9**) with features of double-niche Ushak and 'Transylvanian' field designs, which sold for $23,650 in Wiesbaden (May 1993, lot 13).

Wholly different in style, and in clientele, are Kum Kapı silk and metal thread prayer rugs. A turn of the century example (**6**) fetched $76,845 at Christie's, London in October 1993 (lot 428), while a later piece (Sotheby's, London, April 1993, lot 103), attributed to Tossounian and probably made between the wars, fetched $23,470. Another, said to be from the Zareh Penyamian atelier, made $55,050 at Christie's in London in April 1994 (lot 419).

THE CAUCASUS

Caucasian rugs on the market fall into loosely defined 'early' (17th/18th century) and commercial period (last third 19th century onwards) weavings. The Caucasian attribution for the so-called 'classical' carpets is contentious – to view the Caucasus, parts of northwest Persia and eastern Anatolia as entirely separate is anachronistic, and the majority of early examples have been found in Anatolia. Not so many years ago, 19th century Caucasian rugs, loosely divided by design, materials and according to supposed region and even town of origin, were the the staple diet of Western collectors. This is still true to a large extent, with rare and beautiful pieces commanding market attention, but the leading edge of serious collecting has moved on to other fields. There have also been pockets of demand for Caucasian rugs in countries which have otherwise largely ignored oriental rugs – they have long been the scatter rugs of Paris intellectuals and of Harley Street physicians. Perhaps because they are bought by collectors and also have a role as elite furnishings, they are rather less affected by recession or fashion than tribal and nomad rugs.

10.

The nomenclatura of 19th century Caucasian rugs are the 'Star' and 'Pinwheel' Kazaks. Once thought to be very old (in no other rugs were inscribed dates, usually random combinations of the Arabic numerals 0, 1, 2 and 3, so consistently misread), it is now clear that most are from the second half of the 19th century. At least in the case of the Pinwheel Kazaks, the reputation for rarity is also enormously exaggerated. While most recently a Star Kazak was sold at Sotheby's, New York in April 1993 for $68,500 (**11**), the past two years have seen one Pinwheel sold at Rippon Boswell, Wiesbaden (November 1992, lot 103) for $30,835, and three at Sotheby's New York – December 1992, lot 62, $48,400 (**12**); April 1993, lot 118, $29,900; December 1993, lot 144, $33,350. Sotheby's in London sold a lesser rug in April 1994 for $13,800 (lot 32) and another in the

11.

12.

10. Marasali Shirvan prayer rug, east Caucasus, first half 19th century. 1.04 x 1.29m (3'5" x 4'3"). Rippon Boswell, Wiesbaden, 15 May 1993, lot 159. Estimate DM33,000, sold for DM48,720 ($30,310).

11. Star Kazak rug, west Caucasus, mid 19th century. 1.27 x 1.91m (4'2" x 6'3"). Sotheby's, New York, 15 April 1993, lot 132. Estimate $40,000-$60,000, sold for $68,500.

12. Pinwheel Kazak rug, west Caucasus, second half 19th century. 1.96 x 2.54m (6'5" x 8'4"). Sotheby's, New York, 10 December 1992, lot 62. Estimate $30,000-$35,000, sold for $48,400.

13. Shirvan prayer rug, east Caucasus, 19th century. 0.85 x 1.64m (2'10" x 5'5"). Sotheby's, London, 20 October 1993, lot 37. Estimate £5,000-£8,000, sold for £5,175 ($7,765).

13.

14. Lenkoran rug, southeast Caucasus, early 19th century. 1.43 x 2.87m (4'8" x 9'5"). Rippon Boswell, Wiesbaden, 30 May 1992, lot 137. Estimate DM85,000, sold for DM98,600 ($61,435).

15.

16.

same month at Christie's, London (lot 454) made $11,220.

A beautiful small blue-ground Kuba rug (**1**) sold extremely well at Rippon Boswell in May 1993, making $23,095, although the price was only half of the $46,200 paid for a similar piece, credibly dated 1230 AH (1815 AD), at Sotheby's in New York in December 1987.

Among the best east Caucasian prayer rugs on the market in this period was a finely-woven Marasali Shirvan (**10**) sold for $30,310 at the same Rippon Boswell May auction (lot 159), while one of the undoubted bargains was a lovely lattice design ivory-ground Shirvan (**13**), with extremely thick, luscious pile, which went almost unnoticed at Sotheby's in London in October 1993 (lot 37), making a miserly $7,765.

One of the highest recent prices for a 19th century Caucasian rug was the $61,435 paid for a Lenkoran rug (**14**) at Rippon Boswell (May 1992, lot 137), which compares with $27,500 paid at Sotheby's New York (December 1992, lot 39) for a long rug of similar design but lesser quality. It may be a truism to say that quality is all-important in such rugs, but it was not always so. In many cases price differences between excellent and good rugs of similar type have widened greatly as the market has grown more knowledgeable and discerning.

Of three of the most interesting rugs at these auctions, we know little more than that they were probably woven in the Caucasus. The first was a colourful late Dragon carpet (**15**) sold at Rippon Boswell in Wiesbaden in May 1993 (lot 126) for $72,165. The foreshortened 'dragons' and rudimentary lattice containing horsemen, peacocks and lumbering dinosaur-like beasts with tripod feet were drawn in a manner closer to flatwoven Dragon sumakh rugs than 'classical' Dragon carpets. The second belongs to a small group of finely woven silk-wefted prayer rugs with inscribed dates between 1800 and 1815. While there is some doubt about the dates and the weaving area, there is none about their jewel-like quality. Equally uncertain is the origin of the beautifully coloured and drawn 18th century Azerbaijan rug (**16**) sold by Sotheby's in London in April 1993 (lot 60), for $41,530. With a central *göl*-like medallion within an octagonal surround, details clearly related to Azerbaijan embroideries of the period, and precursor to 19th century commercial rugs such as Alpan Kubas, it had been snapped up some months before at an English country auction for under $1,500.

15. Dragon carpet, Karabagh (?) south Caucasus, 19th century. 1.90 x 3.51m (6'3" x 11'6"). Rippon Boswell, Wiesbaden, 15 May 1993, lot 126. Estimate on request, sold for DM116,000 ($72,165).

16. Azerbaijan rug, south-east Caucasus, 18th century. 1.33 x 2.10m (4'4" x 6'11"). Sotheby's, London, 28 April 1993, lot 60. Estimate £15,000-£18,000, sold for £26,450 ($41,530).

PERSIA

17.

17. Heriz silk prayer rug, northwest Persia, late 19th century. 1.42 x 1.83m (4'8" x 6'0"). Christie's, London, 21 October 1993, lot 551. Estimate £4,000-£6,000, sold for: £9,775 ($15,055).

18. Varamin *saf*, possibly Afshar tribe, northwest Persia, 19th century. 1.63 x 2.93m (5'4" x 9'7"). Rippon Boswell, Wiesbaden, 15 May 1993, lot 56. Estimate DM18,500, sold for DM15,080.

Persian carpets on the international market comprise several separate areas of interest. Highest individual prices at auction are usually achieved by 'classical' period weavings exported from the skilled master workshops of the Safavid court during the 16th and 17th centuries, or by luxury weavings of the more recent Qajar and Pahlavi periods (19th and 20th century). But alongside this small and rarefied sector are several others. The largest of all in terms of volume and value consists of high quality decorative carpets, in both wool and silk, made for export in the villages since the so-called revival period of the second half of the 19th century almost until the present day. Results in this sector have been much affected, both inside the USA and elsewhere, by the continuing American embargo on imports of Iranian goods, including antiques. Tribal and nomad rugs, the colourful rural weavings of Iran, are the most diverse, and in many cases the least expensive sector of the market. The best examples have long been widely collected in the West. These rugs, covers, bags and trappings were woven in large quantities throughout Iran, by a plethora of different peoples – Persian, Turkic, Kurdish – who until quite recently continued to lead a traditional lifestyle in which carpet products, both functional and ceremonial, played a major part.

The highest ever auction price for a Persian carpet was paid at a jubilant Christie's in London in April 1993 for lot 432, the longer of the two 'Polonaise' silk and metal-thread carpets that had once belonged to King Umberto of Italy (see pp.222-3). Made in the workshops established by the Safavid Shah Abbas in his new capital, Esfahan, at the beginning of the 17th century, and doubtless originally exported from Persia as a diplomatic gift or princely commission, at $691,390 this lavish carpet realised more than three times the $210,950 it had made at Sotheby's, London, in 1984, when the smaller Umberto carpet cost $245,650.

The price is by no means out of line with those for others of the genre in the past dozen years. In 1982 a 'Polonaise' made $397,000 at Sotheby's, London, while in June 1988 a leading Italian dealer paid $264,000 for a long rug at Sotheby's, New York (SNY). In and around the momentous 'Getty' sale in the same rooms (December 1990), SNY sold two small rugs for $506,000 and $440,000. But Christie's carpet, with its glowing emerald green and scattering of seed pearls, is arguably the best of these, always excepting the brilliant Czartoryski small rug, which was controversially withdrawn from a Christie's, London sale in October 1990.

Also very likely from workshops in Safavid Esfahan, red-ground wool carpets such as lot

18.

19.

19. Kerman 'Vase' carpet, south-central Persia, late 17th or early 18th century. 1.73 x 2.69m (5'8" x 8'10"). Sotheby's, New York, 15 April 1993, lot 83. Estimate $15,000-$20,000, sold for $120,750.

20. 'Baluch' *sofreh*, Khorasan, northeast Persia, 19th century. 0.73 x 1.15m (2'5" x 3'9"). Rippon Boswell, Wiesbaden, 14 November 1992, lot 99. Estimate DM6,000, sold for DM10,440 ($6,610).

21. Sehna prayer kilim, Sanandaj region, Persian Kurdistan, second half 19th century. 1.22 x 1.78m (4'0" x 5'10"). Christie's, London, 29 April 1993, lot 386. Estimate £5,000-7,000, sold for £9,430 ($14,770).

22. Qashqa'i 'Khan' carpet, Fars Province, southwest Persia, first half 19th century. 1.64 x 2.67m (5'5" x 8'9"). Rippon Boswell, Wiesbaden, 15 May 1993, lot 132. Estimate DM68,000, sold for DM58,000 ($36,075).

23. Khorasan carpet fragment, east Persia, 17th century. 1.14 x 2.52m (3'9" x 8'3"). Sotheby's, New York, 16 December 1993, lot 156. Estimate $20,000-$25,000, sold for $23,000.

20.

239 at SNY in September 1993, which sold for $101,500, are regaining the values they commanded earlier this century, when they were popular among wealthy American collectors. Three related pieces in the 1990 'Getty' sale made prices between $82,500 and $121,000.

A magnificent example of the 'Vase' group, true to the name in both design and technique (**19**), sold at SNY for $120,750 in April 1993. Closely comparable to a carpet in the Historical Textile Museum, Lyon, it belongs to a sub-group which also includes carpets in museums in London (Victoria & Albert) and Glasgow (Burrell Collection), and the marvellous Jacoby-Altman-McMullan carpet in the Harvard University Collection, Cambridge, Massachusetts. A number of Safavid fragments also sold during this period, including pieces of Esfahan and 'vase' carpets, but most notable was a large section of a *jufti*-knotted Khorasan carpet (**23**) at SNY in December 1993 (lot 156) for $23,000. This had failed to sell in Sotheby's London rooms in 1992, but another, slightly larger piece, without the spectacular trefoil border, had sold there in October 1991 for $53,900.

Of two 18th/19th century Kurdish 'Garden' carpets, the earlier, and better, was at Rippon Boswell in Wiesbaden in May 1992 (lot 126), where it made $355,250. The other, one of two

21.

once belonging to the collector Hagop Kevorkian (its companion is in the Islamic Art Museum at Berlin-Dahlem), was sold by Sotheby's, London, in October 1993 for $109,500. It had appeared in the same rooms at least twice before – first in the 1969 Kevorkian sale, when it was acquired by The British Rail Pension Fund, and again in 1987, when it failed to sell.

Ultra-fine Sehna kilims from Persian Kurdistan, with their dense all-over designs based on 18th century Persian textiles, are widely collected. A prayer rug in Christie's 'Polonaise' sale (lot 386) made $14,770 (**21**), while a leading German dealer paid $17,215 for the rather idiosyncratic lot 1121 at Nagel, Stuttgart in May 1994. Also in the 'Polonaise' sale, a silk Heriz prayer rug (lot 551), about a century old, with beautiful colour and in perfect condition, was a bargain at $15,055 (**17**). An equally good buy at Rippon Boswell in May 1993 (lot 56) was one of the more unusual 19th century rugs on offer, a *saf* (multiple-niche prayer carpet), of uncertain tribal origin, from the Varamin region of northern Persia (**18**). Closely resembling a flatweave sold in 1991 in Stuttgart for $10,860, it made $10,220.

So-called 'Baluch' tribal rugs were made by a motley assortment of nomads, semi-nomads and villagers in eastern Iran and Afghanistan. They have enjoyed burgeoning popularity among collectors who rightly see them as authentic 'tribal' weavings, offering both material and artistic quality at accessible prices. A pilewoven *sofreh* or eating rug (**20**) sold in Wiesbaden in November 1992 (lot 99) for $6,610, is comparable to a similar piece in the same rooms in March 1992 for $7,705 (lot 100). Equally rooted in the semi-nomad tradition, but combined with the urban sophistication of settled Turkish-speaking Qashqa'i weavers in Fars Province, is a finely woven silk-wefted 'Khan' carpet (**22**), sold in May 1993 for $36,075 at Rippon Boswell in Wiesbaden (lot 132). Also perhaps woven to honour a tribal khan was a spectacular Feraghan horse-cover (**2**) with a complex all-over floral design, which sold at Christie's in New York in February 1993 for $6,050 (lot 11).

22.

21.

CENTRAL ASIA

The great mass of Central Asian weaving on the market consists of the rugs, tent furnishings, transport bags, covers and animal trappings, both functional and ceremonial, produced in the 18th and 19th centuries by the various Turkoman tribes. The best of them are of superb technical and material quality, and these sombre, predominantly red, carpet products have been avidly collected at various times, particularly in Germany. The results of some recent sales have suggested that Turkoman rugs have re-emerged from the doldrums of the past few years. Not, of course, that the committed specialists ever abandoned their faith, with top of the range pieces and examples of rare types and formats consistently causing great excitement among dealers and private collectors alike and achieving very substantial prices at auction. During the period under review, the sale in December 1993 at Sotheby's in New York of sixty-one Turkoman rugs and trappings belonging to the well-known English collector/scholar Dr Jon Thompson was of particular significance, as it confirmed a revival in this highly specialised market that had begun in Germany in the summer of 1993.

While a good early Salor *chuval* (large tent-bag) in good condition fetched $10,470 at Sotheby's, London (April 1993, lot 42), at the Thompson sale (Sotheby's, New York, December 1993), lot 60, a superb fragment representing less than half of a chuval of similar design (**28**), was sold for $12,075, and two complete Salor *chuvals* (lots 55 and 57) for $17,250 and $14,375 respectively. Two very desirable Salor wedding camel trappings with the *kejebe* design, lots 53 and 58 (**24**) were much more expensive, selling for $46,000 and $51,750 respectively. Decorative trappings of other Turkoman tribes do not reach these prices.

24. Salor Turkoman animal trapping, first half 19th century. 2.13 x 0.79m (7'0" x 2'7"). Sotheby's, New York, 16 December 1993, lot 58. Estimate $40,000-$60,000, sold for $51,750.

25. Chodor Turkoman animal trapping, first half 19th century. 1.68 x 0.66m (5'6" x 2'2"). Sotheby's, New York, 16 December 1993, lot 37. Estimate $15,000-$20,000, sold for $24,150.

24.

25.

26.

26. Tekke Turkoman *uuk-bash*, **first half 19th century. 0.61 x 0.63m (2'0" x 2'1"). Sotheby's, New York, 16 December 1993, lot 8. Estimate $2,000-$3,000, sold for $12,650.**

27. Turkoman Eagle-*göl* group 2 main carpet, first half 19th century. 1.89 x 3.12m (6'2" x 10'3"). Nagel, Stuttgart, 23 June 1993, lot 3195. Estimate DM58,000, sold for DM51,750 ($30,300).

28.

28. Salor Turkoman *chuval* **fragment, first half 19th century. 0.61 x 0.66m (2'0" x 2'2"). Sotheby's, New York, 16 December 1993, lot 60. Estimate $4,000-$5,000, sold for $12,075.**

27.

Lot 37 in the same sale, a very beautiful Chodor trapping with *ertmen güls* (**25**) fetched $24,150, while lot 31, an Arabachi *kejebe* design trapping (**30**), an appreciably scarcer type on the market than the Salor examples, fetched only $14,950.

So-called Eagle-*göl* carpets have retained the prestige that followed the publication in 1990 of a monograph defining the group and its sub-groups. Two main carpets of group 2 were sold in Germany in 1993 – by Nagel, Stuttgart, in June (lot 3195) for $30,300 (**27**) and by Rippon Boswell, Wiesbaden, in November (lot 76) for $34,370. By contrast, a main carpet of this group at the Sotheby's, New York, December sale (lot 50) made only $10,350.

Very similar prices were paid for two outstanding Saryk *ensis* (tent door rugs), now in two German private collections: lot 103 at Rippon Boswell's November 1993 sale (**29**) went for $61,580, while lot 23 at the SNY Thompson auction made $57,500.

29.

30.

31.

29. Saryk Turkoman *ensi*, 18th or 19th century. 1.40 x 1.76m (4'7" x 5'9"). Rippon Boswell, Wiesbaden, 13 November 1993, lot 103. Estimate DM65,000, sold for DM99,760 ($61,580).

30. Arabachi Turkoman animal trapping, first half 19th century. 1.52 x 0.53m (5'0" x 1'9"). Sotheby's, New York, 16 December 1993, lot 31. Estimate $8,000-$10,000, sold for $14,950.

31. Tekke Turkoman *khalyk*, second half 19th century. 0.63 x 0.37 (2'1" x 1'3"). Rippon Boswell, Wiesbaden, 13 November 1993, lot 106. Estimate DM12,500, sold for DM17,400 ($10,740).

Most Turkoman tribes wove small tent-bags (*torbas*) with 'Memling' güls, but old Yomut pieces are virtually unknown, and the $10,925 paid for lot 48 in the SNY sale (3) was well above average. Among interesting small Tekke pieces, *uuk-bash* (tent-strut covers), especially those which have survived complete, are rare, and the $12,650 paid for lot 8 at SNY was not too high (26). On the other hand, the $10,740 at Rippon Boswell (November 1993, lot 106) for a *khalyk* (camel breast trapping) of standard design (31) was close to a record.

CHINA

The myth, current for many decades, that the Chinese did not produce carpets until the 18th century, has withstood both facts and arguments, but at last seems on the way out. At least partly responsible for this new-found enlightenment has been the presence in the USA since 1993 of a representative of the Chinese government, which has been feeding a steady stream of Ming and early Qing carpets, as well as later decorative furnishings, directly onto the international auction market, thereby bypassing Hong Kong middlemen.

A magnificent 16th century 'throne or dais carpet' made of camel-wool on silk warps and showing a dragon looking towards the rectangular re-entrant niche, was sold at Christie's, New York in December 1993 (lot 19). The low price of $11,500 was accounted for by the severe damage the carpet had suffered and doubts whether it could be adequately restored. The overall condition of an Imperial Dragon carpet (**32**) from the same source raised no such questions, though the loss of its borders distorts the original format, and it contained a substantial area of reweave in the field. It was bid up to $68,500 at Sotheby's, New York, in September 1993 (lot 219). This carpet too is Ming and is documented as originating in the Imperial palace in Beijing. Similar in period, and in the loss of its borders, was yet another Ming carpet offered by Nagel in June 1993 (lot 3260). But its price of $30,300 reflected the recognition that even a four hundred year old rug can be pretty ordinary.

A rather worn but very good 17th/18th century Ningxia medallion carpet (**33**) was sold at Sotheby's, New York in December 1993 (lot 63, $32,200). The fact that it made only half the price of a very decorative early 19th century Ningxia rug in the same rooms in October 1993 (lot 39, $60,250) demonstrates the market's uncertainty. Buyers who are at home with good and excellent Chinese decorative weavings are simply not used to dealing with the much more splendid, but damaged, earlier carpets and fragments.

32. Imperial Chinese Dragon carpet, Beijing (?), 16th or 17th century. 3.15 x 4.47m (10'4" x 14'8"). Sotheby's, New York, 22 September 1993, lot 219. Estimate $60,000-$80,000, sold for $68,500.

33. Ningxia carpet, western China, 17th or 18th century. 1.60 x 2.54m (5'3" x 8'4"). Sotheby's, New York, 16 December 1993, lot 63. Estimate $15,000-$20,000, sold for $32,200.

32.

33.

THE COVER STORY AT SOTHEBY'S

Each season Sotheby's brings out the best in rugs, carpets, tapestries and textiles in London and New York. The rugs shown here span five centuries of weaving, come from nomadic tribes, villages, city and court workshops and range in price from £3,100 ($4,500) to £345,000 ($500,000).

To find out more about buying or selling rugs and carpets at Sotheby's, please call:

Jacqueline Bing
in London on (44 71) 408 5152
Sotheby's, 34-35 New Bond Street,
London W1A 2AA or

Mary Jo Otsea
in New York on (212) 606 7996
Sotheby's, 1334 York Avenue,
New York NY 10021

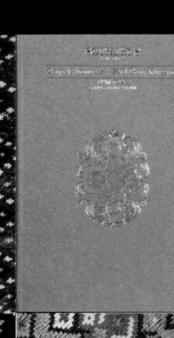

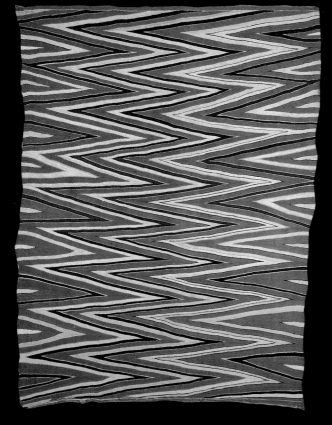

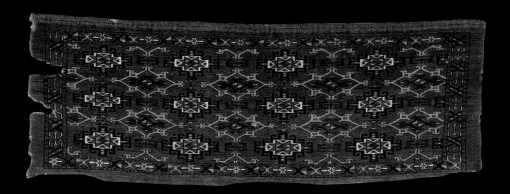

ISLAMIC ART

A week of sales of Islamic and Indian Art
is held bi-annually in London in April and October

A Kashan lustre pottery bowl depicting a camel and
camel-driver, Persia, early 13th century, 15.2cm diameter.
Sold in London on 28th April 1994 for £41,100.

For further information, please contact John Carswell or Brendan Lynch on (071) 408 5154

SOTHEBY'S, 34-35 NEW BOND STREET, LONDON W1A 2AA.

SOTHEBY'S

FOUNDED 1744

Carpets at Christie's

It's not by magic that Christie's sold the worlds's most expensive Oriental rug as well as the world's most expensive European rug at auction last year...

A Louis XIV Savonnerie carpet, circa 1680, approximately 17ft.5in. x 9ft.7in. (5m.31cm. x 2m.92cm.). Sold at Christie's New York on 30 October 1993 for $728,500. **1993 record price for any European carpet.**

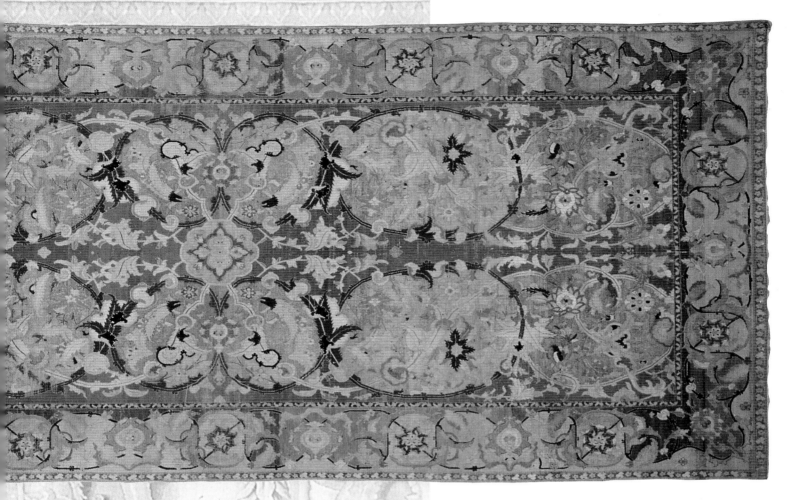

A Polonaise silk and metal thread carpet, 17th century, 162 x 169in. (410x176cm.) Sold at Christie's London on 29 April 1993 for £441,500. **1993 record price for any Oriental carpet.**

...over 200 years auction experience and commitment to our clients, be they buying or selling, means that although we cannot guarantee our carpets to fly, we do our best to make each sale a soaring success.

If you would like any further information, please contact James A. Ffrench in New York on (212) 546 1187 or William Robinson in London on (4471) 389 2370.

For catalogue subscriptions please contact New York, (718) 784 1480 or London (4471) 389 2820.

CHRISTIE'S

502 Park Avenue, New York, NY 10022
Tel: (212) 546 1000 Fax: (212) 980 8163

8 King Street, St. James's, London SW1Y 6QT
Tel: (4471) 839 9060 Fax: (4471) 389 2215

85 Old Brompton Road, London SW7 3LD
Tel: (4471) 581 7611 Fax: (4471) 321 3321

This magnificent Small-Medallion Ushak rug, west Anatolia, mid 16th century, 1.14 x 1.78m (3'9" x 5'10") was sold in Wiesbaden on 13 November 1993 for DM208,800 (approx. $124, 285).

We have established a reputation for achieving record prices including the Mughal Star-Lattice carpet, second half 17th or early 18th century, which was sold in Wiesbaden on 18 November 1989 for DM1,322,400 (approx. $718,700) and the magnificent Double-Niche Ushak rug, mid 16th century, which was sold in Wiesbaden on 11 May 1991 for a record price for the type of DM220,400 (approx. $127,400).

We are always looking for exceptional Oriental and European rugs, carpets, flatweaves and textiles. We hold regular specialist auctions in the Spring and Autumn and are now accepting entries for our future auctions.

We also offer evaluation services worldwide and restoration and conservation of antique carpets and textiles at our workshop.

Please contact Christa or Detlef Maltzahn for detailed information.

RIPPON BOSWELL & CO.

established 1884 in England
International Auctioneers of rare Oriental Carpets
Gesellschaft zur Organisation von Auktionen mbH

65185 Wiesbaden · Friedrichstrasse 45 · Telephone (49-611) 37 20 62 · Telefax (49-611) 30 73 69

TAPIS, initiation sarong , (detail)
Paminggir people, Lampung, Sumatra, Indonesia
Cotton, silk, mica shist mirrors
Embroidery, ikat
53" x 24 $^1/_2$" (135cm x 62cm), detail 14 $^3/_4$" x 8" (37.5cm x 20cm)
19th cent.

ESOTERIC SCULPTURE & TEXTILES

THOMAS MURRAY

ASIATICA – ETHNOGRAPHICA

P.O. BOX 1177 . MILL VALLEY, CA 94942 . TEL 415.679.4940 . FAX 415.453.8451

CARPETS

A gallery that has grown on the same site since 1920, through dedication and the quality of service.

GALERIE NEIRIZ BERLIN

KILIM, before 1800, South Persia, Fars Region, Luri, 304 x 142cm

KURFÜRSTENDAMM 61 · 10707 BERLIN · TEL/FAX: 030-882 3232

Rascid
Rahaim & C.

Director: Dell'Orto Franco
ANTIQUE ORIENTAL CARPETS

BAKHSHAISH, North Persia, second half 19th century, 410 x 275m

VENEZIA   VIA XXII MARZO, 2380   TEL. (041) 5224736   FAX. (041) 5228033

A complete cij (Reed screen from a Kirgiz Yurt), Central Asia, turn of the century. 127x780cm

ALBERTO
BORALEVI
THE CARPET STUDIO
CULTURA ED ARTE
NEL TAPPETO ANTICO

THE CARPET STUDIO DI ALBERTO BORALEVI & C.S.A.S.

50123 FIRENZE, VIA MONALDA 15/R
(TORRE DEGLI STROZZI). TEL. & FAX 055-21 14 23

VICENZA, ITALY.
NOT ONLY THE TOWN OF PALLADIO

PASHÀ GROUP OF HASAN PASHAMOGLU
ORIENTAL CARPETS AND KILIMS

Corso Palladio 138/A,
36100 Vicenza, Italy
Tel.: (39 444) 320101 - Fax: (39 444) 320106

Istanbul - Turkey
Nuruosmaniye Cad. 63/3 - Cagaloglu
Tel: (90 212) 527 3686 Fax: (90 212) 511 6477

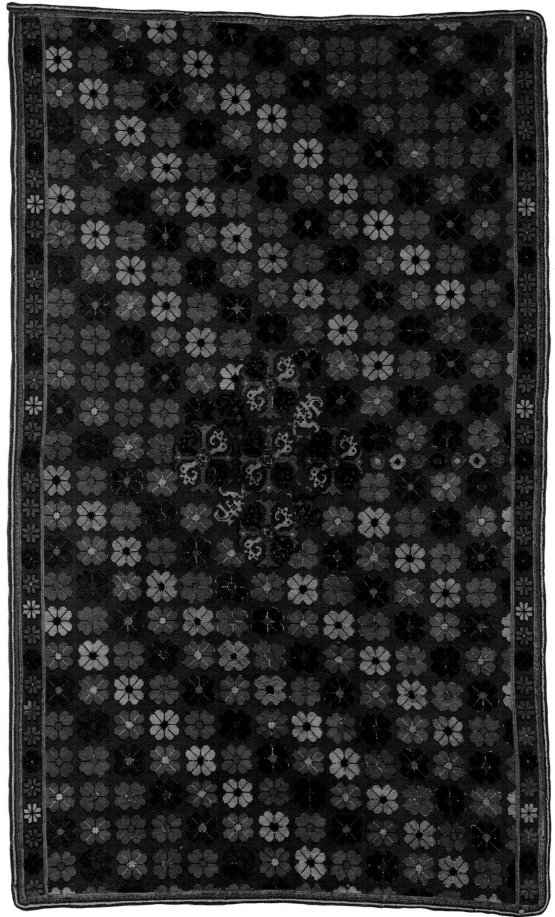

DERBENT SILK EMBROIDERY ON A BACKING OF RUSSIAN EXPORT COTTON
1'5" x 2'7"
18th century

MARK KESHISHIAN & SONS, INC.

RARE ORIENTAL RUGS & TAPESTRIES

4505 STANFORD STREET, CHEVY CHASE, MD 20815, USA.   TEL: (301) 951-8880, FAX: (301) 907-8236.

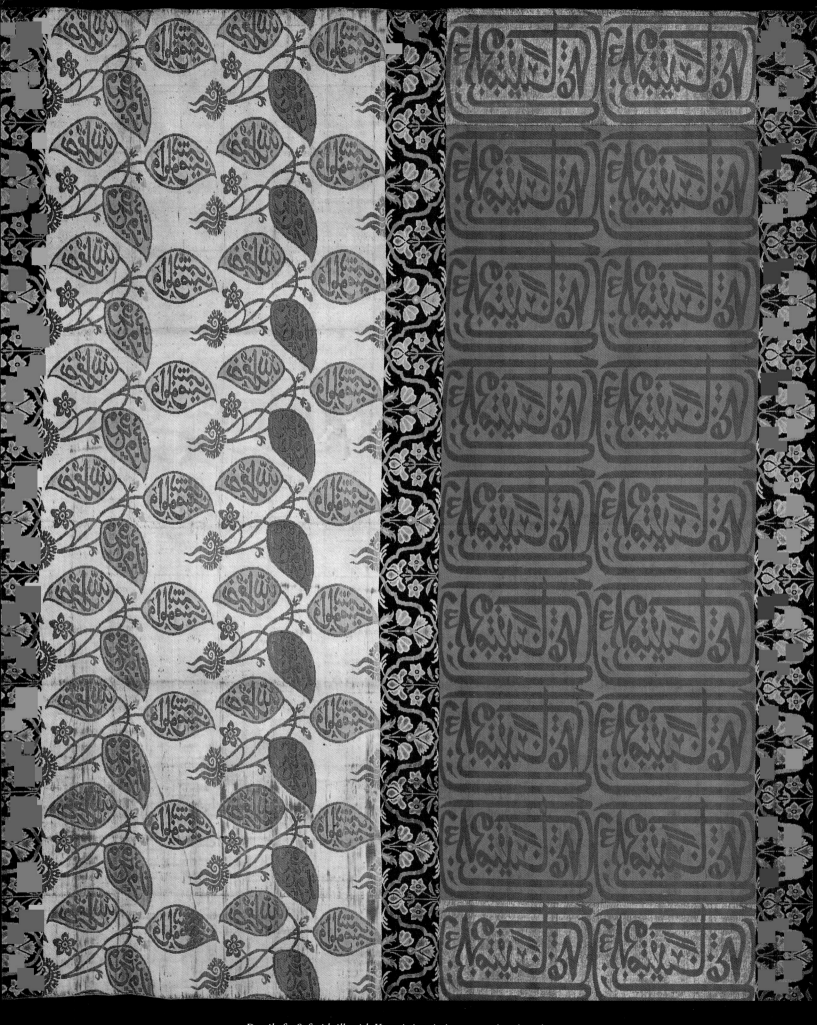

Detail of a Safavid silk with Koranic inscriptions woven in mirror image.
Persia, late 17th century. 34 1/2 x 192 1/2 in (88 x 489 cm)

FRANCESCA GALLOWAY
21 Cornwall Gardens London SW7 4AW Tel: 071-937 3192 Fax: 071-937 4958

Konya carpet
Central Anatolia
circa 1800
102 x 160cms

Gallery: 10123 Turin, Via Cavour 17/a, Tel. 011 5626268 Telefax 011 502226
Restoration Studio and Gallery: 10121 Turin, Corso Re Umberto 2, Tel. 011 547774

"For the New Galleries of the 90s Small ... is Beautiful"

New York Times
April 22, 1994

By Barbara Z. Sedlin
April 30, 1994

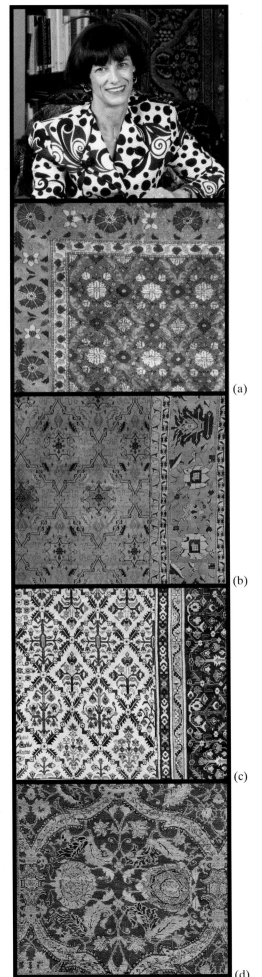

A week ago, the lead article in the *New York Times Weekend* section, which features the arts, opened its two page coverage of semi-private galleries with the above headline. The story reported the burgeoning of the semi-private art gallery, lying midway between the conventional extremes of the spacious well-lighted gallery with scary overheads and the frequently idiosyncratic private dealer, as the recent, major phenomenon in the New York art world.

The context in which business and art transactions occur is rapidly changing, stimulated by the low cost availability of the fax, mobile phone, micro-computer and soon-to-be interactive video. Properly employed, this technology permits one or two people to accomplish the tasks of a sophisticated multiperson staff – all without even being permanently tied to a specific location.

Both the office and the selling function are being decentralized, removed from the core to be "taken on the road" or "brought to the home." For example, elite agricultural products, from premium fruit to fine wines, are purveyed by direct marketers. Inventories are warehoused until sales orders are received, rather than displayed and sold in retail stores, and then delivered direct to customers.

Pondering the implications of converging technology and trends led to the realization that the large gallery with centralized functions is currently not necessary. As a result of the combined impact of interactive Video, CD Rom and International Art Fairs, it may ultimately become obsolete.

So, I came to the dramatic decision to terminate operations at our 5,000 square foot state-of-the-art gallery space on East 57th Street. It was closed quitely without the customary fanfare of an inventory clearance (sale?) because the integrity of the collections did not deserve such cavalier treatment.

We are now functioning for an interim period as a private dealer, only by appointment, (call 212-722-1235), but plan to inaugurate a semi-private exhibition suite within a noteworthy Manahattan Art Deco building in the autumn of 1994. Operation as a semi-private gallery means general public access will be scheduled for a limited period during the week and the remainder of time will be available by pre-scheduled appointment. This brings us full circle – we started as a semi-public gallery in 1973; subsequently opened a showroom in an antiques center in 1976 and then built a major, independent gallery in 1990.

In contrast to most private dealerships, whose restricted hours are associated with a limited inventory, our semi-private dealership enjoys the benefit of more than two decades on the scene as a prominent public gallery. Our collections have breadth, depth and diversity and superb quality. We believe we are the only dealership in the U.S. – perhaps the world – which has consistently pursued a high-level, broad-spectrum inventory of rugs, carpets, tapestries and textiles encompassing *the classical, the collectible* and *the decorative.*

To illustrate this range and level, we have depicted details of selected pieces from our Indian collection.

Example (a): From a silk Lahore collection rug, 18th c.

Example (b): From a fine, large mid-19th c. Lahore echoing diaper motif of 17th/18th c.

Example (c): From a late 19th c. oversize Agra, a design employing variation of plant motif of 16 c.

Example (d): From an outstanding classical furnishing carpet, 18th c., an interpretative design of important 16th c. collection rug

We will continue to eschew regional or formal specialization and focus on esthetics, authenticity, diversity, and historical heritage whenever and wherever it appears in textile art forms. We do intend to devote more effort to exhibition and other forms of marketing of collection pieces.

We invite you to visit us "At Home" or "On Location."

If we don't match your decor, we will match your mood...

THE GHIORDIAN KNOT

212 371 6390   New York City   212 722 1235

1636 Third Avenue New York NY 10128 (Mailing address only)

(a)

(b)

(c)

(d)

A Z E R İ ™

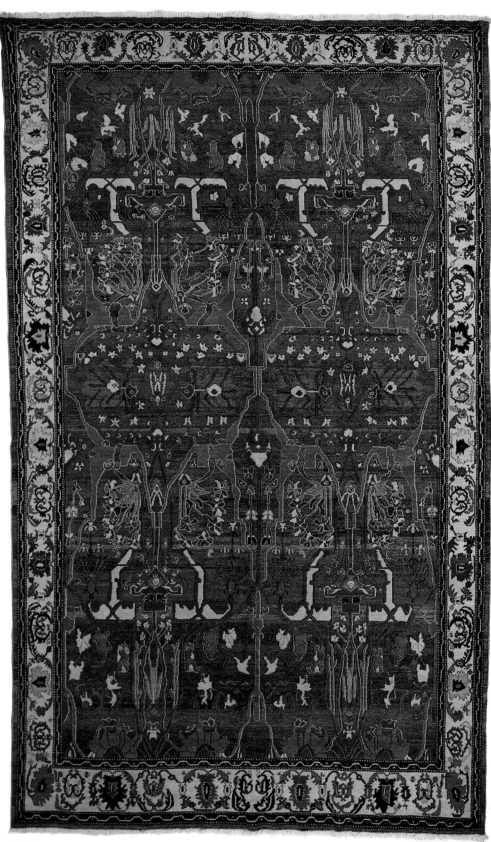

N°532B. 11'5" x 19'10" ~ 348 x 604cm.

WOVEN LEGENDS, INC.

4700 Wissahickon Avenue
Nº106
Philadelphia, Pennsylvania 19144
Telephone 215.849.8344
Facsimile 215.849.8354

ORITOP AG

Zollfreilager, Freilagerstrasse 47
Block 1, Kabine 140
CH-8043 Zurich
Telephone 01.491.9393
Facsimile 01.491.5333

Anglo Persian Carpet Company *(Founded 1910)* South Kensington Station Arcade London SW7 2NA Telephone 071 589 5457 Fax 071 589 2592

Orient Stars
A Carpet Collection

**Published by E. Heinrich Kirchheim
and Hali Publications Ltd.**

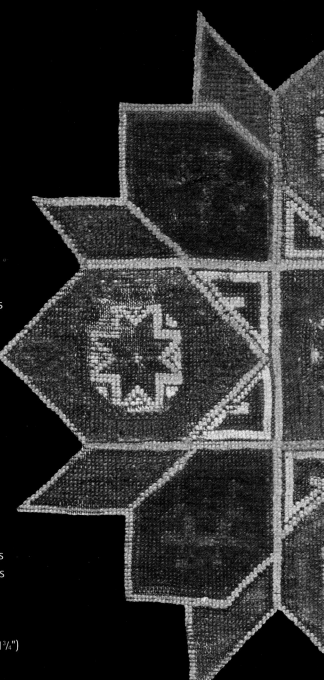

The Collection
- 231 oriental carpets and textiles
- 41 carpets pre-dating 1600
- 5 carpets from 12th to 14th centuries
- Over half previously unpublished

The Authors
The text comprises eighteen
essays, with captions and extensive
notes, by Heinrich Kirchheim,
Michael Franses, Friedrich Spuhler,
Jürg Rageth, Garry Muse and
Eberhart Herrmann.

The Book
- Separate English and German editions
- 394 pages with over 250 colour plates
- Almost 200,000 words
- Over 700 encyclopaedic notes
- A comprehensive list of works cited
- Large format, 360 x 300 mm (14" x 11¾")
- 170gsm high quality art paper
- Hardbound in cloth with slipcase
- Numbered limited edition

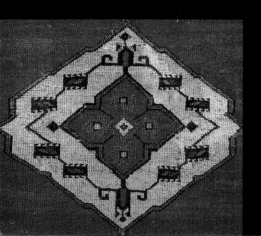

Price: £160 $240 DM385
Please use the ORDER CARD provided for the English and German editions.

Order extra copies now!

Subject to availability: individually numbered, special hardbound edition of 500 copies.

Softbound Price: **£34 $55 DM87**
Hardbound Price: **£44 $72 DM113**
Plus Postage and Packing
£5 $10 DM15

Extra Copies

For further information call Ashley Spinks on 44 71 328 1998.

THE HALI ANNUAL makes a superb and original gift.

Subject to availability: individually numbered, special hardbound edition of 500 copies.

Softbound Price: **£34 $55 DM87**
Hardbound Price: **£44 $72 DM113**
Plus Postage and Packing
£5 $10 DM15

Gift

For further information call Ashley Spinks on 44 71 328 1998.

If you have enjoyed THE HALI ANNUAL, start a subscription to HALI, *The International Magazine of Antique Carpet and Textile Art.*

	1 Year (6 Issues)	2 Years (12 Issues)
UK	**£56**	**£102**
GERMANY	**DM178**	**DM332**
REST OF EUROPE	**£60**	**£108**
USA & CANADA	**$104**	**$189**
*REST OF THE WORLD	**$75**	**$138**
GERMAN SUPPLEMENT	**DM24**	**DM42**

*Airmail rates available on request

HALI
The International Magazine of Antique Carpet and Textile Art

Subscription

For further information call Ashley Spinks on 44 71 328 1998.

If you are not sending your order card in an envelope, please delete whichever address is not applicable

UK, Europe and Rest of World
THE HALI ANNUAL
Circulation Department
Kingsgate House
Kingsgate Place
London NW6 4TA
United Kingdom

USA and Canada
THE HALI ANNUAL
c/o I.M.D. Limited
P.O. Box 966
Rochdale Village Station
Jamaica, New York 11434-0966
USA

UK, Europe and Rest of World
THE HALI ANNUAL
Circulation Department
Kingsgate House
Kingsgate Place
London NW6 4TA
United Kingdom

USA and Canada
THE HALI ANNUAL
c/o I.M.D. Limited
P.O. Box 966
Rochdale Village Station
Jamaica, New York 11434-0966
USA

UK, Europe and Rest of World
THE HALI ANNUAL
Circulation Department
Kingsgate House
Kingsgate Place
London NW6 4TA
United Kingdom

USA and Canada
THE HALI ANNUAL
c/o I.M.D. Limited
P.O. Box 966
Rochdale Village Station
Jamaica, New York 11434-0966
USA

Thomsons roll out the RED carpet for HALI

and the blue and brown, green and mauve. . . .

Thomson ▰ Colour Printers Ltd, 14 Carnoustie Place, Glasgow G5 8PB. Tel: 041-429 1094. Fax: 041-429 5638.

As one of the premier graphic reproduction companies in the United Kingdom, our job is the capture and manipulation of colour originals.

We are dealing with an increasingly broad client base throughout the United Kingdom and Continental Europe, who all have one thing in common: an enthusiastic involvement with their product.

As a prerequisite to success in our business we believe it is essential that we share our clients' enthusiasm, thereby achieving our aim of helping to bring their concepts into print - literally the mass production of ideas.

The passion of HALI exceeds enthusiasm, so the work on our first issue of the magazine, Number 64 in June 1992, was a baptism into a fascinating and to us unknown colourful world of antique rugs and textiles.

The magazine's extremely well informed readership treat it as a definitive reference work, their Bible, so enormous care is taken throughout the production process to ensure colour accuracy.

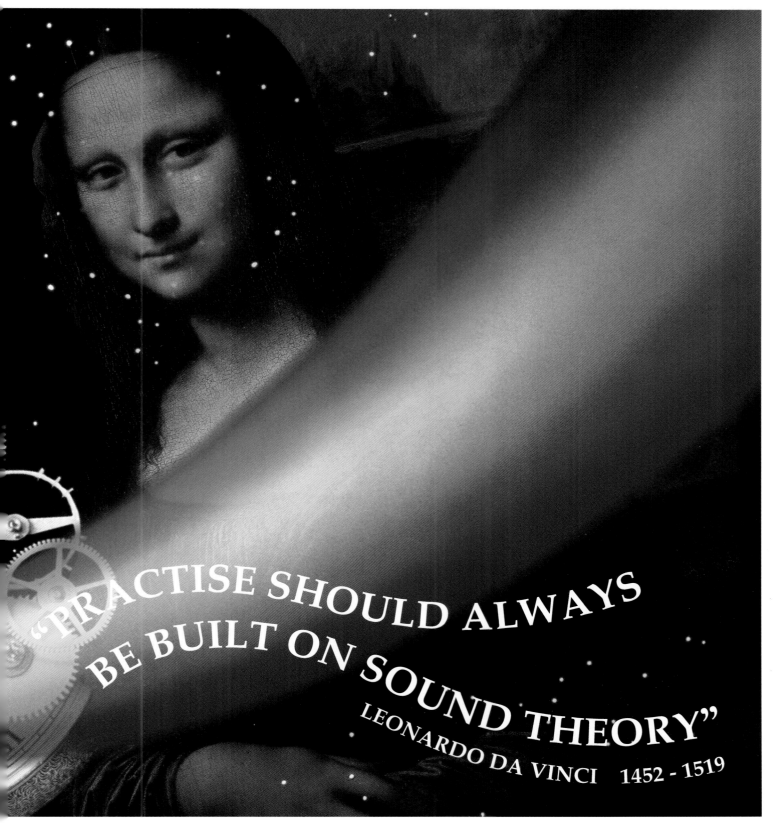

"PRACTISE SHOULD ALWAYS BE BUILT ON SOUND THEORY"

LEONARDO DA VINCI 1452 - 1519

To accomplish this we use some of the most powerful electronic image capture and manipulation equipment available to our industry today.

It is intriguing to consider that some of the most powerful and sophisticated computer equipment of modern times is used to bring to you examples of one of the most ancient achievements of man: the woven fabric.

Every issue of HALI brings a new challenge. We hope we can continue to meet those challenges and help bring Vision to the voice of textile art.

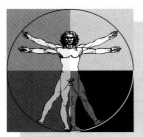

VISION REPRODUCTIONS LIMITED, 15 Carters Lane, Kiln Farm, Milton Keynes, MK11 3ER. England.
Telephone (44-908) 260006 Fax (44-908) 260003

APPENDIX

Endnotes, bibliographies and acknowledgements

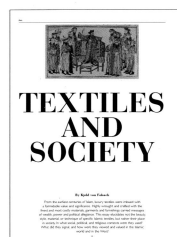

See pages 8-23

This is an abridged version of the essay that first appeared in Kjeld von Folsach & Anna-Maria Keblow Bernsted, *Woven Treasures, Textiles from the World of Islam*, Copenhagen 1993, in which several authors contributed complementary studies on Islamic textiles, focusing on the holdings of the David Collection, Copenhagen.

1. R.B. Serjeant, *Islamic Textiles*, Beirut 1972, p.14.
2. Maurice Lombard, *Les textiles dans le monde musulman du VIIe au XIIe siècle*, Paris 1978, p.178.
3. Serjeant, op. cit., pp.214-215.
4. E.J. Brill's First Encyclopaedia of Islam, 1913-1936, Reprint Leiden 1987, [hereafter *EoI 1*] vol.V, p.743: *Libas*.
5. Florence E. Day, 'The Inscription of the Boston "Baghdad" Silk: A Note on Method in Epigraphy', in *Ars Orientalis*, I, 1954, pp.191-194.
6. Something to this effect was attempted by Eliyahu Ashtor, for example, in his 'Essai sur les prix et les salaires dans l'empire califien', in *Rivista degli studi orientali*, XXXVI, 1961, pp.19-69.
7. Ashtor, op.cit., pp.43-44.
8. According to Walther Hinz, *Islamische Währungen des 11. bis 19. Jahrhunderts umgerechnet in Gold*, Wiesbaden 1991, p.1, the dinar corresponds to ca. 4.23g of pure gold. On January 5, 1993, the price of gold was $329 per 1 troy ounce, or to 31.1g, which would mean that the dinar would be worth $44.68.
9. Ashtor, op.cit., pp.49 and 54.
10. Serjeant, op.cit., pp.145-146.
11. See e.g. Serjeant, pp.157 ff.
12. *The Encyclopaedia of Islam: New Edition*, Leiden 1960, [hereafter *EoI 2*] vol.V, pp.736-737: *Libas*.
13. Serjeant, op.cit., p.10.
14. The concept is discussed in *EoI 1*, cit., vol.VIII, pp.785-793: *Tiraz*; in Serjeant, op.cit., pp.7-27; in Lombard, op.cit., pp.219-222; in Lisa Golombek & Veronika Gervers, 'Tiraz Fabrics in the Royal Ontario Museum', in *Studies in Textile History, in Memory of Harold G. Burnham*, Veronika Gervers (ed.), Toronto 1977, pp.82-93; and in addition it is mentioned in nearly all publications that deal with early Islamic textiles. It does not seem to the author that there is unanimity in the literature on whether the inscriptions in *tiraz* had to have a specific character, or whether any inscription, even the simplest, could be accepted as designating *tiraz*. The concept is used most often in connection with early textiles, but in which epoch does a textile with an inscription stop being *tiraz*? Must the inscription be embroidered or woven in a material and technique different from that of the ground weave?
15. Serjeant, op.cit., pp.7-9.
16. See e.g. Ernst Kühnel & Louisa Bellinger, *Catalogue of Dated Tiraz Fabrics*, The Textile Museum, Washington DC 1952, p.1.
17. Serjeant, op.cit., pp.172-173. For the role of the *muhtasib*, see also under *Hisba* in *EoI 2*, vol.III, pp.485-493.
18. *EoI 1*, vol.VIII, p.790: *Tiraz*; Serjeant, op.cit., p.141.
19. *EoI 1*, vol.VIII, p.790: *Tiraz*.

20. Anne E. Wardwell, 'Panni tartarici: Eastern Islamic silks woven with gold and silver (13th and 14th centuries)', in *Islamic Art III, 1988-1989*, Genoa 1989, pp.108-109.
21. Richard Ettinghausen, 'An Early Ottoman Textile', in *First International Congress of Turkish Art, Ankara, 1959: Communications*, Ankara 1961, pp.134-140.
22. See the discussion of this silk in Kjeld von Folsach, Anna-Maria Keblow Bernsted, *Woven Treasures, Textiles from the World of Islam*, Copenhagen 1993, pp.104-105.
23. Golombek/Gervers, op.cit., p.85. Ibn Khaldun's description, see Serjeant, p.7, indicates that the inscription and ground weave should be of different materials.
24. Serjeant, op.cit., pp.7-8.
25. See Kjeld von Folsach, *Fabelvaesener fra Islams verden*, David Collection, Copenhagen 1991, pp.4-6.
26. See Robert Sabatino Lopez, 'Silk Industry in the Byzantine Empire', in *Speculum*, XX, no.1, 1945, pp.20-22.
27. *EoI 2*, vol.V, p.6: *Khil'a*. This article and L.A. Mayer, *Mamluk Costume: A Survey*, Geneva 1952, are the primary sources for the following.
28. Muhammad Manazir Ahsan, *Social Life under the Abbasids*, London 1979, p.40.
29. Serjeant, op.cit., p.24.
30. Mayer, op.cit., p.63.
31. Mayer, op.cit., pp.58 ff.
32. Alfred Leix, 'Frühorientalische Stoffe', in *Ciba-Rundschau*, 56, 1942, p.2074.
33. Lopez, op.cit., p.14.
34. *EoI 2*, vol.V, p.736: *Libas*.
35. Mayer, op.cit., pp.12 and 15.
36. *EoI 2*, vol.V, p.734: *Libas*.
37. Lombard, op.cit., p.177. If one uses the conversion method mentioned in note 8 above, 4,000 dinars would correspond to about $180,000.
38. *EoI 2*, vol.V, p.749: *Libas*.
39. Serjeant, op.cit., p.11.
40. *EoI 1*, vol.VIII, p.788: *Tiraz*; *EoI 2*, vol.IV, p.317: *Ka'ba*; Serjeant, op.cit., p.215.
41. Serjeant, op.cit., p.22.
42. Lombard, op.cit., p.180.
43. *EoI 2*, vol.III, p.360: *Hidjab*.
44. Serjeant, p.142.
45. *EoI 2*, vol.III, p.209: *Harir*.
46. *EoI 2*, vol.III, pp.359-361: *Hidjab*.
47. A.S. Tritton, *The Caliphs and their non-Muslim Subjects*, London 1970, p.119. Tritton counters the earlier presumption that the *ghiyar* laws went back to the Caliph 'Umar b. al-Khattab (634-644) because at this early date Muslims and *dhimmis* anyway dressed differently. Also *EoI 2*, vol.II, pp.227-231: *Dhimma*, and Bat Ye'or, *The Dhimmi: Jews and Christians under Islam*, London 1985.
48. *EoI 2*, vol.II, p.1075: *Ghiyar*.
49. Tritton, op.cit., pp.121 and 120. For conditions under the Mamluks, see Mayer, op.cit., pp.65-68.
50. Falke did the classical pioneering work on the history of silk weaving: Otto von Falke, *Kunstgeschichte der Seidenweberei*, 2 vols., Berlin 1931. Leonie von Wilckens, *Die textilien Künste der Spätantike bis um 1500*, Munich 1991 is one of the newest surveys that deals with the Medieval period, and Agnes Geijer, *A History of Textile Art*, reprint, London 1982, and Brigitte Tietzel, *Geschichte der Webkunst*, Cologne 1988, discuss the history of these textiles in general.
51. See Manuel Gomez-Moreno, *El panteon real de las Huelgas de Burgos*, Madrid 1946.
52. See e.g. Brigitte Tietzel, *Italienische Seidengewebe des 13., 14. und 15. Jahrhunderts*, Deutsches Textilmuseum, Krefeld, Cologne 1984, cat.nos. 85, 95, and 104.

LOVE AND UNDERSTANDING
A Personal Choice from the Orient Stars Collection

By John Mills

Heinrich and Waltraud Kirchheim's Orient Stars Collection of Eastern carpets, kilims and embroideries, which was exhibited in Hamburg and published during 1993, has been hailed as a significant milestone in the evolution of love and understanding of certain types of oriental carpets, especially early material from Anatolia. Here, one of the most widely respected of current writers on the subject discusses aspects of the collection and the multi-author catalogue, and their longer-term relevance to carpet studies.

See pages 24-33

1. Heinrich Kirchheim, Michael Franses, Friedrich Spuhler, Jürg Rageth, Garry Muse and Eberhart Herrmann, *Orient Stars: A Carpet Collection*, London & Stuttgart 1993.
2. John Mills, 'Early Animal Carpets in Western Paintings – A Review', HALI 1/3, 1978, p.234.
3. 'Zahhak Enthroned', from the Demotte *Shahnameh*, Freer Gallery, Washington DC, inv.no. 23.5. See Richard Ettinghausen, 'New Light on Early Animal Carpets', *Festschrift für Ernst Kühnel*, Berlin 1959, pp.96-113. For the 'Seljuk' carpets see Oktay Aslanapa, *One Thousand Years of Turkish Carpets*, Istanbul 1988, pp.13-35.
4. Nobuko Kajitani et al, *Gionmatsuri 'Yama' 'Hoko' Kensohin Chosa Hokokusho: Torai Senshokuain no Bu*, Kyoto 1992, nos. 40, 42, 47, 48.
5. John Mills, 'Carpets in Paintings: The Bellini, Keyhole or Re-entrant Rugs', HALI 58, 1991 pp.86-103.
6. Mills 1991, loc.cit.
7. Belkis Balpinar and Udo Hirsch, *Carpets of the Vakıflar Museum Istanbul*, Wesel 1988, pls.18, 19 and 20, pp.212-217.
8. For examples see Yetkin, op.cit, pl.35, and Onno Ydema, *Carpets and Their Datings in Netherlandish Paintings 1540-1700*, Zutphen 1991, p.35, fig.24.
9. Ydema, op.cit., calls the border type the 'a93 border' and discusses its appearances in blue-ground Lotto rugs in the paintings on pp.36-37.
10. Balpinar and Hirsch, op.cit., pp.280-281, pl.52.

TRACING THE DRAGON
The Stylistic Development of Designs in Early Chinese Textiles

By Jacqueline Simcox

What did extremely rare, early Chinese textiles have begun to appear more frequently on the international market in recent years, many emerging from centuries of storage in Tibetan monasteries. The small output of surviving silk embroideries, brocades and tapestries represents a mere fraction of the products of one of the most important of Chinese industries but it nonetheless provides enough information to trace the development of particular motifs, and thus to establish a chronology of style and technique.

See pages 34-47

1. Maryta M. Laumann, *The Secret of Excellence in Ancient Chinese Silk*, Taipei 1984. The author describes how members of the nobility were required by the emperor to buy luxurious silks, thereby forcing them to spend their wealth and decreasing their potential threat to him as ruler. This in turn led to aristocrats vying with each other to acquire the finest and most innovative designs.
2. Irene M. Franck and David M. Brownstone, *The Silk Road, A History*, New York & Oxford 1986.
3. Anne E. Wardwell, Curator, Textile Department, *The Bulletin of the Cleveland Museum of Art* vol.79, no.10, December 1992.
4. Dieter Kuhn, *Textile Technology: Spinning and Reeling* in Joseph Needham (ed.), *Science and Civilisation in China*, part IX, vol.5, Cambridge 1988.
5. Sae Ogasawara, 'Chinese Fabrics of the Song and Yuan Dynasties Preserved in Japan', *Orientations*, vol.20, no.8, August 1989.
6. I am indebted to Anne Wardwell for this information.

7. Jessica Rawson, *Chinese Ornament: The Lotus and the Dragon*, London 1984, p.101.
8. Ta-Ming Hui-tien, published reprint Taipei, 1963 Tung-nan Shu-pao-she; Ray Huang, *1587 A Year of No Significance*, New Haven 1981, p.54.
9. Pratapaditya Pal, *Tibetan Paintings*, London 1984.
10. Huang Nengfu (ed.), *The Great Treasury of Chinese Fine Arts, vol.6, Printing, Dyeing, Weaving and Embroidery*, Beijing 1990, pls.191 and 193; R. Soame Jenyns, *Chinese Art: The Minor Arts II*, London 1965, pp.70 & 71.

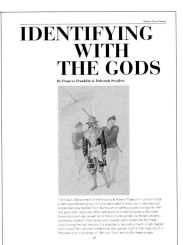

IDENTIFYING WITH THE GODS

By Frances Franklin & Deborah Swallow

The Indian Department of the Victoria & Albert Museum in London holds a well-documented group of richly decorated formal court costumes and simple everyday textiles from Burma which were acquired during the 19th and early 20th centuries. With reference to contemporaneous Burmese books and paintings, as well as to the accounts written by British soldiers, diplomats, traders, missionaries and travellers who visited the Burmese court during the last century, it is possible to reconstruct with a high degree of accuracy the costume conventions that applied both at the royal court in Mandalay and in all strata of 18th and 19th century Burmese society.

See pages 48-61

1. T.A. Trant, *Two Years in Ava (1824-1826)*, London, 1827, p.297.
2. John Crawfurd, *Journal of an Embassy to the Court of Ava*, London, 1834, Part I, p.230.
3. Henry Yule, *A Narrative of the Mission of the Governor General of India to the Court of Ava in 1855*, London, 1858, p.26.
4. Crawfurd, op.cit., Part II, p.100.
5. Lieutenant-General Albert Fytche, *Burma Past and Present*, 1878, p.64.
6. Bertha and Max Ferrars, *Burma*, London, 1901, p.60, pls.136 & 379; see also Trant, op.cit., p.214.
7. Shway Yoe (J. George Scott), *The Burman: His Life and Notions*, 1882, reprinted New York 1963, p.72.
8. Ferrars & Ferrars, op.cit., p.59, comment: "The piece is doubled and its edges sewn together along one side; the turn of the cloth serves as a bag or wallet, according as the piece is draped; it has no lining."
9. *British Burma Gazetteer*, Rangoon, 1880, Part I, p.402.
10. Yule, op.cit., 1858, p.111.
11. Shway Yoe, op.cit., p.467. By 1901, however, the *hta-mein* and *pah-soe* were superseded by the more convenient *longye* (tubular sarong) for ordinary wear. See Ferrars & Ferrars, op.cit., p.60.
12. Some of these horizontal running patterns have been given names, some simply descriptive (four-stripe, five-stripe, seven-stripe, six-twist stripe etc), others appearing to indicate reservation for the use of particular royal persons, e.g. *taba htet tin* = princess pattern, or *taik kaung tin pan khet* = chief queen's floral garland. Many *acheik-luntaya* consist of a series of different horizontal designs.
13. Manipur paid tribute and offered wives to Burma following its conquest by King Bayinnaung in 1556. In the 18th century the Naga king of Manipur invaded Burma, and, in turn, after his death, the Burmese invaded Manipur. With the help of the British the Manipuris negotiated a treaty of alliance in 1762. According to Yule the Manipuris were descendants of 'unfortunates' who were carried off in droves from their country by the Burmans in the time of King Mentaragyi and his predecessors. Yule, op.cit., pp.153-4.
14. Pamphlet published to coincide with an exhibition of traditional *acheik*, by the Mandalay Division of Co-operatives, 1985.
15. Yule, op.cit., p.153.
16. Xia Nai, *Jade and Silk of Han China*, The Franklin D. Murphy Lectures III, University of Kansas, 1985, p.59.
17. Reigned 1698-1714, Toungoo Dynasty, Ava.
18. Jane Terry Bailey, 'Burmese Paintings: Sagaing, Pagan and Amarapura', in *Artibus Asiae*, 1978, vol.XL, p.42, fig.3.
19. Bailey, op.cit., p.48, fig.18.
20. It is interesting to note that the Thai Lue people of Phrae and Nan in north Thailand, who were moved into Thailand from Yunnan in China at the turn of the 18th and 19th centuries, use a simple tapestry weave. See Susan Conway, *Thai Textiles*, London 1992, p.93, and Sylvia Fraser-Lu, *Handwoven Textiles of South East Asia*, Singapore 1988, p.117, pl.14.
21. Personal communication, Paothong Thonchua, Chiengmai University, 1990.
22. Michael Symes, *An Account of an Embassy to the Kingdom of Ava*, 1800, reprinted Farnborough 1969, p.31.

23. From a manual by Wanthok Rhweton Noauratha, dated 1816, quoted by Yi Yi in 'The thrones of the Burmese Kings', *Journal of the Burma Research Society*, XLIII, ii, Dec. 1960, p.67.

24. Charles Duroiselle, *Guide to the Mandalay Palace*, Calcutta, 1931, p.38.

25. Symes, op.cit., p.413.

26. Crawfurd, op.cit, Part I, p.230.

27. Yule, op.cit., p.86.

28. Yule, op.cit., p.80.

29. Symes, op.cit., p.310.

30. A gold chain consisting of a number of strings distinguished different ranks of nobility – three strings indicated relatively low rank, twelve was the optimum and the king alone wore twenty four. Trant op.cit., p.269.

31. Yule, op.cit., p.80.

32. Two of these form part of the V&A collection: IM 320-1924 and IS 45-1981.

33. See for example Robyn Maxwell, *Textiles of Southeast Asia: Tradition, Trade and Transformation*, Melbourne, 1990, p.176 ff. 34. S.P. Sen, 'The Role of Indian Textiles in Southeastern Trade in the 17th Century', *Journal of Southeast Asian History*, 1962, vol.III, no.2, pp.92-110.

35. Henry Burney (Resident to the Court of Ava – 1830-36), 'Some account of the wars between Burmah and China', *Journal of the Asiatic Society of Bengal*, vol.IV, 1837, pp.544-5.

36. J. Horton Ryley, *Ralph Fitch. England's Pioneer to India and Burma: His Companions and Contemporaries, with his own remarkable narrative told in his own words*, London, 1899, p.165.

37. Yule, op.cit., p.84.

38. *Zar* = gold; *dozi* = to lay upon. The term incorporates a range of different applications and techniques: *satara* (silver gilt spangles or sequins); *badla* (narrow strips of crinkled gold); kalabato (twisted silver-gilt wire). See Charu Smita Gupta, 'The Gilded Thread', in *The India Magazine*, vol.12, December 1991, pp.138-9. Veronica Murphy in *The Indian Heritage*, Victoria & Albert Museum, London 1982, p.92, writes that *zardosi* work is "now looked on as a typically Indian court style but considered by some to have been learned from the Portuguese". Unlike other parts of Southeast Asia, the Burmese do not seem to have adopted the use of gold thread for decorative supplementary weft weaving. 39. John Lowry, *Burmese Art*, London 1974, p.2.

40. Yi Yi, 'Life at the Burmese Court Under the Konbaung Kings', in *Journal of the Burma Research Society*, vol.XLIV, Part I, June 1961, p.121.

See pages 138-149

These essays are extracted from the longer text that appeared in Donald King and Santina Levey, *The Victoria & Albert Museum's Textile Collection: Embroidery in Britain from 1200 to 1750*, London 1993.

1. M. Calberg, 'Tissus et broderies attribuées aux Saintes Harlinde et Relinde', in *Bulletin de la Société Royale d'Archéologie de Bruxelles*, October 1951, pp.1ff.

2. C.F. Battiscombe (ed), *The Relics of Saint Cuthbert*, 1956, pp.375ff.

3. Sir Frank Stenton, *The Bayeux Tapestry*, 1957.

4. The standard work on English embroidery of the 12th to 14th century is Mrs A.F.I. Christie, *English Medieval Embroidery*, 1938. Donald King, *Opus Anglicanum*, 1963, is an exhibition catalogue describing many English embroideries of the 11th to 16th century.

5. A surviving English secular embroidery of the 14th century, in the Musée de Cluny, Paris, is described by D. King, op.cit., item 76.

6. 'The Hardwick Hall Inventory of 1601', edited by Lindsay Boynton, *The Journal of the Furniture History Society*, vol.VII, 1971.

See pages 78-83

This is an edited version of the account that originally appeared in *Textile Conservation Symposium*, Los Angeles County Museum of Art 1986, pp.63-67. I would like to acknowledge Ann Svenson, Assistant Textile Conservator, and John Gebhart, Conservation Photographer, for their indispensable help with this project.

1. See Michael Brand and Glenn D. Lowry, *Akbar's India: Art from the Mughal City of Victory*, exhibition catalogue, New York 1985.

2. While Gatorfoam continues to be used by conservators, today there are alternatives including Corrulite and Coroplast (rigid plastic corrugated boards), paper honeycomb and also metal honeycomb boards.

3. Since long-term off-gassing is the concern for most new and relatively untested materials, barrier materials such as Mylar and the newer laminates continue to be popular.

4. Pellon, a non-woven polyester material used in clothing construction, contains an acrylic foam binder that will yellow over time. The manufacturer now produces a similar product for conservation use called Axcel, made from 100% polyester without binders or sizings.

5. Paper conservators have demonstrated, however, that fibres in contact with acrylic sheeting can sustain microabrasion.

See pages 158-163

This is an edited and augmented version of the account that originally appeared in *The Pacatnamu Papers. Volume 1*, Christopher B. Donnan and Guillermo A. Cock, (eds.), Museum of Cultural History, University of California, Los Angeles 1986.

BIBLIOGRAPHY

Benson, Elizabeth P., and William J. Conklin, *Museums of the Andes*, Tokyo 1981.

Cieza de Leon, Pedro de, *La Cronica del Peru*, Vol.1, Fondo Editorial Pontificia Universidad Catolica del Peru – Academia Nacional de la Historia, Lima 1984 [1553].

Cock, Guillermo A., *From the Powerful to the Powerless: The Jequetepeque Valley Lords in the 16th Century*, Peru, M.A. thesis, Archaeology Program, University of California, Los Angeles 1985; 'Power and Wealth in the Jequetepeque Valley during the Sixteenth Century', in *The Pacatnamu Papers. Volume 1*, Christopher B. Donnan and Guillermo A. Cock, (eds.), Los Angeles 1986.

Netherly, Patricia Joan, *Local Level Lords in the North Coast of Peru*, Ph.D. dissertation, Cornell University, Ithaca, New York 1977.

Ramirez-Horton, Susan, 'Retainers of the Lord or Merchants: A Case of Mistaken Identity', in *Hombre y su Ambiante en Los Andes Centrales*, Luis Milliones and Hiroyasu Tomoeda, (eds.), Senri Ethnological Studies 10,

National Museum of Ethnology, Osaka 1982.

Rostworowski de Diez Canseco, Maria, 'Pescadores, Artesanos y Mercaderes Costenos en el Peru Prehispanico', in *Revista del Museo Nacional 1*, Museo de la Cultura Peruana, Lima 1975.

Schmidt, Max, *Kunst und Kultur von Peru*, Berlin 1929.

1. This textile was excavated by Mary E. Doyle and was cleaned, blocked, and mounted by Sharon Gordon Donnan. The drawing (Fig. 4) was made by Alana Cordy-Collins and Genaro Barr.

2. One small fragment of a textile nearly identical to this one was found at Pacatnamu by Giesela and Wolfgang Hecker in 1962, almost exactly 400 metres northwest of where this textile was found. It consists of a narrow strip of cloth, which appears to be a vertical piece of the same, or at least a very similar, textile. It does not appear to add any new iconographic details to those visible on this piece. As with this fragment, it was found near the surface of the ground and appeared to have been looted. There were no clearly associated artefacts.

3. The identification of this animal as a llama is based on the cloven hoofs, long head, relatively small ears, and a downward curving tail.

4. Two other textiles depicting looms and bobbins have been reported. One is in the Amano Museum in Lima (Benson and Conklin 1981: pp.56-57), and has no provenance. The other is in the Museum für Völkerkunde in Berlin (Schmidt 1927: p.492 right) and is said to come from Pachacamac, on the Central Coast of Peru. All three share many technological and stylistic features with the one excavated at Pacatnamu, and they may all have been woven at or near that site.

5. The sacrificed llama with white fur was found carefully buried beneath a floor in the elevated architecture.

6. Cieza 1984 [1553]:Ch. LXVII, p.205; Cock, 1986.

7. Cieza 1984 [1553]:Ch. XI, pp.191-192.

8. A discussion of these sources and the information they provide is available in Rostworowski 1975; Netherly 1977; Ramirez-Horton 1982: Cock 1985, 1986.

FROM THE INFINITE BLUE

Mapuche Textiles from Southern Chile

By Vanessa & Andrés Moraga

When seen at a distance, from across the horizon of the Pampas or the undulating heights and valleys of the lower Sierras, the monumental blue and white geometric forms of Mapuche chief's ponchos must have had a striking visual impact. Radiating power, they proclaimed at a glance the identity and status of their owner. But these dynamic textiles were more than visual insignia or badges of prestige. As the most highly developed and pre-eminent Mapuche art form, they were invested with the deepest spiritual and cultural ideas of the people. Like all Andean textiles, they eloquently and elegantly transcended their utilitarian role, mediating between the living and the dead, and encoding a vision of the sacred and the mythic. In so doing, Mapuche textile artists created a singular abstract language that explored the essential nature of colour, shape and the geometry of space.

See pages 164-179

1. See John Cooper, 'The Araucanians' *in Handbook of South American Indians*. Vol. 2. Steward (ed.). Washington DC., 1946, p.690.

2. The Mapuche never actually formed a single nation or political unit. The name Araucanian or Mapuche therefore indicates several distinct but related groups who inhabited different geographical regions of south/central Chile. These comprised the *Picunche* (in the north); the *Mapuche* (in the heartland); the *Huilliche* (of the south) and the *Pehuenche* (of the Andean cordillera); as well as the Argentine *Araucanians*. See Cooper, pp. 690-694.

3. From Fray Diego de Rosales' *Historial General del Reino De Chile* (1674) quoted in Aureliano Oyarzun and Ricardo Latcham, *Album de Tejidos y Alfareria Araucano* Santiago, 1929.

4. A very early example of this motif in a textile is seen in a fibre bag from Arica, Northern Chile dating to 800-500 BC. (Alto Ramirez phase).

5. The advent of the repeating Winchester rifle greatly facilitated this process.

6. Ruth Corcuera, *Herencia Textil Andina*. Buenos Aires, 1987, p.92.

7. Montell, Gosta. *Dress and Ornaments in Ancient Peru*. London: Oxford University Press, 1929. All subseqent references are to the chapter 'The Post-Columbian Age', pp.237-244.

8. As Gina Laczko notes, "Originally the *chamal* referred to any rectangular piece of textile intended for clothing, the woman's chamal being a *kepam*, or wrap-around dress, and the man's chamal being a *chiripa*, or breechcloth." See 'The Weaver. The Araucanians of Chile', in *The Ancestors, Native Artisans of the Americas*, A. Roosevelt (ed.). New York, 1979, p.139. The garments were differentiated only by colour: all women's textiles were dyed a very deeply saturated shade of indigo that appeared almost black, and the men's garments were left undyed, or possibly even bleached. The man's *chiripa* fell into disuse in the late

19th century, replaced by European style pants, but some of these ancient garments survive into the 20th century. Photographs of men playing the ritual hockey game *chueca* show them wearing the chiripa.

9. L. Adelson and A. Tracht, *Aymara Weavings, Ceremonial Textiles of Colonial and 19th century Bolivia*. Washington DC 1983, p.65.

10. Joseph H. Claude, *Los Tejidos Araucanos*, Santiago 1928.

11. According to Gina Laczko, this type of poncho was "so rare that apparently it has no specific name", op.cit, p.143.

12. Pedro Mege Rosso. "Los simbolos envolventes: una etnoestetica de las mantas mapuches" in *Boletin del Museo Chileno de Arte Precolombino*. No 3, 1989. Santiago de Chile.

13. From the field notes of Samuel Lothrop, an eminent Americanist and Anthropologist who collected Mapuche Textiles for the Museum of American Indian/Heye Foundation. Quoted in Laczko, op.cit., p.143

14. Ann Pollard Rowe, *Warp Patterned Weaves of the Andes*, Washington DC 1977, p.20.

15. Most pre-Columbian examples are brown ikat on white cotton. Rowe publishes an ikat fragment from northern Peru, Late Intermediate Period, that has a field of repeat stepped diamond or cross motifs, identical in concept and design to Mapuche ikat ponchos. See Rowe, op.cit., fig.4, p.18.

16. See 'Observations on the Painted Designs of Patagonian Skin Robes' by Carl Schuster, in *Essays in Pre-Columbian Art and Archaeology* by Samuel K. Lothrop et al., Cambridge, Mass. 1964, and Samuel K Lothrop, *Polychrome Guanaco Cloaks of Patagonia. Contributions from the Museum of the American Indian*, Vol. VII, #6. New York 1929.

17. Schuster, op. cit., pp.424-5

18. Angelika Gebhart-Sayer, *The Cosmos Encoiled: Indian Art of the Peruvian Amazon*, New York 1984., pp.7, 9.

19. Schuster, op.cit., p.448.

20. Cooper notes that "Personal rank and prestige was derived chiefly from martial prowess and from wealth; generous hospitality, and eloquence in speech were other well-recognized avenues to status." From "The Araucanians" p.727.

21. Louis Faron, *The Mapuche Indians of Chile*, in the series *Case Studies in Anthropology*, Spindler (ed.), New York 1968, p. 67.

22. In the 19th century, Mapuche chiefs were buried with their horses. E.R. Smith. an English traveller, described the burial site as follows: "At both the head and foot of this grave was an upright, forked stick, supporting a transverse pole, over which was hung the skin of the chieftain's favourite horse, while a long bamboo lance, planted in the ground, with a little white pennant fluttering in the wind, denoted the rank of the deceased." *The Araucanians*. London 1855, p.172.

23. Faron, op.cit., p.102. The shamanistic aspects of the Mapuche religion have strong affinities with the practices of the northernmost Pacific cultures, such as the Inuit (Eskimo) and Siberian people. These include trance, divination and curing ceremonies, involving incantations and ritual drumming. Wooden masks are worn during ritual hockey games. The shaman is known as the *machi*. This role is usually filled nowadays by a woman, but in the past male transvestites performed the ritual acts. The two most important items of shamanistic paraphernalia are a painted drum, which symbolically depicts the four quarters and centre of the Mapuche universe, and strongly resembles Siberian examples, and the *rewe*, a totemic notched effigy post.

SEEING AND BELIEVING

Navajo Blankets
By Joshua Baer

Between 1820 and 1880, a group of weavers living in what is now the Four Corners region of the American Southwest produced a body of artwork that is thought by connoisseurs to rank among the finest aesthetic accomplishments of the 19th century. The author looks briefly at the history of Navajo weaving before turning his attention to the more elusive question of what it means to 'see' a Navajo blanket.

See pages 180-193

This article is excerpted from a work in progress entitled *Space And Design – The Art and the History of the Navajo Blanket.*

INDEX TO ADVERTISERS

Whilst every care is taken by the publishers, the descriptions and attributions of pieces advertised are the sole responsibility of the individual advertisers.